THE POLITY OF CHRIST

T&T Clark Enquiries in Theological Ethics

Series editors
Brian Brock
Susan F. Parsons

THE POLITY OF CHRIST

Studies on Dietrich Bonhoeffer's Chalcedonian Christology and Ethics

Ulrik Nissen

LONDON • NEW YORK • OXFORD • NEW DELHI • SYDNEY

T&T CLARK
Bloomsbury Publishing Plc
50 Bedford Square, London, WC1B 3DP, UK
1385 Broadway, New York, NY 10018, USA
29 Earlsfort Terrace, Dublin 2, Ireland

BLOOMSBURY, T&T CLARK and the T&T Clark logo are
trademarks of Bloomsbury Publishing Plc

Copyright © Ulrik Nissen, 2020

First published in Great Britain 2020
This paperback edition published in 2021

Ulrik Nissen has asserted his right under the Copyright, Designs and
Patents Act, 1988, to be identified as Author of this work.

For legal purposes the Acknowledgements on p. ix constitute
an extension of this copyright page.

All rights reserved. No part of this publication may be reproduced or
transmitted in any form or by any means, electronic or mechanical,
including photocopying, recording, or any information storage or retrieval
system, without prior permission in writing from the publishers.

Bloomsbury Publishing Plc does not have any control over, or responsibility for, any
third-party websites referred to or in this book. All internet addresses given in
this book were correct at the time of going to press. The author and publisher
regret any inconvenience caused if addresses have changed or sites have
ceased to exist, but can accept no responsibility for any such changes.

A catalogue record for this book is available from the British Library.

Library of Congress Control Number: 2019955006

ISBN: HB: 978-0-5676-9159-0
PB: 978-0-5676-9899-5
ePDF: 978-0-5676-9161-3
ePUB: 978-0-5676-9160-6

Typeset by Integra Software Services Pvt. Ltd.

To find out more about our authors and books visit www.bloomsbury.com
and sign up for our newsletters.

For Sarah, Emilie, Ditte and Selma

CONTENTS

Acknowledgements	ix
List of Abbreviations	xi

Chapter 1
INTRODUCING CHRISTIAN ETHICS BETWEEN UNIVERSALITY AND SPECIFICITY

	1
Is there a third position?	4
Chalcedonian Christology as a foundation for social ethics	8
Why choose a Chalcedonian approach?	13
Content and structure of the book	19

Chapter 2
THE SIMULTANEITY OF DIVINITY AND HUMANITY IN LUTHER'S SOCIAL ETHICS

	23
From two kingdoms doctrine to three estates	24
Chalcedonian motifs in Luther's theology and ethics	27
Luther's social ethics between universality and specificity	32
Conclusion	37

Chapter 3
THE CHALCEDONIAN CHRISTOLOGY IN BONHOEFFER'S ETHICS

	39
The who, how and where in the 'Lectures on Christology'	41
God revealed in flesh as the holy mystery of Christmas	46
The *cantus firmus* and polyphony of the Christian life	47
Conclusion	48

Chapter 4
THE CHRISTOLOGICAL SHAPING OF CENTRAL CONCEPTS IN BONHOEFFER'S ETHICS

	49
Reality as the contradictory Christ-reality	50
The secular as *saeculum*	55
Christonomy as the foundation of the human condition	60
The Christological ontology of reason	65
Responsibility and Christological responsiveness	70
Conclusion	77

Chapter 5
BONHOEFFER'S SOCIAL ETHICS BETWEEN UNIVERSALITY AND SPECIFICITY 79
- Christian political thought as a contradictory affirmation of reality 82
- Christian ethics between participation and witness 85
- Natural law Christologically reshaped 90
- Conclusion 94

Chapter 6
POLITICAL THOUGHT IN THE POLITY OF CHRIST 95
- Law and justice between universality and specificity 95
- A Chalcedonian affirmation of Christian humanism 106
- Communicative responsibility Christologically reshaped 112
- Conclusion 119

Chapter 7
LIVING IN THE *SAECULUM* AND BEARING WITNESS TO CHRIST 121
- The Christian's dual citizenship 123
- Conversation and the polyphony of life 127
- Bearing witness over contentious issues 134
- Conclusion 140

CONCLUSION 143

Bibliography 148
Index 163

ACKNOWLEDGEMENTS

When a book like the present one is completed, there are several people who have encouraged, supported and in many other ways furthered the work. The list of people to whom I am indebted in gratitude by far exceeds both the reasonable limits of these acknowledgements and my inadequate attempt to remember them all.

I do wish to express particular gratitude, however, to Carlsbergfondet (The Carlsberg Foundation) for providing the grant in 2003 that made this project possible. Without this grant the present book would probably never have been realized. I also wish to thank Det Frie Forskningsråd – Kultur og Kommunikation (The Danish Council for Independent Research – Humanities) for a grant in 2007 which made it possible for me to have a sabbatical in which I could finish the project. Finally, I wish to thank the Faculty of Theology (now part of the Faculty of Arts) at Aarhus University for granting me a three-month sabbatical in the final stages of the project. The present book was first defended as a doctoral dissertation (dr. theol.) at the Faculty of Arts, Aarhus University in March 2014. I wish to thank Kirsten Busch Nielsen, Bernd Wannenwetsch and Svend Andersen who served as the assessment committee for this defence. Before the publication of this book, the entire manuscript was revised, and new studies and publications have been included where it was deemed relevant. The original dissertation was comprised of a plurality of studies and a summary of these studies. I acknowledge with gratitude the permission to reuse parts of these studies for this book:

- 'Between Unity and Differentiation. On the Identity of Lutheran Social Ethics'. In *The Sources of Public Morality – On the Ethics and Religion Debate*. Edited by Ulrik Nissen, Svend Andersen and Lars Reuter, 152–71. Societas Ethica. Europäische Forschungsgesellschaft für Ethik, 2003.
- 'Reconciliation and Public Law. Christian Reflections about the Sources of Public Law'. *Studia theologica* 58, no. 1 (2004): 27–44.
- 'Dietrich Bonhoeffer and the Ethics of Plenitude'. *Journal of the Society of Christian Ethics* 26, no. 1 (2006): 97–114.
- 'Disbelief and Christonomy of the World'. *Studia theologica* 60, no. 1 (2006): 91–110.
- 'The Christological Ontology of Reason'. *Neue Zeitschrift für systematische Theologie und Religionsphilosophie* 48, no. 4 (2006): 460–78.
- 'Responding to Human Reality. Responsibility and Responsiveness in Bonhoeffer's Ethics'. In *Being Human, Becoming Human: Dietrich Bonhoeffer and Social Thought*. Edited by Brian Gregor and Jens Zimmerman, 203–25. Eugene, OR: Wipf & Stock Publishers, 2010.

- 'Being Christ for the Other: A Lutheran Affirmation of Christian Humanism'. *Studia theologica* 64, no. 2 (2010): 177–98.
- 'Letting Reality Become Real: On Mystery and Reality in Dietrich Bonhoeffer's Ethics'. *Journal of Religious Ethics* 39, no. 2 (2011): 321–43.
- 'Responsibility and Responsiveness: Reflections on the Communicative Dimension of Responsibility'. *Neue Zeitschrift für systematische Theologie und Religionsphilosophie* 53, no. 1 (2011): 90–108.
- 'Social Ethics Between Universality and Specificity. Outline of a Chalcedonian Social Ethic'. *Dialog* 51, no. 1 (2012): 83–91.

Particular gratitude is also extended to everyone who has given me comments on various versions of the articles over the years. Some of the papers were first presented at different conferences or seminars, e.g. The Society of Christian Ethics. I wish to thank both the participants at these occasions for their comments and the anonymous reviewers of the articles submitted to the journal. Also, I wish to express my gratitude for the comments and suggestions for improvements from the reviewers at all the other journals where the articles have been submitted. Finally, special thanks go to those who gave me comments on parts of the final dissertation manuscript – Bo Kristian Holm, Christopher R. J. Holmes, Kees van Kooten Niekerk and Christine Schließer. I am deeply grateful to all of you.

These acknowledgements would be far from complete if I were not to mention my gratitude to my parents for first leading me to Christ and being the first examples in my life of what it means to follow Christ. I am deeply grateful to you, my dear mother, Aase Birk Nissen, and father, Steen Holst Nissen (in memoriam), for showing me what it means for Christ to be the way, and the truth, and the life. This book would never have been written if it had not been for you.

Last – but not least – I wish to thank my wife and our four daughters for their continuous support. Judith, Sarah, Emilie, Ditte and Selma – you have all been an incredible support throughout the work on this book. Judith, you have always been patient, encouraging and supportive in so many different ways. Sarah, Emilie, Ditte and Selma – you have always reminded me of the things in life that really matter. Thank you for always being there, whenever I turned off my computer and was reminded of the sheer pleasure of being together. I dedicate this book to you with the hope and prayer that you may all grow and become faithful followers of Christ in faith, hope and love. It goes for all of you that the many hours I needed to spend on my own to finish this book filled me with feelings of failed priorities. I know you will not hold it against me and that we all look forward to having more time being together.

Risskov, August 2019

ABBREVIATIONS

The following abbreviations refer to standard works of Luther and Bonhoeffer. A complete list of references and full bibliographic details are found in the Bibliography. Quotations from the Bible are from the New Revised Standard Version unless otherwise noted.

BSELK   *Die Bekenntnisschriften der Evangelisch-Lutherischen Kirche.* Herausgegeben von Irene Dingel im Auftrag der Evangelischen Kirche in Deutschland. Vollständige Neuedition.

DBW   *Dietrich Bonhoeffer Werke.* Herausgegeben von Eberhard Bethge, Ernst Feil, Christian Gremmels, Wolfgang Huber, Hans Pfeifer, Albrecht Schönherr and Heinz Eduard Tödt. Band 1–17.

DBWE   *Dietrich Bonhoeffer Works.* General Editor, Wayne Whitson Floyd, Jr. Vols 1–17. English-language edition of *Dietrich Bonhoeffer Werke.*

LW   *Luther's Works.* Edited by Jaroslav Pelikan et al. Vols 1–55. American edition.

WA   *D. Martin Luthers Werke: Schriften.* Band 1–73. Kritische Gesamtausgabe. Weimarer Ausgabe.

Chapter 1

INTRODUCING CHRISTIAN ETHICS BETWEEN UNIVERSALITY AND SPECIFICITY

Just as in Jesus Christ God and humanity became one, so through Christ what is Christian and what is worldly become one in the action of the Christian. They no longer battle like eternally hostile principles. The action of the Christian instead springs from the unity of God and world brought about in Jesus Christ.[1]

In Christ we are invited to participate in the reality of God and the reality of the world at the same time, the one not without the other. The reality of God is disclosed only as it places me completely into the reality of the world. But I find the reality of the world always already borne, accepted, and reconciled in the reality of God. That is the mystery of the revelation of God in the human being Jesus Christ.[2]

In these two quotations from Dietrich Bonhoeffer's *Ethics* and the implications following from them, the theme of the present book is summarized. What are the ethical implications of the reconciliation of the world and God in Jesus Christ? Can we extrapolate inferences of relevance for the contemporary debate on Christian ethics, particularly with regard to the question about the role of Christian voices in public?

It is now almost twenty years ago since, in autumn 2001, I made the first outline for a project on social ethics, which has now found the form of the current book. I was a theology student during the 1990s and moved on to PhD studies, which I finished in summer 2001. Only a few months later, the Western world was trembled by the attack on the Twin Towers of the World Trade Center on 11 September 2001. That attack, and the subsequent political and cultural

---

1. Dietrich Bonhoeffer, *Ethics* (ed. Clifford J. Green; trans. Reinhard Krauss, Charles C. West and Douglas W. Stott; Dietrich Bonhoeffer Works; vol. 6; Minneapolis, MN: Fortress Press, 2005) (DBWE 6), 238. Quotations from Bonhoeffer's writings will be from the English-language edition of *Dietrich Bonhoeffer Werke*. References without quotations will be to the original German text. The pages in the German original can be followed in the margins of the English edition. The same principle also applies to references to Martin Luther's writings.

2. DBWE 6, 55.

reactions in Western and Middle Eastern countries, only seemed to make the project's aim and intentions more urgent still. Since then, the media and public debate have relentlessly returned to 'armed intervention', criteria for just war, terror legislation, national surveillance of citizens and related topics. Meanwhile, issues such as insulting cartoons, headscarves and religious symbols in public received similar attention. From a Danish perspective, the 'cartoon crisis' that developed in December 2005 and early 2006 produced an unprecedented awareness of the role that religious motifs and sensibilities can play in a political context. In all of these debates, the relationship between religion and politics has been a constantly recurring issue. In some of these debates the argument goes that, in order to uphold social cohesion, religion should play no role in public life (or at least a very limited role). Religion should be regarded as a private matter. The presumption seems to be that public debate should be conducted according to criteria that are acceptable to all reasonable citizens, and which are therefore assumed to hold a common or universal validity. Religion is seen as the source of a particular or specific understanding of authority that can only play a guiding role for those who hold this worldview. In Denmark in 2006, this line of argument was endorsed by the prime minister of the day.[3] Not long afterwards, the underlying viewpoint was debated by several Danish theologians.[4] It is difficult not to see the rise of nationalist movements in many European countries as late repercussions of these events of the early years of the first decade of the second millennium, a factor which was documented in an article right before the elections for the European Parliament in May 2019.[5] Also, the British 'Brexit' movement and the North American 'Make America Great Again' under the current US president appear to be expressions of similar tendencies. Rather than placing an emphasis on what we have in common and thereby sharing responsibilities for a better world for all of humanity, these movements are emphasizing what is particular to the various nationalities and what makes them different from others. Some of these movements and things being said in the media and in political campaigns give rise to the question of whether we are in some ways reaching a new Bonhoeffer moment.[6]

This growing diversity poses a political challenge to maintain a given society's unity, or social cohesion, and at the same time to acknowledge the validity and legitimacy of diverse worldviews. This task has also stimulated a theoretical discussion about the relationship between the common or universal versus a specific or particular foundation of philosophical and theological ethics. Various representatives of both a universal and a more identity-specific approach to ethics have formulated theories and positions that wrestle with this dilemma. These

---

3. Anders Fogh Rasmussen, 'Fogh: Hold religionen indendørs', *Politiken* (2006), 6.

4. Peter Lodberg, *Sammenhængskraften: Replikker til Fogh* (Højbjerg: Univers, 2007).

5. BBC.com, 'Europe and Right-Wing Nationalism: A Country-by-Country Guide', https://www.bbc.com/news/world-europe-36130006 (accessed 22 July 2019).

6. Lori Brandt Hale and Reggie L. Williams, 'Is This a Bonhoeffer Moment?', sojo.net, https://sojo.net/magazine/february-2018/bonhoeffer-moment (accessed 22 July 2019).

two dimensions are often seen as inherently contradictory. On the one hand, the universal approach has a sound and reasonable claim in its argument for a common morality, as this seems to be increasingly important in a political and cultural climate that is constantly exhibiting signs of conflict and collision. On the other hand, the theorists who argue in favour of a more particular understanding of ethics place a valid emphasis on the importance of the different identity-formative contexts, traditions and communities that are inescapable for any political citizen.

Against this backdrop, the present book seeks to promote an understanding of the foundation of political thought that moves beyond a tendency to separate its universal and its specific dimension. My wish is to contribute to a *third position* where, in their relation, the universal and specific dimensions of a Christian social ethic are continuously seen as a unity, even as they remain distinct from each other. From this third position's perspective, the universal and specific dimensions rest in a differentiated unity.

Apart from its general background – namely the debate on the sources and the identity of a contemporary Christian (social) ethic – this book also has its background in my own earlier research. In two previous studies I have worked with the Lutheran understanding of natural law.[7] Partly because of this background, and partly because the book's topic can be seen as particularly pertinent to the Lutheran tradition, this book focuses on the Lutheran tradition in its engagement with its subject. Many relevant conclusions could be drawn from the two previous studies, but I shall mention only two inferences, both of which are seminal to this book:

1. The natural law tradition is an essential and necessary part of a Lutheran social ethic. The importance of this theme in Martin Luther's social ethic makes the concept unavoidable, assuming that one wishes to maintain continuity with the Lutheran tradition in a contemporary context. At the same time, the concept of natural law provides this tradition with an inevitable universal dimension. Hence this book's emphasis on the universal dimension of social ethics.
2. Natural law is characterized by a simultaneous 'natural' and 'divine' dimension. This was not just part of the Lutheran tradition's understanding of natural law. Rather, it was a commonly held understanding of natural law prior to the contractarian theories of the early seventeenth century. Most of

---

7. Ulrik Nissen, *Påberåbelsen af lex naturalis i diskussionen om statsmagtens legitimitet i det 16. århundredes lutherske, reformerte og anglikanske teologi, og denne diskussions betydning for opkomsten af den moderne idé om samfunds-kontrakten* (Aarhus: AU Library Scholarly Publishing Services, Aarhus Universitet, 2019); Ulrik Nissen, *Nature and Reason: A Study on Natural Law and Environmental Ethics* (Aarhus: AU Library Scholarly Publishing Services, Aarhus Universitet, 2019). Although the two studies mentioned here serve as part of the background, they are not included in the book itself. If I refer to these studies or briefly quote a passage from them, a clear reference will be given.

those holding such positions found it unthinkable that the universal, 'natural' dimension of natural law could be separated from its specific, 'divine' origin or source. It was not until Hugo Grotius presented his so-called impious hypothesis that this indissoluble link was questioned – and even Grotius maintained that the connection cannot be questioned 'without the utmost wickedness'.[8] In the present context, the important conclusion to be drawn from Luther's understanding of natural law is that the link between the natural and the divine dimension of natural law is still contended. Consequently, this book cannot confine itself to merely endorsing the universal dimension in the identity of Lutheran social ethics. This would imply disregard for an essential part of the understanding of natural law within the Lutheran tradition. Instead, I endeavour to present arguments supporting the simultaneous unity and difference of the universal and the specific dimension. As this book seeks to demonstrate, Bonhoeffer also argues in favour of such a unity and difference simultaneously coexisting in his understanding of the origins of Christian ethics. Bonhoeffer also offers a critique of understanding ethics as something separate from the divine will, maintaining that both the 'natural' and the 'divine' dimension are essential to a Christian, theological understanding of reality.

Is there a third position?

The central question of the book is whether there is a third position between universality and specificity which makes it possible to affirm all that we have in common as human beings and, at the same time, makes it possible for Christians to live faithful lives bearing witness to Christ in public. More specifically, the outlined background propels the book's *central question* into the foreground: is it possible – on the basis of select theorists (primarily from within the Lutheran tradition) – to determine a foundation for a Christian social ethic that enables us simultaneously to maintain the unity and the difference between the universal and specific validity? In other words, the book asks whether it is possible to overcome the traditional dichotomy between a universal and a more specific foundation of a Christian social ethic by endorsing a differentiated unity between the two. This leads to the book's *thesis*: that there are central Chalcedonian motifs in the Lutheran tradition – not least in Bonhoeffer's Christological ethic – that may provide a basis for reformulating the foundation of a Lutheran social ethic pertaining to the crucial question of how the relationship between the universal and the specific dimension of a Christian social ethic can be understood; and that these motifs

---

8. Hugo Grotius, *Prolegomena to the Law of War and Peace* (Library of Liberal Arts; Indianapolis, IN: Bobbs-Merrill Co., 1957), § 11.

may be appropriated for the purpose of endorsing a differentiated unity of the universal and specific foundation, and hence validity of a Christian social ethic.

The book's focus on the Lutheran tradition should not be understood as an expression of a firm confessionalism. Rather, the emphasis is 'critical-constructive'.[9] This means that the book attempts to focus on the context and tradition within which it seeks to contribute, critically and constructively, to a new understanding. This is not to suggest that its results are irrelevant outside this tradition, nor to suggest in any way that other traditions would be less relevant to the topic at hand. Indeed, the book's central question would render such an assumption absurd. However, simply aiming to contribute to Christian social ethics in general would broaden the book's topic beyond all practicable limits. The focus on the Lutheran tradition is also due to an inherent tension, and maybe even problem, within this tradition, which also means that this tradition may hold a key to the solution.[10]

The title of the book is inspired by Ernst Wolf's essay with the same title, which was first published in 1948 and later in the first volume of his collected essays, *Peregrinatio*.[11] In this essay, Wolf argues that there is a problem in Lutheran social ethics derived from a tendency to interpret Luther's theology in an individualistic sense. Rather, faith calls Christians to live faithful lives as reconciled and created beings in the midst of the world.[12] In this understanding there is a tension between the Christian faithfulness and the worldly life of the Christian. This is a tension which we also find in Bonhoeffer and not least in his Christology and his Christological ethics. It is the aim of this book to show that this understanding can be viewed in light of a differentiated unity as described above, based on a Chalcedonian Christology. In other words, I contend that Bonhoeffer's ethic can contribute to reformulating a contemporary Lutheran social ethic. I base this on the Lutheran background of his ethic, and that in much of the recent Lutheran social ethics debate Bonhoeffer has, to some extent, been overlooked for such a systematic-theological purpose.

Because this book wishes to promote an understanding of the foundation of social ethics that moves beyond a tendency to separate its universal and specific dimensions, it is important to clarify what I mean by 'social ethics'. This is particularly crucial here, as Bonhoeffer regards the concept of 'social ethics' as

---

9. We can differentiate between at least seven different interpretations of what it means for a position to be 'Lutheran': the genetic, contextual, philological, institutional, substantial, confessional or critical-constructive. For further elaboration, see the section 'Defining Lutheranism' in Ulrik Nissen, *Between Universality and Specificity: A Study of Christian Social Ethics with Particular Emphasis on Dietrich Bonhoeffer's Ethics* (Aarhus: Aarhus University, 2014), 17–19.

10. For the methodological reflections behind the book, see ibid., 15–17.

11. Ernst Wolf, 'Politia Christi: Das Problem der Sozialethik im Luthertum', in *Peregrinatio* (ed. Ernst Wolf; München: Chr. Kaiser, 1962), 214–42.

12. Ibid., 228.

an ethical aporia.¹³ Bonhoeffer makes this comment in reference to Reinhold Niebuhr's *Moral Man and Immoral Society*.¹⁴ According to Bonhoeffer, that work represents an abstract split between individual and society. In contrast to Niebuhr's understanding, Bonhoeffer regards human beings as indivisible wholes inseparable from the human and created community to which they belong.¹⁵

Within the concept of 'social ethics', we can distinguish between a broader and a narrow understanding.¹⁶ Whereas the former designates all of the ways in which human beings can have relations with each other, the latter is concerned with institutional – meaning social, political and economic – issues. Bonhoeffer's critique of social ethics places him within the broader understanding of social ethics. This is also apparent from the centrality of sociality throughout Bonhoeffer's theology and ethics.¹⁷ However, Bonhoeffer's *Ethics* also reveals his engagement with social ethics in the narrower sense, as he is concerned with the social and political implications of Christian faith.

This book uses 'social ethics' in both senses of the phrase. The broader notion is apparent when the book seeks to contribute to understanding the foundation of a Christian social ethic that makes it possible to maintain simultaneously the differentiated unity of its universal and specific dimensions. The narrower understanding, on the other hand, is implicit when the book submits its topic as relevant to contemporary debates on the conditions and criteria governing public discourse, and on the relationship between religion and politics. Albeit both notions are therefore represented in the book, the broader notion is particularly important given the book's overall aim.

It is similarly important to define the concepts of 'ethics' and 'Christian ethics', not least because Bonhoeffer apparently dismisses both concepts. Due to his situationist approach to ethics – an understanding we also find applied in his notion of responsibility in *Ethics*¹⁸ – Bonhoeffer rejects the idea of a 'Christian ethic' in his Barcelona lecture from 1929, 'Basic Questions of a Christian Ethic'.¹⁹

13. Dietrich Bonhoeffer, *Ethik* (herausgegeben von Ilse Tödt, Heinz Eduard Tödt, Ernst Feil und Clifford Green; Dietrich Bonhoeffer Werke; band 6; Gütersloh: Chr. Kaiser, 2nd rev. edn, 1998) (DBW 6), 36.

14. Reinhold Niebuhr, *Moral Man and Immoral Society: A Study in Ethics and Politics* (New York: Charles Scribner, 1960).

15. DBW 6, 38.

16. Brian Hebblethwaite, 'Sozialethik', in *Theologische Realenzyklopädie* (ed. James K. Cameron Horst Balz et al.; vol. 31; Berlin/New York: W. de Gruyter, 2000), 497–527.

17. Clifford J. Green, *Bonhoeffer. A Theology of Sociality* (Grand Rapids, MI: W. B. Eerdmans, rev. edn, 1999).

18. DBW 6, 260, 287.

19. Dietrich Bonhoeffer, *Barcelona, Berlin, Amerika. 1928–1931* (herausgegeben von Reinhart Staats und Hans Christoph von Hase in zusammenarbeit mit Holger Roggelin und Matthias Wünsche; Dietrich Bonhoeffer Werke; band 10; München: Chr. Kaiser, 1991) (DBW 10), 323–45.

It is not the aim of a Christian ethic to formulate specific principles. Rather, it is in the concrete moment that the responsibility for the other arises and the Christian seeks the will of God. Therefore, Bonhoeffer can even argue that Christianity is fundamentally amoral,[20] and that it is the aim of Christian ethics to dissolve the notion of ethics.[21] It is also obvious, however, that Bonhoeffer acknowledges a place for ethical reflection on issues pertinent to a Christian theology. This follows from his understanding of Christian ethics as reflecting ethical issues in light of fundamental Christian notions.[22] Or, as he expresses it in *Ethics*: 'The subject matter of a Christian ethic is God's reality revealed in Christ becoming real [*Wirklichwerden*] among God's creatures ...'[23] Finally, there is the obvious fact that *Ethics*, in its entirety, is precisely such a sustained reflection on ethical issues as seen in light of Christian theology.

These deliberations also serve as the background for understanding Christian ethics in the present book. In this context, Christian ethics is understood as a theological discipline constituted by a critical reflection on fundamental ethical issues and contemporary moral challenges in light of Christian theology, faith and tradition. This implies that Christian ethics engages in a conversation with other disciplines – from the humanities, social sciences and life sciences. In this conversation, Christian ethics maintains a self-awareness of being embedded in a particular tradition, even while it continuously seeks to go beyond this tradition in its endeavours to further the conversation with other disciplines, traditions and worldviews. In this understanding of Christian ethics, the book seeks to position itself between universality and specificity.

This leads us to the two central concepts in the book: universality and specificity. These two terms are not sharply differentiated from similar word pairs such as 'common' and 'particular'. Readers of the articles that are part of the book will therefore find the word pairs universal/common versus specific/particular used interchangeably. These notions provide the terminological context within which the book wishes to engage in the classical and contemporary debate about the relationship between a universal (common) morality versus a specific (particular) understanding of Christian ethics. This debate plays a central role, for instance in the contemporary debate on the relationship between a liberal democratic understanding of the construction of ethics (as in John Rawls, for example) and more particularistic views (as expressed by Stanley Hauerwas and others). These positions are often considered contradictory – as is indeed the case for the two representatives of these standpoints mentioned here. Likewise, natural law, according to the classical view, is often understood as a universal foundation of ethics, and therefore as a significant example of a moral tradition in which the particular dimension plays a lesser role. As noted, the present book aims to go

---

20. Ibid., 326.
21. DBW 6, 301.
22. DBW 10, 323.
23. DBWE 6, 49.

beyond this dichotomous view and contribute to a third position: a position that has no sharp division between the universal and specific dimensions. Rather, these dimensions are seen as resting in a differentiated unity. As this book proposes, it is this differentiated unity that may be endorsed in light of a Chalcedonian Christology – which is why that approach is clarified in the following section.

Chalcedonian Christology as a foundation for social ethics

As already mentioned, it is the thesis of the book that the Chalcedonian Christology in Lutheran theology particularly exemplified by Bonhoeffer's Christological ethics provides a way forward for an understanding of social ethics between universality and specificity. In order to see how the book hereby contributes to the current understanding of Lutheran social ethics, a brief overview of the literature is hereby attempted.

It would be too ambitious (and it is not the aim of the book) to map the contemporary landscape of Lutheran social ethics. Instead, the aim is more modest, focusing on the specific topic of the book. Therefore, the present overview will point to significant positions in Lutheran social ethics since the mid-1960s. When this juncture is chosen as the point of departure, it has to do with the publication of two works that are both central to the book. The well-known Lutheran theologian Paul Althaus published a monograph on Luther's ethics in 1965.[24] Despite the book's merits, the Christological motifs play a secondary role. There is no mention of Christ in the list of contents, and no entry in the index indicating an interest in Christology. The understanding of the justification by faith and what this implies for the Christian is of course related to Jesus Christ, and as such it plays a role in, for example, Althaus' explanation of the two kingdoms doctrine and the life of the Christian. But the understanding of Christ and its ethical implications is not a topic in itself and as such it remains in a secondary role. Around the same time, the Lutheran World Federation (LWF) concluded a study process on the relationship between Christ and humanity which was begun in 1963.[25] The study theme of the committee was 'The Quest for True Humanity and the Lordship of Christ' – a theme which was partly ecumenically motivated. Therefore, it was a central issue of the study process to reflect on the relationship between the doctrine of the two kingdoms and the 'lordship of Christ'. This led the committee to reflect on the question of the relationship between the 'universally human [and] specifically Christian in ethics',[26] whereby it approaches the central issue of the present book. The tension between Althaus' book on Luther's ethics and the LWF study report signals a problem within Lutheranism concerning the

---

24. Paul Althaus, *Die Ethik Martin Luthers* (Gütersloh: Gütersloher Verlagshaus Gerd Mohn, 1965).
25. Ivar Asheim, ed., *Christ and Humanity* (Philadelphia, PA: Fortress Press, 1970).
26. Ibid., x.

1. Introducing Christian Ethics between Universality and Specificity 9

place and role of Christological motifs in Lutheran social ethics. The present book places itself in this continuous discussion.

The question about the role of the lordship of Christ in a Lutheran social ethic was also raised in the already mentioned essay by Ernst Wolf.[27] In this essay, written not long after Bonhoeffer's *Ethik*, Wolf examines different models of Lutheran social ethics and argues that the importance of maintaining that being in the world for the Christian is always related to the kingdom of Christ and vice versa.[28] This implies that the *iustitia civilis* and the *iustitia christiana* are organically related to each other,[29] which is why Wolf can speak of the Christian being in the world (*das christliche Dasein in der Welt*) as political worship (*politischen Gottesdienst*).[30] For a contemporary Lutheran ethicist, Hans G. Ulrich, the influence from Wolf is found in several places in a recent outline of protestant ethics.[31] Ulrich also uses the concept of the polity of Christ (*politia Christi*) to express the central concern of a protestant social ethic.[32] In distinction from Wolf, however, Ulrich has a stronger emphasis on the witness:

> In evangelical social ethics the witness of the existential life form [i.e. the new creation in Christ] has been called 'politia Christi': It is the public expression, testing, and communication of the human existential life form, as it is determined in Christ. In Jesus Christ it is revealed how human existence is fulfilled. *Therefore* the evangelical ethic and social ethic is witness. It is a witness of this new creation in Christ.[33]

Even if both Wolf and Ulrich argue for the centrality of Christological motifs for a Lutheran social ethic, we do not find any attempt to make use of Chalcedonian motifs in either of them, nor do we find an explicit attempt to argue for a differentiated unity of universality and specificity.

The ambivalent status of Christological motifs in Lutheran social ethics is probably the reason why they do not play a significant role in either an anthology on Lutheran ethics from the late 1990s or two relatively recent overviews of core issues in Luther's ethics.[34] Also, despite their differences, in the two most recent

---

27. Wolf, 'Politia Christi'.
28. Ibid., 230.
29. Ibid., 237–38.
30. Ibid., 239.
31. Hans G. Ulrich, *Wie Geschöpfe leben. Konturen evangelischer Ethik* (Münster: LIT, 2005).
32. Ibid., 42–44.
33. Ibid., 42 (my translation).
34. Karen L. Bloomquist and John R. Stumme, *The Promise of Lutheran Ethics* (Minneapolis, MN: Fortress Press, 1998); Max Josef Suda, *Die Ethik Martin Luthers* (Forschungen zur systematischen und ökumenischen Theologie, 108; Göttingen: Vandenhoeck & Ruprecht, 2006).

and significant contributions to a Lutheran political ethic, the Christological motifs have not been treated as a central issue.[35] However, several studies testify to the centrality of Christological themes and motifs in Luther's ethics, even if they are based on different approaches and arguments.[36] In neither of these studies, however, do we find an attempt to elaborate upon a Chalcedonian structure in Luther's theology and ethics. This may come as somewhat of a surprise, as the Chalcedonian Christology – not least the *communicatio idiomatum* – has been shown to play a central role in Luther's theology.[37] These studies, however, do not focus explicitly on the ethical implications of this motif in Luther.

As this brief overview shows, the Chalcedonian Christology plays a central role in Luther's theology. However, this motif has not caught the attention it rightly deserves in the deliberations on the foundation of Luther's social ethic or political thought. The present book hopes to contribute to the ongoing discussion on the foundations of Lutheran social ethics by elaborating upon this Chalcedonian motif in Luther's theological ethics.

35. Whereas Andersen attempts to read Luther in light of a Rawlsian perspective, Laffin explicitly wishes to free Luther from a modern political narrative, see Svend Andersen, *Macht aus Liebe. Zur Rekonstruktion einer lutherischen politischen Ethik* (Berlin/New York: W. de Gruyter, 2010); Michael Richard Laffin, *The Promise of Martin Luther's Political Theology: Freeing Luther from the Modern Political Narrative* (ed. Brian Brock and Susan F. Parsons; T&T Clark Enquiries in Theological Ethics; London: Bloomsbury T&T Clark, 2016).

36. Tuomo Mannermaa, *Der im Glauben gegenwärtige Christus. Rechtfertigung und Vergottung. Zum ökumenischen Dialog* (Arbeiten zur Geschichte und Theologie des Luthertums; N.F., band 8; Hannover: Lutherisches Verlagshaus, 1989); Dietmar Lage, *Martin Luther's Christology and Ethics* (Texts and Studies in Religion; Lewiston, NY: Edwin Mellen Press, 1990); Antti Raunio, *Summe des christlichen Lebens: die 'Goldene Regel' als Gesetz der Liebe in der Theologie Martin Luthers von 1510 bis 1527* (Reports from the Department of Systematic Theology; vol. 13; Helsinki: University of Helsinki, 1993); Oswald Bayer, *Freiheit als Antwort: zur theologischen Ethik* (Tübingen: Mohr, 1995); Veli-Matti Kärkkäinen, "'The Christian as Christ to the Neighbour": On Luther's Theology of Love', *International Journal of Systematic Theology* 6, no. 2 (2004), 101–17; Antti Raunio, 'Faith and Christian Living in Luther's Confession Concerning Christ's Supper (1528)', *Lutherjahrbuch* 76 (2009), 19–56.

37. Kjell Ove Nilsson, *Simul. Das Miteinander von Göttlichem und Menschlichem in Luthers Theologie* (Göttingen: Vandenhoeck & Ruprecht, 1966); Johann Anselm Steiger, 'Die communicatio idiomatum als Achse und Motor der Theologie Luthers: Der "fröhliche Wechsel" als hermeneutischer Schlüssel zu Abendmahlslehre, Anthropologie, Seelsorge, Naturtheologie, Rhetorik und Humor', *Neue Zeitschrift für systematische Theologie und Religionsphilosophie* 38, no. 1 (1996), 1–28; Johann Anselm Steiger, *Fünf Zentralthemen der Theologie Luthers und seiner Erben: Communicatio, Imago, Figura, Maria, Exempla* (Studies in the History of Christian Thought; vol. 104; Leiden: Brill, 2002); Oswald Bayer, *Creator est creatura: Luthers Christologie als Lehre von der Idiomenkommunikation* (Theologische Bibliothek Töpelmann; 138; Berlin: W. de Gruyter, 2007).

When we turn to Bonhoeffer, the picture immediately changes. Whereas the Christology apparently plays an ambivalent role in Luther's theology and ethic, it has almost become a commonplace to state that Bonhoeffer's ethic fundamentally is a Christological ethic. Several studies demonstrate the central role Christological motifs play in his ethic.[38] Even if these studies all demonstrate the inevitability of Christological motifs in an understanding of Bonhoeffer's ethics, we do not find a focused attempt to demonstrate the Chalcedonian theme and an elaboration of its potential in Christian social ethics. Apparently, only two works (apart from the current book and the articles it is based on) have focused explicitly on Chalcedonian motifs in Bonhoeffer's theology and ethics.[39] However, neither of these have an explicit interest in its ethical implications, nor do they attempt constructively to engage with these themes in order to contribute to a contemporary understanding of the foundation of Lutheran social ethics. In Holmes' book on ethics and the presence of Christ, the emphasis is on a Christological ethic, but it is not a study on Bonhoeffer, even if he does play a central role.[40]

38. Jürgen Moltmann, *Herrschaft Christi und soziale Wirklichkeit nach Dietrich Bonhoeffer* (Theologische Existenz heute; vol. 71; München: Chr. Kaiser, 1959); Jürgen Weissbach, *Christologie und Ethik bei Dietrich Bonhoeffer* (Theologische Existenz heute; vol. 131; München: Chr. Kaiser, 1966); John A. Phillips, *The Form of Christ in the World: A Study of Bonhoeffer's Christology* (London: Collins, 1967); R. F. Kohler, 'Christocentric Ethics of Dietrich Bonhoeffer', *Scottish Journal of Theology* 23, no. 1 (1970), 27–40; Larry L. Rasmussen, *Dietrich Bonhoeffer: Reality and Resistance* (Studies in Christian Ethics; Nashville, TN: Abingdon, 1972); Oswald Bayer, 'Christus als Mitte. Bonhoeffers Ethik im Banne der Religionsphilosophie Hegels', *Berliner Theologische Zeitschrift* 2 (1985), 259–76; James H. Burtness, *Shaping the Future: The Ethics of Dietrich Bonhoeffer* (Philadelphia, PA: Fortress Press, 1985); Martin Honecker, 'Christologie und Ethik: zu Dietrich Bonhoeffers Ethik', in *Altes Testament und christliche Verkündigung* (Stuttgart/Ithaca, NY: Snow Lion Publications; W. Kohlhammer, 1987), 148–64; Hans-Jürgen Abromeit, *Das Geheimnis Christi: Dietrich Bonhoeffers erfahrungsbezogene Christologie* (Neukirchener Beiträge zur Systematischen Theologie 8; Neukirchen-Vluyn: Neukirchener, 1991); Gunter M. Prüller-Jagenteufel, *Befreit zur Verantwortung: Sünde und Versöhnung in der Ethik Dietrich Bonhoeffers* (Ethik im Theologischen Diskurs; Münster: LIT, 2004); Karsten Lehmkühler, 'Christologie', in *Bonhoeffer und Luther. Zentrale Themen ihrer Theologie* (ed. Klaus Grünwaldt, Christiane Tietz and Udo Hahn; Hannover: VELKD, 2007), 55–78.

39. Ronald A. Carson, 'Motifs of Kenosis and Imitatio in the Work of Dietrich Bonhoeffer, with an Excursus on the Communicatio Idiomatum', *Journal of the American Academy of Religion* 43, no. 3 (1975), 542–53; Christopher R. J. Holmes, 'Wholly Human and Wholly Divine, Humiliated and Exalted: Some Reformed Explorations in Bonhoeffer's Christology Lectures', *Scottish Bulletin of Evangelical Theology* 25, no. 2 (2007), 210–25.

40. Christopher R. J. Holmes, *Ethics in the Presence of Christ* (London/New York: T&T Clark, 2012). In the dissertation, upon which the current book is based, the research review is more extensive, including an overview with relation to each of the articles mentioned in the acknowledgements. The reader is kindly referred to this research review for further references, see Nissen, *Between Universality and Specificity*, 27–35.

With regard to the overall aim of the current book, the contribution that comes closest to my own approach is an article by Franklin Sherman on the outline of a Chalcedonian social ethic.[41] In this article Sherman takes his point of departure from the seemingly general difference between a social ethic based on the doctrine of creation (which employs categories such as 'orders of creation', the 'natural order' and natural law), and the other understanding which finds its premises in a Christological foundation. Sherman also refers to these two approaches as the question about the relation between nature and grace. Rather than seeing these two as opposites, Sherman wishes to argue for a Chalcedonian understanding which maintains what is valuable in both the emphasis on continuity and the endorsement of discontinuity between nature and grace. The thesis of his essay is

> that it would be well for all concerned if it were recognized that the term 'christological ethics' is equivocal; that Christology has been employed as an apologia for very different types of ethics, some characterized by a continuity between nature and grace, some by a discontinuity; but that what is valuable in each of these types can be embodied in an ethic that cleaves to the 'vital center' of Chalcedonian Christology.[42]

In light of this thesis, Sherman reflects on Barth's and Bonhoeffer's understanding of the relation between nature and grace. As for Bonhoeffer, Sherman points to the understanding in the later years of his life, where Bonhoeffer argued for the 'continuity between Christian ethics and ordinary human goodness'.[43] Even more central in Sherman's essay, however, is Barth's understanding of the same question. Also, Emil Brunner plays an important role. This leads him to the formulation of the following passage, where he gives a succinct summary of the importance of the Chalcedonian position in the understanding of social ethics:

> [F]rom both sides [i.e. church and state] what is desired is a recognition of the duality between church and world, but without a dualism; and on the other hand, sympathetic identification of the church with the world, but not an identity between the two. It is this which leads us to propose that, if a Christological social ethic is to be formulated, it is a Chalcedonian Christology that is required. For it is precisely these two kinds of error that the Chalcedonian definition of

---

41. Franklin Sherman, 'The Vital Center: Toward a Chalcedonian Social Ethic', in *The Scope of Grace. Essays on Nature and Grace in Honor of Josep Sittler* (ed. Philip J. Hefner; Philadelphia, PA: Fortress Press, 1964), 233–56. Esther Reed also points to the importance of developing a 'Chalcedonian way of thinking' for Christian ethics. Her approach is inspired not least by Karl Barth and Mikhail Bakhtin. See Esther D. Reed, *The Genesis of Ethics: On the Authority of God as the Origin of Christian Ethics* (London: Darton, Longman and Todd, 2000), 186–208.

42. Sherman, 'The Vital Center', 234.

43. Ibid., 236.

the faith was designed to guard against: on the one hand, the 'Nestorian' dualism between the divine and human natures of Christ, and on the other hand, the Eutychian amalgamation of them. Our assumption in saying this, however, is that the Chalcedonian formula did not, as often alleged, perform only the negative function of excluding such aberrations, but is worthy of commendation in its own right as a positive statement of the faith.[44]

Sherman points to Bonhoeffer as a person in whom we find the Chalcedonian position made explicit. It is in a letter to his friend, Eberhard Bethge, that Bonhoeffer uses the metaphor of symphonic music to explain the Christian's relation to the world. Just as polyphonic compositions are characterized by a *cantus firmus* to which other contrapuntal voices are added, loving God should be regarded as a *cantus firmus* to which earthly love is added. The unity and yet differentiation between these two kinds of love is explicitly exemplified by the Chalcedonian Christology, and it is seen as a model of the Christian life.[45]

Even if Sherman's essay in many respects comes close to the aim of the present book, there are some important differences. First, it is not the aim of Sherman to develop a Chalcedonian social ethic within the context of Lutheran ethics. Indeed, it may be questioned whether his essay may even be read as a contribution to a Lutheran understanding of this issue. Therefore, a central figure in his article is Karl Barth and references to the Lutheran tradition (apart from Bonhoeffer) are very limited. Second, Sherman keeps his deliberations at a highly general level and does not show how this influences central ethical concepts such as reason, responsibility etc. In this regard, the title of the article is significant – it acknowledges that it only moves 'toward a Chalcedonian social ethic'. Third, it does not attempt to outline a more constructive understanding of the implications of this Chalcedonian position. We are left with an understanding of potential implications, but we are not provided with an attempt to make this more concrete. In at least these three aspects, the present book contributes a new insight into the implications of a Chalcedonian social ethic.

Why choose a Chalcedonian approach?

A question that could readily arise regarding the aim of this book is: Why did the author choose a Chalcedonian approach to contemporary social ethics? This question is just as pertinent as the answer seems obvious. First, my choice has

---

44 Ibid., 241.

45. Dietrich Bonhoeffer, *Widerstand und Ergebung. Briefe und Aufzeichnungen aus der Haft* (herausgegeben von Christian Gremmels, Eberhard Bethge und Renate Bethge in zusammenarbeit mit Ilse Tödt; Dietrich Bonhoeffer Werke; band 8; Gütersloh: Chr. Kaiser, 1998) (DBW 8), 440-41. We will return to this letter later in the book. See also Chapter 3, particularly the section 'The *Cantus Firmus* and Polyphony of the Christian Life'.

to do with the place and role of Christological thought in a Christian ethic. I contend that the implications of the life, death and resurrection of Jesus Christ can be regarded as the indispensable foundation for any Christian ethic. Without this foundation, it is ultimately meaningless to speak of a Christian ethic. In this sense, the book follows Wolfhart Pannenberg's claim when he submits that the Christology is 'the core of any Christian theology'.[46] The question is not whether a relationship between Christ and Christian ethics exists. Rather, the question is how to determine this relationship and what the implications are. I therefore regard the reflections on the ethical implications of the life, death and resurrection of Jesus Christ as the *conditio sine qua non* of Christian ethics. Hereby, I place myself in continuation with the debate on Christology and ethics, both with regard to the debate in the last half of the twentieth century[47] and the revival of the Christology and ethics discourse in recent years.[48] Second, the role and place of Jesus Christ are central to both Luther's and Bonhoeffer's theology and ethics. In Luther's commentary on the Galatians, he states that the article on Christ fills his heart and all his theological reflections flow from this article, even if he has only managed to see glimpses of its height, breadth and depth.[49] In many other of Luther's writings, the argument can be made

---

46. Wolfhart Pannenberg, *Grundzüge der Christologie* (5; Gütersloh: Mohn, extended edn, 1976), 13 (my translation). See also Christiane Tietz, 'The Role of Jesus Christ for Christian Theology', in *Christ, Church and World. New Studies in Bonhoeffer's Theology and Ethics* (ed. Michael Mawson and Philip G. Ziegler; London: Bloomsbury T&T Clark, 2016), 9–28.

47. See the two republished classical books on Christ and ethics, H. Richard Niebuhr, *Christ & Culture* (New York: HarperOne, 2001); James M. Gustafson, *Christ and the Moral Life* (Library of Theological Ethics; Louisville, KY: Westminster John Knox Press, 2009).

48. See e.g. Oliver O'Donovan, *Resurrection and Moral Order. An Outline for Evangelical Ethics* (Leicester/Grand Rapids, MI: Apollos/W. B. Eerdmans, 2nd edn, 1994); Mark C. Miller, *Living Ethically in Christ: Is Christian Ethics Unique?* (American University Studies Series VII, Theology and Religion; vol. 173; New York: P. Lang, 1999); Andreas Schuele and Günter Thomas, eds, *Who Is Jesus Christ for Us Today? Pathways to Contemporary Christology* (Louisville, KY: Westminster John Knox Press, 2009); F. LeRon Shults and Brent Waters, *Christology and Ethics* (Grand Rapids, MI/Cambridge: W. B. Eerdmans, 2010); Holmes, *Ethics in the Presence of Christ*; Glen Harold Stassen, *A Thicker Jesus: Incarnational Discipleship in a Secular Age* (Louisville, KY: Westminster John Knox Press, 2012); Lisa Sowle Cahill, *Global Justice, Christology and Christian Ethics* (New Studies in Christian Ethics; vol. 32; Cambridge: Cambridge University Press, 2013); Michael Mawson and Philip G. Ziegler, eds, *Christ, Church, and World: New Studies in Bonhoeffer's Theology and Ethics* (London: T&T Clark, 2016); Luke Bretherton, *Christ and the Common Life. Political Theology and the Case for Democracy* (Grand Rapids, MI: W. B. Eerdmans, 2019).

49. Martin Luther, *In epistolam S. Pauli ad Galatas commentarius ex praelectione* (herausgegeben von U. Freitag; Weimar: H. Böhlau, [1531, 1535] 1911) (WA 40 I), 33, 7–11.

that his theology reflects a sustained pondering over the implications of Jesus Christ's life, death and resurrection.[50] As for Bonhoeffer, the Christological motif is apparent throughout his theology, from his early *Sanctorum Communio* to his late *Letters and Papers from Prison*. In *Ethics*, Bonhoeffer focuses on the Christological theme from the opening section onwards. Further, in his lectures on Christology, Bonhoeffer speaks of Christ as the centre of human existence, history and nature.[51] Therefore, several commentators also rightly describe Bonhoeffer's ethic as a Christological ethic.[52] Third, the Chalcedonian motif seems to hold a potential that is fruitful for the book's thesis. It seems that the Chalcedonian motif may make it possible to affirm the book's aim to find a position from which to support a differentiated unity for the universal and specific dimensions of a Christian social ethic. The understanding of the unity and difference between the two natures of Christ, and the relationship between them, seems to buttress the reading of this classical formula as a model for a contemporary understanding of the unity and difference between the universal and specific dimensions of the foundations of a Christian social ethic. I aspire to substantiate this last point in the course of the book.

Even if the above-mentioned arguments for this approach sustain the assumption that this notion may hold valuable potential for the contemporary debate on the foundations of Christian social ethics, the question still remains of how the book understands and employs Chalcedonian Christology. In particular, the question might be raised of whether such an approach to Christology is expedient in a contemporary context.

It should be noted that the book does not focus on the dogmatic or historical understanding and teachings of the identity and relation of the two natures of Christ. Therefore, it does not engage in discussing or analysing the original background or meaning of the Chalcedonian settlement in 451. J. N. D. Kelly's work, *Early Christian Doctrines*, remains a classic in its overview of these debates.[53] However, for the purpose of this introduction to the book, it is worth noting the central theological questions at stake in these first centuries of early Christianity. The controversial question was how one could affirm both the divine and human nature of Jesus Christ without either separating or identifying the two. The debates over this question already have their roots in the writings of the New Testament. John Macquarrie gives a good account of the various accentuations of this early understanding of Christ, as it is portrayed in Paul, the

---

50. Marc Lienhard, *Martin Luthers christologisches Zeugnis: Entwicklung und Grundzüge seiner Christologie* (Göttingen: Vandenhoeck & Ruprecht, 1980).

51. Dietrich Bonhoeffer, *Berlin. 1932-1933* (herausgegeben von Carsten Nikolaisen und Ernst-Albert Scharffenorth; Dietrich Bonhoeffer Werke; band 12; Gütersloh: Chr. Kaiser, 1997) (DBW 12), 306–11.

52. See also Chapter 3.

53. J. N. D. Kelly, *Early Christian Doctrines* (London: A. & C. Black, 5th rev. edn, 1993).

synoptic gospels, John and other New Testament writings.[54] He refers to Martin Hengel saying that, with regard to Christology, more happened in the first two decades than in the whole of the next seven centuries,[55] although Macquarrie amends this to the first four centuries,[56] hereby emphasizing the importance of the Chalcedonian settlement.

The debate leading up to Chalcedon can be summarized as being represented by the schools of Alexandria and Antioch. Whereas the former emphasized the unity of the person of Christ and his divinity, the latter contended the humanity of Christ and the distinction between the two natures in the hypostatic union.[57] Drawing upon a complex philosophical terminology, the debate during these first four centuries tried to establish an understanding of how one could affirm both the true divinity and true humanity of Jesus Christ, how the unity between the two could be maintained without mixing the two (as this would compromise either the divinity or humanity), and how the differentiation could be maintained without separating the two. As an intermediate summary of these debates and an attempt to reach a settlement, the Chalcedonian formulation of 451 was regarded as an ecumenical compromise. Here it was attempted to reach a common acknowledgement, whereby the paradox of maintaining this difference and unity at the same time was stated:

> Therefore, following the Holy Fathers, we all with one accord teach men to acknowledge one and the same Son, our Lord Jesus Christ, at once complete in Godhead and complete in manhood, truly God and truly man, consisting also of a reasonable soul and body; of one substance (*homousios*) with the Father as regard his Godhead; and at the same time of one substance with us as regards his manhood; like us in all respects, apart from sin; as regards his Godhead, begotten of the Father before the ages, but yet as regards his manhood begotten, for us men and for our salvation, of Mary the Virgin; the God-bearer (*Theotokos*); one and the same Christ, Son, Lord, Only-begotten, recognized in two natures, without confusion, without change, without division, without separation; the distinction of nature's being in no way annulled by the union, but rather the characteristics of each nature being preserved and coming together to form one person and subsistence, not as parted or separated into two persons, but one and the same Son and Only-begotten God the Word, Lord Jesus Christ; even as the prophets from earliest times spoke of him, and our Lord Jesus Christ himself taught us, and the creed of the Fathers has handed down to us.[58]

---

54. John Macquarrie, *Jesus Christ in Modern Thought* (London: SCM Press, 3rd impr. edn, 1993), 27–146.

55. Ibid., 145.

56. Ibid., 166.

57. Ibid., 155; Oliver Crisp, *Divinity and Humanity: The Incarnation Reconsidered* (Current Issues in Theology; Cambridge: Cambridge University Press, 2007), 36–40.

58. Cited from Macquarrie, *Jesus Christ in Modern Thought*, 165.

This Chalcedonian settlement remained more or less stable until the challenge of the Enlightenment,[59] even if the theological debate obviously continued regarding a fuller understanding of Jesus Christ.[60] However, at the time of the Reformation, the Chalcedonian Christology was still considered central.[61] Characteristic for the Lutheran understanding was the concept of the *communicatio idiomatum*.[62] Even if both Macquarrie[63] and Oliver Crisp hold a critical understanding of Luther's use of this concept – Crisp even calls it 'fatally flawed'[64] – the centrality of this concept for Lutheran reformers seems beyond dispute.

Crisp distinguishes between two uses of the *communicatio idiomatum* – a weak and a strong meaning – in his analysis of the problems with the doctrine of *perichoresis*.[65] He finds the former in Pope Leo's *Tome*,[66] where the properties of the divine and human nature are both predicated on the person of Christ and yet without transferring properties from one of the natures to the other. The stronger view is represented by Luther. Here, there is 'a real transfer of (some) properties from the divine to the human nature, and vice versa'.[67] Crisp regards this as flawed, as no natures can share all properties and yet remain distinct entities. Crisp acknowledges the centrality of this concept in Lutheran theology, and yet he maintains his critique of this position as being logically impossible. Even if Crisp may be right that this is logically impossible, the question may be raised as to whether this is a sufficient criterion for the critique that he raises. Rather than seeking the logical plausibility, it is important to recognize the paradox in this position. When Luther argues for the *communicatio idiomatum*, his concern seems to be a theological truth rather than a logical truth. The centrality of this concept in Luther's theology is therefore an expression of the essential theological implications this holds for his ethics, the Eucharist, anthropology, pastoral counselling, theology of nature and rhetoric.[68] The paradoxical or mysterious nature of this reality is also an understanding that we find returning in Bonhoeffer, as we shall see later in the book.

The bulk of the book is concentrated on Bonhoeffer's Christological ethic. As he was writing his *Ethics* in the years 1940–43, his constructive attempt to formulate the ethical implications of the reconciliation of the reality of the world with the reality of God in the reality of Christ may be seen as an attempt to understand the

---

59. Ibid., 172.
60. Ibid., 165ff.
61. Ibid., 171.
62. See Chapter 2.
63. Macquarrie, *Jesus Christ in Modern Thought*, 171.
64. Crisp, *Divinity and Humanity*, 22.
65. Ibid., chapter 1 (1–33).
66. Ibid., 7.
67. Ibid., 9.
68. Steiger, 'Die communicatio idiomatum'; Steiger, *Fünf Zentralthemen*, 3–106.

meaning and significance of Jesus Christ in his days. In this sense, Bonhoeffer's question from his prison letters – 'who is Christ actually for us today?'[69] – reflected his work on *Ethics* in the immediately preceding years. It remained a central question, just as it is a central question for contemporary theology.[70] The mentioned renewed reflection on the ethical implications of Christology has also shed new light on Bonhoeffer's ethics.[71] It may be argued that Bonhoeffer's emphasis on *who* Christ is, rather than *what* Christ is seems to ponder the question in an expedient manner, given the challenges of modernity. In this sense, Bonhoeffer's emphasis could be said to reflect the Melanchthonian 'principle of reserve', when he contends that 'The mysteries of the Godhead are not so much to be investigated as adored. It is useless to labour long on the high doctrines of God, his unity and trinity, the mystery of creation, the mode of incarnation … To know Christ is to know his benefits, not to contemplate his nature or the modes of his incarnation.'[72]

However, when the book maintains interest in the Chalcedonian Christology, this is due to its centrality for the Lutheran tradition and the contention that the understanding of the unity and difference in the two natures of Christ as it is depicted in the formula of Chalcedon – and particularly in the Lutheran use of the *communicatio idiomatum* – may be fruitful for the reformulated understanding of the sources of Christian social ethics between universality and specificity. The focus on the Lutheran tradition does not, however, demarcate the book's topic from the challenge of modernity. The question here is, how can one argue for the plausibility of a Chalcedonian Christology in light of the Enlightenment? Macquarrie raises this same question, when he – with reference to Chalcedonian Christology – states that even if classical Christology had been relatively stable for thirteen centuries, this changed with the Enlightenment. '[F]rom the Enlightenment onward the situation has changed, and challenges have continually been offered both to the historical trustworthiness of the New Testament and to the theological claim that God was uniquely present and revealed in the person of Jesus Christ.'[73] Even if I widely concur with Crisp, when he states that theology should not be novel for the sake of novelty, and that 'faithfulness to a tradition is surely consistent with

---

69. Dietrich Bonhoeffer, *Letters and Papers from Prison* (ed. John W. De Gruchy; trans. Isabel Best, Lisa E. Dahill, Reinhard Krauss and Nancy Lukens; Dietrich Bonhoeffer Works; vol. 8; Minneapolis, MN: Fortress Press, 2010) (DBWE 8), 362.

70. See e.g. Schuele and Thomas, *Who Is Jesus Christ for Us Today?*

71. Christopher R. J. Holmes, '"The Indivisible Whole of God's Reality": On the Agency of Jesus in Bonhoeffer's Ethics', *International Journal of Systematic Theology* 12 (2010), 283–301; Bernd Wannenwetsch, 'The Whole Christ and the Whole Human Being: Dietrich Bonhoeffer's Inspiration for the "Christology and Ethics" Discourse', in *Christology and Ethics* (Grand Rapids, MI: W. B. Eerdmans, 2010), 75–98; Holmes, *Ethics in the Presence of Christ*; Mawson and Ziegler, *Christ, Church, and World*.

72. Macquarrie, *Jesus Christ in Modern Thought*, 171.

73. Ibid., 24.

new ways of thinking about that tradition",[74] I acknowledge the real challenges that Macquarrie outlines. In his overview of the central challenges to a contemporary Christology, he points to the historical question (whether the biblical sources give us a historically reliable understanding of Jesus Christ), the starting-point of the Christological inquiry (whether today we can do anything but approach Christology 'from below'), the problem of metaphysics (how we are to regard the strong metaphysics in classical Christology), the relation of Jesus Christ to the human race as a whole (the question about the extent and implications of the reconciliation and atonement in Jesus Christ) and, finally, the question of the uniqueness of Jesus Christ (in comparison to other saviour figures).[75]

Even if I consider these challenges to be real, it is not the aim of the book to respond to these questions. Rather, the aim is to ponder a central theological concept in the Lutheran tradition – the potential of the Chalcedonian Christology pertaining to the contemporary debate on the foundations of Christian ethics with regard to its universal and specific validity. In so doing, I conceive of the Chalcedonian Christology in a broad sense with a focus on its theological implications. Therefore, I approach the Chalcedonian Christology in a more *figurative and metaphorical sense*, where I concur with Bonhoeffer when he argues that the strength of the formula of Chalcedon also lies in its transgression of itself.[76] It is not so much the original understanding of the relation between the two substances that is of interest in the present book, but rather that the formula of Chalcedon is read as a theological expression of the differentiated unity of the reality of God and human reality in Christ. In this light the question is raised: What does this imply for the foundation of Christian ethics?

Content and structure of the book

The book is structured around seven chapters. The introductory Chapter 1 sets out the central question of the book and its thesis. In this chapter I outline the aim of the book, which is an attempt to argue for a Christian social ethics between universality and specificity primarily in light of Bonhoeffer's Chalcedonian Christology and ethics, making it possible both to affirm what we have in common as human beings and, at the same time, to call for Christians to live faithful lives bearing witness to Christ in their public lives. I hereby aim to argue for a third position beyond the antagonism of universalistic approaches, on the one hand, that tend to forget the formative role of the Christian's relation to Christ, and specific approaches to Christian ethics, on the other hand, that sometimes seem to forget that Christ was truly human and that a call to follow him is also a call to live truly human lives.

74. Crisp, *Divinity and Humanity*, xiii.
75. Macquarrie, *Jesus Christ in Modern Thought*, 339–47.
76. DBW 12, 328.

Chapter 2 moves on to Luther's social ethics and shows how the Chalcedonian Christology and particularly the *communicatio idiomatum* plays a central role in his ethics and his political thought. This lays the ground for a simultaneity of divinity and humanity in his ethics. The chapter shows what this implies with relation to his two kingdoms doctrine. During most of the twentieth century Luther's two kingdoms doctrine has played a significant role for the interpretation of his political thought. This has been at the expense of the equally (if not more) important doctrine of the three estates. Recent Luther scholars have argued for a re-appropriation of the three estates. I follow these recent readings and argue that the doctrine of the three estates substantiates a Christological interpretation of Luther's political thought. Further, I show in this chapter how the Chalcedonian motifs play a central role in Luther's theology and ethics. In an engagement with several Luther studies since the early 1990s, I argue for the centrality of both Chalcedonian motifs for Luther's theology as a whole and for the centrality of the *communicatio idiomatum* for his theological ethics. In the last part of Chapter 2 I show this reading supports an interpretation of Luther's social ethics between universality and specificity.

The following three chapters, Chapters 3–5, constitute a core contribution of the book. Within these chapters I explore more deeply Bonhoeffer's theology and ethics, and hereby argue for a reading of his texts that supports the aim of the book. Chapter 3 follows up on the interpretation of Luther's ethics and investigates if we can find a Chalcedonian Christology underlying Bonhoeffer's ethics as well. Bonhoeffer's Christology has been interpreted differently, even if all seem to argue that it plays a pivotal role for his thought. This chapter argues with reference to three specific writings of Bonhoeffer for a Chalcedonian reading and indicates the significance of this for key concepts in his ethics.

In Chapter 4 the book investigates Bonhoeffer's Christological ethics with particular focus on select central concepts in his ethic – his understanding of reality, the secular, Christonomy, reason and responsibility. The primary focus in this chapter is on his *Ethics*, which is read as a hermeneutical starting point for other texts and parts of his theology. The aim in this chapter is to see how these key concepts in Bonhoeffer's ethics can be read in light of his Chalcedonian Christology and how this supports the aim of the book to establish a position for Christian ethics between universality and specificity. With regard to reality, the book analyses different meanings of reality in Bonhoeffer and shows how he makes use of a spatial, temporal and ontological understanding of this concept. With regard to all of them we find an emphasis on a Chalcedonian understanding. When we turn to his concept of the secular, we find this motif returning. Bonhoeffer holds a positive concept of the secular, but it is important that this is understood Christologically. For Bonhoeffer, the secular is intimately related to his understanding of the Christological mystery of reality, which implies for him that there is a fullness or plenitude of reality that affirms his theological appropriation of the secular. His concept of Christonomy is closely related to his Christological interpretation of autonomy. Bonhoeffer does not endorse an autonomy separate from the Christ reality. Rather, there is only one Christ reality. Therefore the human being should rather be understood as having a Christonomy, understood as a freedom in Christ which is not in contrast to human reality. When we turn to reason as the source of moral normativity, it is essential for Bonhoeffer that reason is not understood separately from Christ. He understands Christ as the origin, centre and power of reason. This leads to an understanding of a Christological ontology as the source of reason in Bonhoeffer. The last part of this chapter turns to responsibility, where we find Bonhoeffer's understanding shaped by a deep acknowledgement of Christ as the source and form of the responsible life. Also in his understanding of responsibility we find the Chalcedonian motif recurring and shaping his understanding of responsibility as a concept that implies both an affirmation of responding to the other (and hereby the common human reality) and the Christological shaping of this response, so that the Christian bears witness in being with and for the other.

In the next chapter, Chapter 5, the explicit Bonhoeffer part of this book is brought to an end. In this chapter we investigate the implications of the differentiated unity of universality and specificity for Bonhoeffer's political thought. Here we particularly focus on the contradictory affirmation of reality, Christian ethics between participation and witness, and his Christological reshaping of natural law. Common to these themes, on the one hand, is the continuous affirmation of worldly life and human reality. On the other hand, this affirmation is never separate from its specific foundation and qualification in Christ. It is in Christ that the reality of God and the reality of the world continuously are held together in a polemical unity giving rise both to the foundation and the implications of his social ethics and political thought. In other words, Bonhoeffer's incarnational Christology reappears in his political thought as the interpretative scheme, making it possible for him to endorse a position between radicalism and compromise.

The last two chapters of the book, Chapters 6 and 7, take the argument in a constructive direction. In these last two chapters we look at the implications of our findings for the contemporary debate on Christian political thought and the question about the role of Christian voices in public. In Chapter 6 the book explores how a Christologically saturated understanding of law and justice leads to an affirmation of both the universal and specific dimensions. The chapter shows how both of these aspects are essential for the Lutheran tradition. Both are necessary and yet neither is sufficient in itself. The Lutheran understanding of natural law is read as an example of how the universal and specific dimensions are related to each other in a differentiated unity. Likewise, the humanist tradition, in some of its enlightenment and secular versions, has been read in opposition to religious forms of humanism. In light of the Chalcedonian Christology, however, this chapter argues that there is a simultaneous deep affirmation of both humanism and a Christological understanding of human reality. Finally, the chapter reflects on the concept of responsibility as an idea that can be reformulated in communicative terms. The communicative reshaping of responsibility opens up for integrating the responsive understanding of responsibility found in dialogical approaches to responsibility, and the communicative dimension implicit in the Chalcedonian understanding of the *communicatio idiomatum*.

In the final Chapter 7 an attempt is made to take a step beyond the Chalcedonian understanding of the differentiated unity between universality and specificity and hereby transcend these concepts. This is done in continuation of Bonhoeffer's recognition of the formulations of Chalcedon, and yet he points to its strength in transcending itself. The book hereby also points to the limitations of these concepts. Even if both of them express important dimensions of a Christian ethic, they are also insufficient in themselves. This points to the necessity of a 'third position'. The chapter focuses on the contemporary implications of this differentiated unity pertaining to the question of the Christian's dual citizenship, the conversation in public and how the Christian is called to bear witness also over contentious issues. The last chapter of the section demonstrates what some of the implications of the book's findings are with regard to two concrete questions: human dignity and the question of bioethics in public (with particular reference to the debate on abortion). The first topic is seen as an example, where the book substantiates a constructive conversation with other views and hereby furthers the understanding of human dignity in public. This is seen as an expression of the book's recognition of the universal dimension. The second topic is taken as a controversial question, where it is not likely that the understanding of this question will be significantly furthered in the foreseeable future, even if we aim to engage in a constructive conversation with each other. To a large extent it seems that the significant arguments have been put forward; however, this does not mean that the Christian voice no longer plays a role. The chapter argues that a Christian voice in public may still play an important role in a specific and distinctive critique of prevailing wrongs. Hereby, these two last examples demonstrate how the book's findings lead to a position between universality and specificity and how these dimensions are understood as being in a differentiated unity with each other.

The Conclusion summarizes the book's main findings as a whole.

Chapter 2

THE SIMULTANEITY OF DIVINITY AND HUMANITY IN LUTHER'S SOCIAL ETHICS

The book situates its reflections on the differentiated unity between universality and specificity in the Lutheran tradition. This is due to several circumstances. Apart from the reasons mentioned in the introduction – the particular pertinence of this topic to the Lutheran tradition, the Lutheran background of Bonhoeffer's theology and the immediacy of this background for the author – the emphasis on this tradition follows from its significance for the contemporary debate. The Lutheran reformation marks a watershed in Western political thought in the understanding of the relation between the ecclesial and worldly authorities. This is a reasonable claim, even if we do not hereby contend that Luther was a particularly clear political thinker.[1] Luther's social ethics is one of those parts of his thought which continues to challenge Luther scholars. His thinking on these issues has been very differently assessed. Critics have argued that Luther was confused and inconsistent.[2] Others have claimed that he was opportunistic.[3] Luther himself was not in doubt concerning the importance of his political thought. According to himself, no one since the apostles had spoken so clearly on the worldly authority. 'Indeed, I might boast here that not since the time of

---

1. For a fine introduction to Luther's role and place in the history of political philosophy and his significance for contemporary political theology, see Michael Richard Laffin, *The Promise of Martin Luther's Political Theology: Freeing Luther from the Modern Political Narrative* (ed. Brian Brock and Susan F. Parsons; T&T Clark Enquiries in Theological Ethics; London: Bloomsbury T&T Clark, 2016), introduction (1–28). Laffin's book as a whole has this as a topic. Some parts of the following chapter draw on Ulrik Nissen, 'Between Unity and Differentiation. On the Identity of Lutheran Social Ethics', in *The Sources of Public Morality – On the Ethics and Religion Debate* (ed. Ulrik Nissen, Svend Andersen and Lars Reuter; Societas Ethica, Europäische Forschungsgesellschaft für Ethik; Münster: LIT, 2003), 152–71.

2. See J. W. Allen, *A History of Political Thought in the Sixteenth Century* (repr., London: Methuen, 1977), 15.

3. See Alister E. McGrath, *Reformation Thought: An Introduction* (Oxford, UK and Cambridge, MA: Basil Blackwell, 2nd edn,1993), 210.

the apostles have the temporal sword and temporal government been so clearly described or so highly praised as by me.'[4] Even if we may agree with Luther – if not on the clarity of his political thought, then at least on the importance of his influence – we still cannot avoid reflecting on some of the tensions within this part of his thought. One of these tensions is the relation between his two kingdoms doctrine and his teaching on the three estates. The relation between these two is discussed in the first part of this chapter. Even if these concepts are central in Luther, the book argues for a reading of Luther where the Chalcedonian motifs are emphasized. This constitutes the focus of the second part of this chapter. These motifs substantiate the book's aim to argue for a 'differentiated unity of universality and specificity' in Luther's social ethics, which is the topic of the last part of the chapter.

From two kingdoms doctrine to three estates

Luther's political thought can be approached by his two uses of the law.[5] These explain how Luther speaks of a political and a theological use of the law. Both are found in one of Luther's central texts, namely his commentary from 1535 on Paul's letter to the Galatians.[6] This is closely related to Luther's understanding of the double concept of justice; that is, his distinction between the outer, political justice *coram hominibus* and the inner, spiritual justice *coram Deo*.[7] This distinction enables Luther to argue that the law is good and useful. The double use of the law, like the corresponding notion of a double concept of justice, is closely related to his understanding of the two kingdoms (*Reiche*)[8] or governments

---

4. Martin Luther, *Whether Soldiers, Too, Can Be Saved* (ed. and rev. Robert C. Schultz; trans. Charles M. Jacobs; Luther's Works 46: The Christian in Society III; Philadelphia, PA: Fortress Press, [1526] 1967) (LW 46), 95.

5. This brief summary of Luther's political thought draws upon the findings in my previous study on the reformers' political thought and the rise of early modern contractarianism, see Ulrik Nissen, *Påberåbelsen af lex naturalis i diskussionen om statsmagtens legitimitet i det 16. århundredes lutherske, reformerte og anglikanske teologi, og denne diskussions betydning for opkomsten af den moderne idé om samfunds-kontrakten* (Aarhus: AU Library Scholarly Publishing Services, Aarhus Universitet, 2019), 24–76.

6. Martin Luther, *In epistolam S. Pauli ad Galatas commentarius ex praelectione* (herausgegeben von U. Freitag; Weimar: H. Böhlau, [1531, 1535] 1911) (WA 40 I), 429–30; WA 40 I, 479–80; WA 40 I, 485, 23ff.; WA 40 I, 528, 6ff.

7. WA 40 I, 40ff.; WA 40 I, 208–09; WA 40 I, 393, 21ff.; WA 40 I, 554, 15ff.

8. Martin Luther, *Von weltlicher Oberkeit, wie weit man ihr Gehorsam schuldig sei* (Weimar: H. Böhlau, [1523] 1900), WA 11, 251, 1–8; Martin Luther, *Ein Sendbrief von dem harten Büchlein wider die Bauern* (Weimar: H. Böhlau, [1525] 1908) (WA 18), 389, 14–26.

(*Regimente*)⁹ (without making any sharp terminological distinction between the two): a worldly and a spiritual, respectively.¹⁰ As there are two kingdoms, there also must be two forms of government. This plays a central role in Luther's writing on worldly authority, *Temporal Authority: To What Extent It Should Be Obeyed*.¹¹ The worldly government is instituted by God in order to uphold the world.¹² This government is part of God's *creatio continua*, His continuous presence and creative work within creation. Here the law assumes its political use (*usus politicus*) in upholding worldly order and peace. The spiritual government is upheld by the word. It is the kingdom of mercy and compassion.¹³ In this kingdom, love (and not law) is the rule. Here the law assumes its theological use (*usus theologicus*) where it leads to Christ. Just as when he explains the two uses of the law, so Luther also stresses the necessity of a sharp distinction when dealing with the two kingdoms and governments.¹⁴ They are not to be confused. Both are divine orders, although quite different from one another.¹⁵ They describe two very different ways in which God is at work in the world.

It is important to note that the two kingdoms are differentiated, and yet both are derived from the will of God. Therefore, there is an underlying unity between the two. Hereby, Luther can maintain the worldly use of the law as differentiated from its spiritual use, just as he can maintain the differentiation of the worldly kingdom from the spiritual. But even if they are differentiated, Luther still understands the two uses of the law and the two kingdoms as having the same origin, the same source – i.e. the will of God. In this sense, we can speak of a 'theonomy' in Luther, i.e. the will of God as the source and origin of the law. It is this understanding which also lies behind Luther's understanding of the worldly

9. WA 11, 251, 15–21; Martin Luther, *Ob Kriegsleute auch in seligem Stande sein können* (Weimar: H. Böhlau, [1526] 1908) (WA 19), 629, 17–25.

10. I do not find a consistent use of the distinction between these two concepts in Luther, see Nissen, 'Between Unity and Differentiation', 155. But even if the terminology is not consistent in Luther, there is a duality between the two regiments/governments. Laffin introduces a new and fruitful understanding of Luther's two *ecclesiae* based on a reading of his Genesis lectures and shows how this sheds a new light on his two kingdoms doctrine, see Laffin, *The Promise of Martin Luther's Political Theology*, 98–111. For a wider discussion of 'the doctrine of the two', see Oliver O'Donovan, *The Desire of the Nations: Rediscovering the Roots of Political Theology* (Cambridge: Cambridge University Press, 1996), 193–211.

11. Martin Luther, *Temporal Authority: To What Extent It Should Be Obeyed* (ed. and rev. Walther I. Brandt; trans. J. J. Schindel; Luther's Works 45: The Christian in Society II; Philadelphia, PA: Mühlenberg Press, [1523] 1962) (LW 45), 75–129.

12. WA 11, 247, 21ff.

13. WA 18, 389, 19ff.; WA 19, 629, 18ff.

14. WA 11, 249–53, 262, 3–15.

15. WA 11, 252, 12–23.

authority as the masks of God, *larvae Dei*[16] or *Gottes mummerey*.[17] The worldly authority is understood as God's servant,[18] or God's instruments or co-operators (*cooperatores*).[19] He can even speak of the political rulers as gods.[20] Hereby, Luther emphasizes that, even in their human and worldly appearances and functions, they are expressions of the will of God[21] – and God may be regarded as present within these orders.

In Luther's political thought there is an equally important – or, some would argue, an even more fundamental – concept: the understanding of the three estates.[22] Here, Luther's main idea is that no calling is particularly sacred, or particularly worldly. The spiritual calling is not confined to the priestly order, but extends into the 'secular' realm. Likewise, the worldly calling is not restricted to the 'secular' realm. Rather than speaking of two orders, one should instead speak of the spiritual calling that covers three areas of life, or three estates. Luther distinguishes between the estates of *ecclesia*, *oeconomia* and *politia*. These three estates have different functions. For the church (*ecclesia*), the primary function is to preach the word of God. The church is defined by this preaching. For the household (*oeconomia*), the main task is to nurture and provide for the family. This estate concerns the relations between parents and children, between family and work, and so on. For the political order (*politia*), the main concern is governing the common, public life and civic order. Luther's understanding of the origin and relation between the three estates can be summarized with a reference to his exegesis of Gen. 2.16, in which the *ecclesia* is regarded as the basic estate, and as the one preceding the other two estates. The *oeconomia* and *politia* are thus defined by their relation to God:

> Here we have the establishment of the church before there was any government of the home and of the state; for Eve was not yet created. Moreover, the church is established without walls and without any pomp, in a very spacious and very delightful place. After the church has been established, the household government is also set up, when Eve is added to Adam as his companion. Thus

---

16. WA 40 I, 175, 17ff.; WA 40 I, 176, 27ff.

17. Martin Luther, *Der 127. Psalm ausgelegt an die Christen zu Riga in Liesland* (Weimar: H. Böhlau, [1524] 1899) (WA 15), 373, 5–17.

18. WA 11, 257, 29ff.; Martin Luther, *Vorlesung über die Stufenpsalmen. Psalmus CXXVII* (herausgegeben von U. Freitag; Weimar: H. Böhlau, [1532/33, 1540] 1930) (WA 40 III), 210, 34; Martin Luther, *Auslegung des 101. Psalms* (herausgegeben von E. Thiele and O. Brenner; Weimar: H. Böhlau, [1534–35] 1914) (WA 51), 254, 18ff.

19. WA 40 III, 210, 35ff.; WA 40 III, 214, 20ff.; WA 40 III, 236, 29ff.

20. Martin Luther, *Der 82. Psalm ausgelegt* (herausgegeben von E. Thiele; Weimar: H. Böhlau, [1530] 1913) (WA 31 I), 191, 22; 192, 4; 192, 12; 201, 19; 202, 1; 202, 4.

21. WA 11, 247, 21; WA 19, 629, 14ff.; WA 19, 653, 5ff.; WA 31 I, 190ff.; WA 40 III, 208, 31f.; WA 40 III, 267, 30ff.; WA 51, 238, 19ff.

22. Oswald Bayer, *Freiheit als Antwort: zur theologischen Ethik* (Tübingen: Mohr, 1995), 121.

2. The Simultaneity of Divinity and Humanity in Luther's Social Ethics

the temple is earlier than the home, and it is also better this way. Moreover, there was no government of the state before sin, for there was no need of it. Civil government is a remedy required by our corrupted nature. It is necessary that lust be held in check by the bonds of the laws and by penalties.[23]

In Luther's understanding of these fundamental traits in his political thought, the 'worldly' and the 'spiritual' are distinguished – or differentiated – but are not separated. The two uses of the law are both understood as expressions of the will of God and in this sense have a common foundation. Likewise, the two kingdoms are distinguished from each other and yet both have their source in the will of God. Lastly, the three estates are understood with regard to their different functions, but they still have a common basis in their relation to God's will. Therefore, the worldly or mundane dimension of the will of God is of no lesser concern to Luther than the spiritual or ecclesial function of the law. Rather, these two dimensions may be seen as resting in a differentiated unity that could be seen as an expression of the Chalcedonian motif, which is so central to Luther's theology and ethics.

Chalcedonian motifs in Luther's theology and ethics

Several studies demonstrate the centrality of Christological themes in Luther's ethics, despite their different accentuations.[24] Marc Lienhard follows this observation when he opens his study on Luther's Christology with a quotation from Luther's commentary to the Galatians: 'For in my heart only this article rules, namely faith in Christ, from whom, by whom and to whom all my theological thoughts flow back and forth night and day. Still, I do not believe to have comprehended more than the weakest and lowliest beginning, indeed, only

---

23. Martin Luther, *Lectures on Genesis, Chapters 1–5* (ed. Jaroslav Pelikan; trans. George V. Schick; Luther's Works 1; Saint Louis, MO: Concordia Publishing House, 1964) (LW 1), 103–4.

24. Tuomo Mannermaa, *Der im Glauben gegenwärtige Christus. Rechtfertigung und Vergottung. Zum ökumenischen Dialog* (Arbeiten zur Geschichte und Theologie des Luthertums; N.F., band 8; Hannover: Lutherisches Verlagshaus, 1989); Dietmar Lage, *Martin Luther's Christology and Ethics* (Texts and Studies in Religion; Lewiston, NY: Edwin Mellen Press, 1990); Bayer, *Freiheit als Antwort*; Antti Raunio, *Summe des Christlichen Lebens: die 'Goldene Regel' als Gesetz der Liebe in der Theologie Martin Luthers von 1510–1527* (Veröffentlichungen des Instituts für Europäische Geschichte Mainz, Abteilung für abendländische Religionsgeschichte; 160; Mainz: Philipp von Zabern, 2001); Veli-Matti Kärkkäinen, '"The Christian as Christ to the Neighbour": On Luther's Theology of Love', *International Journal of Systematic Theology* 6, no. 2 (2004), 101–17; Antti Raunio, 'Faith and Christian Living in Luther's Confession Concerning Christ's Supper (1528)', *Lutherjahrbuch* 76 (2009), 19–56.

a small part of the height, breadth, and depth of this wisdom.'[25] This is essential in his understanding of justification by faith and in several other crucial debates. One of the sustained characteristics of his theology is the affirmative view on Chalcedonian Christology.[26] Several relatively recent Luther studies demonstrate the centrality of this motif for Luther's ecclesiology, theology, political thought etc., not least the *communicatio idiomatum*.[27]

> Luther was the first one to place it into the center of Christology, indeed, in that of theology as a whole. For him the communication of attributes is articulated and becomes the central concept for describing and articulating the person of Jesus Christ and the work that was completed by him – neither the person nor the work is ever to be isolated from the other![28]

What is important to note is that the *communicatio idiomatum* is not just central for Luther's Christology, but is an underlying mode of thought for his theology as a whole. Therefore, we find this concept as a recurring motif pertaining to several issues.

When it comes to the doctrine of the *communicatio idiomatum*, Luther stands on the foundation laid by the theology of the early church. Yet at the same time, he carries this doctrine to its peak and radicalizes it as he makes it the

---

25. WA 40 I, 33, 7ff. (my translation). See Marc Lienhard, *Martin Luthers christologisches Zeugnis: Entwicklung und Grundzüge seiner Christologie* (Göttingen: Vandenhoeck & Ruprecht, 1980), 9.

26. See Nissen, 'Between Unity and Differentiation'; Ulrik Nissen, 'Reconciliation and Public Law: Christian Reflections about the Sources of Public Law', *Studia theologica* 58, no. 1 (2004), 27–44; Ulrik Nissen, 'Social Ethics Between Universality and Specificity: Outline of a Chalcedonian Social Ethic', *Dialog* 51, no. 1 (2012), 83–91.

27. Kjell Ove Nilsson, *Simul. Das Miteinander von Göttlichem und Menschlichem in Luthers Theologie* (Göttingen: Vandenhoeck & Ruprecht, 1966); Johann Anselm Steiger, 'Die communicatio idiomatum als Achse und Motor der Theologie Luthers: Der "fröhliche Wechsel" als hermeneutischer Schlüssel zu Abendmahlslehre, Anthropologie, Seelsorge, Naturtheologie, Rhetorik und Humor', *Neue Zeitschrift für systematische Theologie und Religionsphilosophie* 38, no. 1 (1996), 1–28; Johann Anselm Steiger, *Fünf Zentralthemen der Theologie Luthers und seiner Erben: Communicatio, Imago, Figura, Maria, Exempla* (Studies in the History of Christian Thought; vol. 104; Leiden: Brill, 2002), 104; Dennis Ngien, 'Chalcedonian Christology and Beyond: Luther's Understanding of the Communicatio Idiomatum', *The Heythrop Journal* 45, no. 1 (2004), 54–68; Bo Kristian Holm, *Gabe und Geben bei Luther. Das Verhältnis zwischen Reziprozität und reformatorischer Rechtfertigungslehre* (Theologische Bibliothek Töpelmann; 134; Berlin: W. de Gruyter, 2006), 190–95; Oswald Bayer, *Creator est creatura: Luthers Christologie als Lehre von der Idiomenkommunikation* (Theologische Bibliothek Töpelmann; 138; Berlin: W. de Gruyter, 2007).

28. Oswald Bayer, *Martin Luther's Theology: A Contemporary Interpretation* [Martin Luthers Theologie] (trans. Thomas H. Trapp; Grand Rapids, MI: W. B. Eerdmans, 2008), 236.

hermeneutical motor of his whole theology, or an axle around which many other theological themes now begin to turn: not only Christology, but also the doctrine of the Lord's Supper, anthropology, the doctrine of justification, scriptural hermeneutics, rhetoric, the theology of pastoral care and the theology of creation.[29]

Hereby, this concept is understood in a broader sense, which is an understanding that we will see reappearing in Bonhoeffer and which becomes central to the book's aim.

The *communicatio idiomatum* is seen throughout Luther's theology, e.g. in early writings such as his treatise on Christian liberty, *The Freedom of a Christian* from 1520,[30] and in later writings such as his *On the Councils and the Church* from 1539[31] and his disputation on the divinity and humanity of Christ from 1540.[32] In the disputation Luther explicitly concurs with the *communicatio idiomatum* in his understanding of the relation between the two natures of Christ and the implication that the things pertaining to man are rightly said of God, and the things pertaining to God are said of man.[33] In *On the Councils* he explicitly reflects on Chalcedon.[34] He affirms the understanding of the two natures of Christ as depicted in the formula of Chalcedon, even if for him the authority does not lie in the council, but rather in Scripture's affirmation of the divine and human idiomata in Christ.[35] The affirmative view on Chalcedon is also found in a sermon on Colossians 1 from 1537.[36] Luther teaches that Paul understands Christ as truly divine and human and yet he is one person, and he emphasizes the importance of this understanding for the life, death and resurrection of Christ. He sums it up with the notion of the *communicatio idiomatum* and shows how this is an expression of the simultaneous unity and difference of the divine and human nature in Christ.

The affirmative understanding of the *communicatio idiomatum* plays a central role in several of his key notions. It has already been mentioned how numerous studies point to the importance of this concept for several topics in Luther's theology. This is not least the case for his understanding of the Lord's Supper.

29. Johann Anselm Steiger, 'The Communicatio Idiomatum as the Axle and Motor of Luther's Theology', *Lutheran Quarterly* 14, no. 2 (2000), 125-58 (125).

30. Martin Luther, *Von der Freiheit eines Christenmenschen* (Weimar: H. Böhlau, [1520] 1897) (WA 7), 12-38.

31. Martin Luther, *Von den Konziliis und Kirchen* (herausgegeben von F. Cohrs and O. Brenner; Weimar: H. Böhlau, [1539] 1914) (WA 50), 488-653.

32. Martin Luther, *Die Disputation de divinitate et humanitate Christi* (Weimar: H. Böhlau, [28 February 1540] 1932) (WA 39 II), 92-121.

33. Ibid., 93, 2-7.

34. WA 50, 592-605.

35. Ibid., 603-6.

36. Martin Luther, *Von Jhesu Christo Warem Gott und Menschen und von seinem Ampt und Reich, so er führt in der Christenheit. Die Ander Predigt, Von der Menschheit Christi und seinem Ampt* (Weimar: H. Böhlau, [1537] 1911) (WA 45), 297-324.

For Luther it was important to maintain that Christ was present 'in, with, and under' the bread and wine.[37] Hereby, he emphasized that the bread and wine did not cease to be bread and wine, just as Christ was not identified with the bread and wine. But at the same time the *est* implied that the bread and wine *is* the blood and body of Jesus Christ, and that there is a real presence of Christ in the bread and wine. As we shall see later, Bonhoeffer refers to this Lutheran understanding of the real presence of Christ in the bread and wine when he applies it to his understanding of the worldly reality. He argues along the same lines – the world remains world, and yet Christ is really present 'in, with, and under' the worldly reality.[38] Further, the *communicatio idiomatum* is central in his *Confession Concerning Christ's Supper* from 1528, where Luther against Zwingli argues for his understanding, how Christ at the same time can be both in heaven and yet present in the bread and wine.[39] In order to explain this simultaneous differentiation and unity, Luther refers to the doctrine of the incarnation. Just as God is different from and yet one with man in Jesus Christ, so it is with the bread and wine. The divinity and humanity of Jesus Christ are different, and yet there is a real communication of properties between them. '[S]ince the divinity and humanity are one in Christ, the Scriptures ascribe to the divinity, because of this personal union, all that happens to humanity, and vice versa.'[40] In the same way, Christ can be present in the bread and wine, even if he is also in heaven. To sustain this viewpoint, Luther distinguishes between three different forms of presence: (1) a locally, circumscribed sense – according to which something is present in a physical sense; (2) a definitive, uncircumscribed understanding – pertaining to which something is present, even if not empirically verifiable; and (3) a repletive or supernatural being – whereby something can be present simultaneously in all places.[41] It is according to this last understanding that Luther can make use of a communication of properties and hereby argue for the simultaneous presence of divinity and humanity in Christ.

> But now, since he is a man who is supernaturally one person with God, and apart from this man there is no God, it must follow that according to the third supernatural mode, he is and can be wherever God is and that everything is full

---

37. Martin Luther, *Deudsch Catechismus (Der Große Katechismus)* (Weimar: H. Böhlau, [1529] 1910) (WA 30 I), 223, 22ff.; Martin Luther, *Die Konkordienformel* (bearbeitet von Irene Dingel; Göttingen: Vandenhoeck & Ruprecht, 2014) (BSELK, 1468–71).

38. See Chapter 4, particularly the section entitled 'Christonomy as the Foundation of the Human Condition'.

39. Martin Luther, *Vom Abendmahl Christi, Bekenntnis* (herausgegeben von E. Thiele and O. Brenner; Weimar: H. Böhlau, [1528] 1909) (WA 26), 318, 1ff.

40. Martin Luther, *Confession Concerning Christ's Supper* (ed. and trans. Robert H. Fischer; Luther's Works 37: Word and Sacrament 3; Philadelphia, PA: Fortress Press, [1528] 1961) (LW 37), 210.

41. WA 26, 327, 20ff.

of Christ through and through, even according to his humanity – not according to the first, corporeal, circumscribed mode, but according to the supernatural, divine mode. Here you must take your stand and say that wherever Christ is according to his divinity, he is there as a natural, divine person and he is also naturally and personally there, as his conception in his mother's womb proves conclusively. For if he was the Son of God, he had to be in his mother's womb naturally and personally and become man. But if he is present naturally and personally wherever he is, then he must be man there, too, since he is not two separate persons but a single person. Wherever this person is, it is the single, indivisible person, and if you can say, 'Here is God,' then you must also say, 'Christ the man is present too.'[42]

In the present book, it is important to note that this concept is also significant for Luther's ethics. Bo Kristian Holm formulates it accordingly: 'Before this background [i.e. the centrality of the *communicatio idiomatum* (my note)] Luther can say that the divinity, which the believer is given, must show itself "*efficax in humanitate*"… As the Christian is helped by Christ, so the Christian must help the neighbour.'[43] This ethical implication of Luther's *communicatio idiomatum* is particularly clear in his *The Freedom of a Christian*, where he explains how the freedom of the Christian is to be understood. He takes his starting point as his famous paradoxical statement: 'A Christian is a perfectly free lord of all, subject to none. A Christian is a perfectly dutiful servant of all, subject to all.'[44] This leads Luther to an understanding of the Christian as having two natures – spiritual and bodily.[45] With regard to the spiritual (inner) nature, the Christian is free from the physical world and is nourished by the gospel. Steiger comments on this passage in Luther, and argues that this is an expression of how the *communicatio idiomatum* substantiates an ethical responsibility, where the Christian becomes like Christ and therefore enters into a change and exchange with the suffering and troubled fellow human being.

> Like Christ, also 'any one Christian person… [is] of two natures'. Christians are Lords and servants, but precisely in their servitude is freedom concrete, a freedom for self-emptying and taking on ethical responsibility… For, to be a Christ to the neighbour always means to enter into a change and exchange with the suffering and troubled, and thus to carry their load (Gal. 6.2) and suffer with them – to exercise sympathy (συμπάθεια, 1 Cor. 12.26).[46]

---

42. LW 37, 218.
43. Holm, *Gabe und Geben bei Luther*, 192 (my translation).
44. Martin Luther, *The Freedom of a Christian* (ed. and rev. Harold J. Grimm; trans. W. A. Lambert; Luther's Works 31: Career of the Reformer 1; Philadelphia, PA: Fortress Press, [1520] 1957) (LW 31), 344.
45. Ibid.
46. Steiger, 'The Communicatio Idiomatum', 134.

In this becoming like Christ and being a Christ for the other as the foundation of Christian ethics, we have a significant motif that we will find returning in Bonhoeffer.[47]

In this exchange with Christ, it is faith alone that justifies and nothing that the Christian can do by him- or herself can justify him or her before God. 'If you believe, you shall have all things; if you do not believe, you shall lack all things.'[48] Luther links this with the so-called 'happy exchange' (*der fröhliche Wechsel*) and argues that this is resembled in the relation between the two natures of Christ.

> Christ is God and man in one person. He has neither sinned nor died, and is not condemned, and he cannot sin, die, or be condemned; his righteousness, life, and salvation are unconquerable, eternal, and omnipotent. By the wedding ring of faith he shares in the sins, death, and pains of hell which are his bride's. As a matter of fact, he makes them his own and acts as if they were his own and as if he himself had sinned.[49]

So just as there is an exchange of properties between the two natures of Christ, in faith there is an exchange between the righteousness of Christ and the sinfulness of the human being. In this sense Luther understands the justification by faith and Christian life in light of a fundamental exchange of properties (*communicatio idiomatum*), which he compares with the relation between the divine and human nature of Jesus Christ.

Luther's social ethics between universality and specificity

Having seen how Chalcedonian Christology, not least the *communicatio idiomatum*, is central to Luther's theology and ethics, we can now ponder the importance of this concept for Luther's social ethics and its pertinence for the attempt to establish a differentiated unity of universality and specificity. We can assess the significance of this motif with regard to central concepts in Luther's social ethics, such as e.g. his understanding of natural law and reason.[50] With regard to the former, it may be argued that in some contemporary interpretations there is a risk of forgetting the dialectic arising from natural law's foundation in the will of God and its universality in all mankind. This is regrettable, as Luther maintains both sides. On the one hand, Luther argues for natural law as being common to all mankind and, in this sense, being universal. This relation is so close that natural law is inseparable

---

47. See Chapter 4, particularly the section entitled 'Responsibility and Christological Responsiveness'.

48. LW 31, 348–49.

49. Ibid., 351–52.

50. See Nissen, 'Between Unity and Differentiation'; Nissen, 'Reconciliation and Public Law'; Nissen, 'Social Ethics Between Universality and Specificity'.

from human nature,⁵¹ and Luther can even speak simply of nature teaching natural law.⁵² However, on the other hand, Luther also emphasizes that this 'naturalness' of natural law cannot be separated from its foundation in the will of God. Natural law is implanted or inscribed in the human being.⁵³

This simultaneous divine and human dimension of natural law is an expression of a unity and yet differentiation which holds an important theological insight in the understanding of God's relation to mankind. This reading also finds support in Kjell Ove Nilsson's *Simul. Das Miteinander von Göttlichem und Menschlichem in Luthers Theologie*, where it is argued that the simultaneity of the divine and the human is a fundamental theme throughout Luther's theology.⁵⁴ Nilsson demonstrates, among other things, that this notion is inspired by a Chalcedonian Christology and implies a continuous unity and difference between the divine and the human.⁵⁵ This is seen e.g. in Luther's understanding of natural law. Luther understands natural law as fundamentally determined by the will of God and therefore not as rationalistic moral principles that may be separated from its divine origins.⁵⁶ 'For Luther natural law is an expression of God's revelation and work and not of human principles. It is not about an autonomous natural knowledge of God and his will, but about God's action and revelation... Luther's understanding of natural law is thoroughly theocentric and religiously determined and an expression of his doctrine of creation.'⁵⁷ At the same time, natural law finds its expression in concrete human relations.⁵⁸ Hereby, the divine and human dimensions of natural law reflect an incarnational motif that reflects the centrality of the *communicatio idiomatum*.⁵⁹ When the universality is endorsed without due consideration of its necessary relation to the will of God, Luther's understanding

---

51. Martin Luther, *Wider die himmlischen Propheten, von den Bildern und Sakrament* (herausgegeben von O. Brenner and H. Barge; Weimar: H. Böhlau, [1525] 1908) (WA 18), 80, 35ff.

52. WA 11, 279, 19f.; Martin Luther, *Ein unterrichtung wie sich die Christen ynn Mosen sollen schicken, gepredigt durch Mart. Luther* (Weimar: H. Böhlau, [1527] 1900) (WA 24), 9, 20.

53. Martin Luther, *Fastenpostille. Am Vierden Sonntag nach Epiphanie. Epistel S. Pauli zu den Romern ca. xiii* (begonnen von E. Thiele, vollendet von G. Buchwald; Weimar: H. Böhlau, [1525] 1927) (WA 17 II), 102, 8; WA 17 II, 102, 39; WA 18, 80, 28ff.; WA 24, 6, 14ff.; WA 24, 9, 20ff.; WA 24, 10, 4ff.; WA 30 I, 192, 19; WA 39 I, 426, 9ff.; WA 39 I, 454, 4f.; WA 39 I, 478, 16ff. See also Nissen, *Påberåbelsen af lex naturalis*, 33–35.

54. Nilsson, *Simul*.

55. Ibid., 28–29.

56. Ibid., 42.

57. Ibid. (my translation).

58. Ibid., 43–44.

59. Ibid., 35–36, 91–96.

of natural law is at risk of being read too modernistically. In contrast to such a reading, the current book argues that the two dimensions of the origin in the divine will and its universal validity are to be seen as resting in a differentiated unity that resembles the relationship between the two natures of Christ in Chalcedon.[60]

Luther's understanding of reason may be said to hold the same pattern as in natural law. Even if Luther's understanding of reason is equivocal, we find an affirmation of both its general ability in ordering worldly affairs and the emphasis that this is due to the will of God.[61] In this sense Luther maintains both its universality and its specific foundation in the divine will. The political and worldly abilities of reason play an important role in Luther's political thought. This endows the human being with a moral capacity pertaining to human affairs which implies a universal dimension of Luther's understanding of reason. However, at the same time he does not give up on the divine foundation of this universality. The human being is capable of judging rightly and justly, because God sustains and upholds the human being in these tasks and responsibilities. It may be contended that this double-sidedness of reason implies a Chalcedonian motif similar to the one found in natural law.

This fundamental theme also has important implications for Luther's understanding of the hidden presence of God within human reality and in the worldly order, as we have seen in the outline of Luther's political thought. This may be read as an incarnational understanding of the relationship between God the creator and the affirmation of the worldly order reflecting the Chalcedonian motif.[62] In the current book this reading is sustained by a focus on three exegetical texts.[63] The focus on these texts is due to (1) their importance for Luther's social ethics; (2) the fact that they are not prone to the same degree of dependence on circumstances, as is the case in many other political writings of his; and (3) the fact that they may contribute to the somewhat overlooked sides of Luther's political thought.

---

60. We can therefore speak of a theonomy behind Luther's understanding of reason. This is also why it is problematic to read Luther as a forerunner of modernity, as we will return to later (particularly in Chapter 6). I am therefore also sympathetic to the aim in Laffin's recent book, where he wishes to disentangle Luther from a modernistic confinement, see Laffin, *The Promise of Martin Luther's Political Theology*.

61. See Ulrik Nissen, 'Letting Reality Become Real: On Mystery and Reality in Dietrich Bonhoeffer's Ethics', *Journal of Religious Ethics* 39, no. 2 (2011), 321–43; Nissen, 'Social Ethics Between Universality and Specificity'.

62. Nilsson, *Simul*, 91.

63. For a more elaborate analysis of these psalms, see Nissen, 'Between Unity and Differentiation'. For an elaborative account of how the Psalms in general can be formative for theological ethics, see Brian Brock, *Singing the Ethos of God: On the Place of Christian Ethics in Scripture* (Grand Rapids, MI: W. B. Eerdmans, 2007). Chapter 7 focuses directly on Luther's exegesis of the Psalms.

We can find the Chalcedonian motif in Luther's social ethics in his exegesis of Psalm 82,[64] Psalm 101[65] and Psalm 127.[66] In Luther's exegesis of Psalm 82 we find some significant passages on Luther's understanding of the political ruler's responsibility for the citizens' spiritual welfare. Psalm 82 does not speak explicitly of the political office. A plain reading of the text says only that God stands as the judge among the gods. God accuses the gods of judging unjustly, for which they shall be punished accordingly. It is not clear who the gods and their obligations are. As such, Psalm 82 is open to interpretation, and this is the point where Luther's exegesis becomes truly interesting. Luther reads the psalm as though it relates to political office. The political rulers are the congregation of gods whom God will judge. If they judge unjustly, they will receive due punishment, and they are to conduct themselves in office in accordance with the will of God.

Luther understands the temporal estate as a divine ordinance, which is why it must be respected and honoured accordingly.[67] The political rulers are to be reminded of the responsibilities that follow from this status. As a divine ordinance the temporal estate is always dependent upon the continuous blessing of God. The political rule is only upheld for as long as it remains in accordance with the will of God.[68]

> Now, because this is not a matter of human will or devising, but God Himself appoints and preserves all authority, and if He no longer held it up, it would all fall down, even though all the world held it fast – therefore it is rightly called a divine thing, a divine ordinance. And such persons are rightly called divine, godlike, or gods; especially is this so when, beside the institution itself, we have a word or command of God for it, as among the people of Israel, where the priests, princes, and kings were appointed by the oral command and word of God.[69]

Therefore, obedience or resistance is not only due to the political ruler, but also to God. God is the qualifier of the political rule. The ordinance is divine – and therefore must be respected – but it is also subordinated to God, as God is the one who has instituted the ordinance. This also implies that all communities and congregations have their source in the will of God – even Nineveh.[70]

This understanding of God as the power who has established the political community, and the power who has instituted the political ordinance, goes to the

---

64. WA 31 I, 189–218.
65. WA 51, 197–264.
66. WA 15, 348–79.
67. WA 31 I, 191, 32ff.
68. Ibid., 191.
69. Martin Luther, *Psalm 82* (ed. Jaroslav Pelikan; trans. C. M. Jacobs; rev. Walther I. Brandt; Luther's Works 13: Selected Psalms II; Saint Louis, MO: Concordia Publishing House, 1956) (LW 13), 44.
70. WA 31 I, 193, 29ff.

very root of the political order. This implies that political leadership is not confined to strictly political issues, but is rather extended to a certain responsibility for spiritual affairs. That is why Luther can also argue that 'the prince' is to be held responsible for the teaching of the church, why the godly prince is also called a 'savior, father, deliverer'.[71] The prince is responsible for advancing the word of God and should not tolerate blasphemy and other ungodliness.[72] By safeguarding the law of God, the prince secures peace for the state.

Turning to Psalm 101, we see how Luther understands this psalm as a mirror of the political authority. His exegesis of this psalm touches upon several ideas central to the aim of the current book. Of particular pertinence is Luther's understanding of the divine constitution of political authority. Luther emphasizes the political authority as being a gift from God.[73] Therefore, it is also an expression of God's good will when he calls and equips the so-called *Wunderleute* (miraculous people) to become particularly good political leaders.[74] These *Wunderleute* can be found in many different contexts, and some of the most outstanding are godless or pagan.[75] These *Wunderleute* know the natural law better than other people.[76] This also implies that the pagan writings and insights with regard to the worldly kingdom often are preferable to those of the Christian. In many ways, the pagan writers are more clever with regard to worldly affairs than many Christians.[77] So even if Luther understands the worldly authority as a gift from God, he goes at length to argue for the naturalness of its praxis. God is at work under disguise and works through the pagan and godless rulers.[78]

Moving on to Luther's exegesis of Psalm 127, the main aim of the text is to deal with covetousness and to turn the attention towards faith in God.[79] In the political realm, too, faith and trust in God should be the guiding principle.[80] Whether a certain community or dominion endures or thrives is down to its faith and trust in God, so ultimately safety, security and happiness all depend on God's gracious blessings. Man cannot ensure these things by worrying about them. Rather, all such things are to be expected as gifts from God. This is the overall theme of this exposition. However, Luther explains how one should commit oneself with diligence in both the private household and in the political realm. Luther even

---

71. LW 13, 58.
72. WA 31 I, 207, 33ff.
73. WA 51, 201, 30ff., 205, 8ff.
74. Ibid., 207, 21ff.
75. Ibid., 207, 30ff.
76. Ibid., 212, 27ff.
77. Ibid., 242.
78. Ibid., 243, 10ff.
79. WA 15, 360, 16ff.
80. Ibid., 370, 5ff.

encourages work as being committed as if there were no God.[81] The official should work as if everything depended upon him, but at the same time he should know that the ultimate sources of welfare are God's blessings. Knowing that in the end everything is due to God's blessings, the official need neither worry nor have cause for arrogance. Here, Luther uses the already mentioned metaphor for the presence of God in the political realm, speaking of the official as one who should regard all of his work as the work of God under a mask (*larva Dei*). God works in disguise through the hard work of the official, and the official's hard work allows God to conceal His own work.[82]

It is common for these exegetical texts not to use an explicit Christological terminology. We do not find an explicit reference to Chalcedonian Christology or the concept of the *communicatio idiomatum*. What we do find, however, is what we can call an incarnational motif that holds a resemblance to the *communicatio idiomatum*. In these texts, we see the understanding that God takes shape in the physical world. God is understood as being present and at work within the physical world, even if he is still considered differentiated from creation. In this sense, God's unity with and differentiation from creation holds a resemblance to the relation between the two natures of Christ. Hereby, these exegetical texts demonstrate the same simultaneity of the divine and human dimension of the political order as we saw in Luther's understanding of natural law. The current book argues that this simultaneity may be seen as an expression of a Chalcedonian motif.

Conclusion

An investigation of Luther's social ethics has shown several traits of pertinence to the book. We have seen how the two kingdoms doctrine and the concept of three estates are central ideas in Luther's political thought. However, we have also seen how the *communicatio idiomatum* plays a central role in Luther's theology and ethics. In addition to several texts in which Luther explicitly makes positive use of this terminology, we saw how this concept plays a significant role in his ethics. In Luther's *The Freedom of a Christian* he makes explicit use of the concept of the exchange of properties between the divine and human nature in Christ in order to explain how the justification by faith unites the Christian with the righteousness of Christ. Hereby, the Chalcedonian understanding of the exchange of properties in the *communicatio idiomatum* is given a central place in Luther's ethics.

With regard to Luther's social ethics, we cannot demonstrate the same explicit Christological terminology underlying Luther's understanding. But the findings support an interpretation of Luther's texts, where it may be argued that we can find an incarnational motif underlying central social ethical concepts. This has been found to be the case in Luther's understanding of natural law and reason. But it is

---

81. Ibid., 373, 3.
82. Ibid., 373, 5ff.

also the case in his understanding of political authority. For these concepts there is a simultaneity of the divine and human dimension which holds a resemblance to the relation between the divine and human nature in Christ.

The Christological motifs in Luther's theology and social ethics point to the viability of reading him in support of the book's overall aim to argue for a differentiated unity of universality and specificity. In Luther's social ethics and political thought there is a strong emphasis on universality – in his understanding of the 'naturalness' of political order and natural law. Luther clearly emphasized this in several of his writings. At the same time, it is never ignored that this universality is derived from a highly specific source – the will of God. It is due to the will of God that this universality is contended, and therefore it becomes an empty abstraction to ignore this specific origin.

Chapter 3

THE CHALCEDONIAN CHRISTOLOGY IN BONHOEFFER'S ETHICS

Bonhoeffer's ethic has been called many different things – e.g. an ethic of freedom,[1] ethical theology,[2] ethic of responsibility[3] and a Christological ethic.[4] All of these descriptions of Bonhoeffer's ethic point to important and central sides of his ethical thought. In the present book, I contend that Bonhoeffer's ethic fundamentally should be read as a Christological ethic, which is apparent from the outset of his *Ethics*. From his Christological starting point, he builds upon this precondition throughout the whole work. However, I also take this reading a step further, as I wish to argue that Bonhoeffer's ethic is shaped by a Chalcedonian Christology, which places him in continuity with Luther's understanding. In this chapter, I will demonstrate this Chalcedonian Christology in three Bonhoeffer texts and then, in the next chapter, show how this Chalcedonian Christology shapes central concepts in his ethics.

The study by Karsten Lehmkühler is particularly interesting for the present book, as Lehmkühler both compares Luther's and Bonhoeffer's theology, and recognizes the centrality of Chalcedonian thought to Luther.[5] With regard to

---

1. Wolfgang Huber, 'Freiheit als Form der Liebe. Die Aktualität christlicher Freiheit in den gesellschaftlichen Herausforderungen unserer Zeit', in *Religion im Erbe. Dietrich Bonhoeffer und die Zukunftsfähigkeit des Christentums* (ed. Christian Gremmels and Wolfgang Huber; Gütersloh: Chr. Kaiser/Gütersloher Verlagshaus, 2002), 17–36 (17).

2. James H. Burtness, *Shaping the Future: The Ethics of Dietrich Bonhoeffer* (Philadelphia, PA: Fortress Press, 1985), 25ff.; Clifford J. Green, 'Ethical Theology and Contextual Ethics: New Perspectives on Bonhoeffer's Ethics', in *Religion im Erbe. Dietrich Bonhoeffer und die Zukunftsfähigkeit des Christentums* (ed. Christian Gremmels and Wolfgang Huber; Gütersloh: Chr. Kaiser, 2002), 255–69.

3. Eberhard Bethge, 'Freiheit und Gehorsam bei Bonhoeffer', in *Schöpferische Nachfolge* (Heidelberg: FEST, 1978), 331–61 (358).

4. Oswald Bayer, 'Christus als Mitte. Bonhoeffers Ethik im Banne der Religionsphilosophie Hegels', *Berliner Theologische Zeitschrift* 2 (1985), 259.

5. Karsten Lehmkühler, 'Christologie', in *Bonhoeffer und Luther. Zentrale Themen ihrer Theologie* (ed. Klaus Grünwaldt, Christiane Tietz and Udo Hahn; Hannover: VELKD, 2007), 55–78.

Bonhoeffer, however, Lehmkühler rightly makes the point that Bonhoeffer emphasizes the promeity of Christ.[6] But this is not in contrast to Luther's emphasis on the *communicatio idiomatum*. Rather, it is to be read as a complementary thought structure (which is astonishingly close),[7] as they both closely relate the person and the work (*Werk Christi*) of Jesus Christ to each other. Lehmkühler argues that Bonhoeffer accentuates the presence (*Gegenwart*) of Christ and how this is closely related to his understanding of the two natures of Christ.[8] With regard to Chalcedon, it is acknowledged that Bonhoeffer affirms its paradoxical formulation of the relation between the two natures of Christ, even if its strength lies in exceeding the objectifying (*dinglich*) understanding of Jesus Christ.[9] The Chalcedonian Christology in Bonhoeffer is also acknowledged in other studies.[10] In neither of these studies, however, is the focus on Bonhoeffer's ethics. This is, however, the case in Clifford Green's article, where we find a similar stance on the Chalcedonian Christology,[11] even if this remains a sporadic observation. Consequently, Green does not show the implications of the Chalcedonian approach in Bonhoeffer's ethic. In a recent contribution to Bonhoeffer's Christological ethics, the emphasis is laid upon three Christological formulae (*Christus totus*, *Christus praesens* and *Christus pro me*).[12] Hereby, Bernd Wannenwetsch wants to steer between what he calls the idealist and foundationalist temptation. Even if I share the intention to argue for 'a Christologically saturated account of the Christian life',[13] our ways of pursuing this goal are different. Wannenwetsch holds a distinct ecclesial approach.[14] Throughout this book it is the aim to argue for a

---

6. Ibid., 59.
7. Ibid., 62.
8. Ibid., 62f.
9. Ibid., 64.
10. Ronald A. Carson, 'Motifs of Kenosis and Imitatio in the Work of Dietrich Bonhoeffer, with an Excursus on the Communicatio Idiomatum', *Journal of the American Academy of Religion* 43, no. 3 (1975), 542–53; Hans-Jürgen Abromeit, *Das Geheimnis Christi: Dietrich Bonhoeffers erfahrungsbezogene Christologie* (Neukirchener Beiträge zur Systematischen Theologie; 8; Neukirchen-Vluyn: Neukirchener, 1991), 190–212; Green, 'Ethical Theology and Contextual Ethics'; Ernst Feil, *Die Theologie Dietrich Bonhoeffers: Hermeneutik, Christologie, Weltverständnis* (Studien zur systematischen Theologie und Ethik; band 45; Berlin: LIT, 5th ext. edn, 2005), 118f., 90f.; Christopher R. J. Holmes, 'Wholly Human and Wholly Divine, Humiliated and Exalted: Some Reformed Explorations in Bonhoeffer's Christology Lectures', *Scottish Bulletin of Evangelical Theology* 25, no. 2 (2007), 210–25.

11. Green, 'Ethical Theology and Contextual Ethics', 257.

12. Bernd Wannenwetsch, 'The Whole Christ and the Whole Human Being', in *Christology and Ethics* (ed. F. LeRon Shults and Brent Waters; Grand Rapids, MI: W. B. Eerdmans, 2010), 75–98.

13. Ibid., 75.
14. Ibid., 84–85.

foundation of Christian ethics between universality and specificity, where the Chalcedonian Christology (in Luther and Bonhoeffer) has proven to be a viable course. Therefore, I find it regrettable that the Chalcedonian Christology is downplayed in Wannenwetsch's article.[15]

Apart from the Christology underlying Bonhoeffer's *Ethics* – which the present book reads as a Chalcedonian Christology – we find an explicit consent to the formula of Chalcedon (even the *communicatio idiomatum*) in three writings: first and foremost, his 'Lectures on Christology',[16] but also in a circular letter from December 1939[17] and one of his prison letters from May 1944.[18]

The who, how and where in the 'Lectures on Christology'

Wannenwetsch and others rightly draw attention to Bonhoeffer's focus on *who* Christ is in his 'Lectures on Christology'.[19] This question also resounds in the often quoted passage from one of Bonhoeffer's prison letters – 'What keeps gnawing at me is the question, what is Christianity, or who is Christ actually for us today?'[20] The emphasis on *who* Jesus Christ is follows from Bonhoeffer's concern with the contemporaneity of Jesus Christ. Therefore, Bonhoeffer also devotes the first main section of his Christology lectures to Jesus Christ as present (*Der gegenwärtige Christus*).[21] Hereby, Bonhoeffer emphasizes both the existential encounter with Jesus Christ and the locus of this encounter, viz. the church. Who Jesus Christ is, is revealed in the church[22] and can, therefore, only be grasped in faith.[23] In this sense there is an ecclesial Christology in Bonhoeffer. One can even argue

---

15. Ibid., 79–80.

16. Dietrich Bonhoeffer, *Berlin. 1932–1933* (herausgegeben von Carsten Nikolaisen und Ernst-Albert Scharffenorth; Dietrich Bonhoeffer Werke; band 12; Gütersloh: Chr. Kaiser, 1997) (DBW 12), 279–348.

17. Dietrich Bonhoeffer, *Illegale Theologen-Ausbildung: Sammelvikariate 1937–1940* (herausgegeben von Dirk Schulz; Dietrich Bonhoeffer Werke; band 15; Gütersloh: Chr. Kaiser, 1998) (DBW 15), 537–43.

18. Dietrich Bonhoeffer, *Widerstand und Ergebung. Briefe und Aufzeichnungen aus der Haft* (herausgegeben von Christian Gremmels, Eberhard Bethge und Renate Bethge in zusammenarbeit mit Ilse Tödt; Dietrich Bonhoeffer Werke; band 8; Gütersloh: Chr. Kaiser, 1998) (DBW 8), 439–42.

19. Wannenwetsch, 'The Whole Christ and the Whole Human Being', 77.

20. Dietrich Bonhoeffer, *Letters and Papers from Prison* (ed. John W. De Gruchy; trans. Isabel Best, Lisa E. Dahill, Reinhard Krauss and Nancy Lukens; Dietrich Bonhoeffer Works; vol. 8; Minneapolis, MN: Fortress Press, 2010) (DBWE 8), 362.

21. DBW 12, 291–312.

22. Ibid., 283, 296.

23. Ibid., 314, 341.

for a eucharistic Christology, as Bonhoeffer points to the sacraments as the place where – according to Luther's theology – Jesus Christ takes shape.[24] This ecclesial background is important for an understanding of Bonhoeffer's Christology. But Bonhoeffer has more to say than that. A close reading shows that he shares the Lutheran understanding of the Chalcedonian Christology. This is not to be read in contrast to the *who*, rather, it is to be understood as a supplement to the *how* within the *who*, just as he can speak of the *where* as a supplementing structure within the *who*.[25] Here, my reading comes closer to that found in Lehmkühler (as already mentioned).

Bonhoeffer's acknowledgement of the Chalcedonian Christology is present in a theological appraisal rather than in an apologetic endeavour. He comments explicitly on the Chalcedonian Christology and the *communicatio idiomatum* in four passages in his lectures: (1) in his reflections on Christ as sacrament;[26] (2) in his historical explanation of the formula of Chalcedon;[27] (3) in his explanation of the Lutheran understanding of the two natures of Christ;[28] and (4) in his summary of the implications of critical Christology.[29] Three observations are common to these four passages: (1) Bonhoeffer acknowledges the Chalcedonian Christology; (2) he does not simply repeat the original formulations of the formula of Chalcedon; and (3) he points to the strength of the Chalcedonian formulation lying in its transgression of itself.

First, the acknowledgement of the Chalcedonian Christology is found in Bonhoeffer's explanation of Lutheran theology.[30] Bonhoeffer gives an account of the Lutheran understanding of the ubiquity of God with regard to the sacraments, and how this implies that God is really present in the bread and wine.[31] The *genus majestaticum* means that there is an actual transfer of the divine properties to the body of Christ.[32] 'This [i.e. the *genus majestaticum*] asserts that the attributes of the divine nature can and must be expressed by the human nature. Jesus is all-powerful; Jesus is ever-present. It is based on the "est" in the doctrine of the Eucharist. The *genus majestaticum* is at the core of Lutheran theology.'[33] Second, Bonhoeffer is also critical of the Chalcedonian formulations as they run the

---

24. Ibid., 303.
25. Ibid., 306.
26. Ibid., 302–4.
27. Ibid., 327–28.
28. Ibid., 330–33.
29. Ibid., 339–40.
30. Ibid., 303–4, 327–36.
31. Ibid., 303.
32. Ibid., 305, 330.

33. Dietrich Bonhoeffer, *Berlin, 1932–1933* (ed. Larry L. Rasmussen; trans. Isabel Best and David Higgins; Dietrich Bonhoeffer Works; vol. 12; Minneapolis, MN: Fortress Press, 2009) (DBWE 12), 345.

risk of reducing the mystery of Christ in an objectifying manner. The relation between the two natures of Christ cannot just be understood as substances or in an otherwise objectifying sense.[34] For Bonhoeffer there is a point in the concept of οὐσία signifying the totality of God. The problem is not so much this concept, but rather the objectifying understanding of it.[35] And, third, Bonhoeffer argues that the formula of Chalcedon transgresses itself and therein lies its real strength.[36] In its paradoxical formulations, it includes all there is to say about Christ and thereby goes beyond itself. 'The Chalcedonian formula is an objective, living assertion about Christ that goes beyond all conceptual forms. Everything is encompassed in its very clear yet paradoxical agility [*Lebendigkeiten*].'[37] In the Chalcedon's *how* it exceeds itself and thereby returns the Christological question to the *who*.[38] In its paradoxical self-transgression the formula of Chalcedon thereby points away from the attempt to explain the mystery of Christ in terms of nature and substances, towards the place where this is proclaimed and believed – the place where the *who* is revealed, i.e. the church. Here, I concur with Wannenwetsch's reading: 'Bonhoeffer insists there can be only one way of accessing the person of Christ, and that is at the very locus of his revealing presence in the here and now: the church.'[39] However, as we have seen, the emphasis on the church as the locus of the revelation of Christ does not imply a rejection of the Chalcedonian Christology and its implications.

With regard to the last point – the self-transgression of the formula of Chalcedon – Bonhoeffer paves the way for an understanding of the Chalcedonian Christology and the *communicatio idiomatum* which interprets this doctrine more figuratively and metaphorically. This proves important, when we turn to his *Ethics*, but already in his lectures on Christology, this observation is significant. When Bonhoeffer ponders the *where* of Christology, he argues that Christ is present as the centre of human existence, history and nature.[40] The centre of human existence is understood in an ontological-theological sense, as it concerns our being persons before God. Christ is understood as the believed centre (*die geglaubte Mitte*), as he is both the end of the law and the beginning of the new existence under justification by faith.[41] In the recognizable sense, only the humanity of Christ is determinable, just as it is only the 'humane' aspect of human existence that is recognizable. However, just as it may be believed that there is more to Jesus of Nazareth than his humanity, it also may be believed that

---

34. DBW 12, 328.
35. Ibid., 339.
36. Ibid., 328.
37. DBWE 12, 343.
38. DBW 12, 336.
39. Wannenwetsch, 'The Whole Christ and the Whole Human Being', 81.
40. DBW 12, 306–11.
41. Ibid., 307.

there is more to human existence than merely its 'humane' reality. Just as it may be believed that Jesus is Christ, it also may be believed that Christ is the centre of human existence – even if neither can be demonstrated.

This also applies to his understanding of history, where we also find some of the more explicit political implications of Bonhoeffer's Christology. Bonhoeffer interprets history Christologically, arguing that history both points forward in its promise of Christ and is a revelation of the fulfilment of the messianic promises. However, the truth of the messianic revelation can only be preached and never demonstrated.[42] Therefore, the church is considered the centre of history.[43] This centre is a hidden centre of the state, as the state forms history. 'The church should be understood as the center of history. The church is the center of a history that is made by the state. The church must be understood to be the center, the hidden center, of the state.'[44] As the hidden centre of the state, the church judges and justifies the state in accordance with the state's fulfilment of the people's purpose.[45] I contend that this may be read as an expression of a Chalcedonian Christology understood in a figurative sense. Just as there is a mysterious and real presence of God in Jesus Christ and in the sacraments, Bonhoeffer's understanding of Christ as the centre of history (and thereby the hidden centre of the State) may be read as an expression of a figurative, Chalcedonian understanding of the mysterious presence of Christ within the political realm. This reading also finds support when we later turn to his *Ethics*.

Finally, Bonhoeffer understands Christ as the centre of nature.[46] This motif will not be pursued further here. However, it is important to notice that Bonhoeffer also here argues that Christ as new creature cannot be demonstrated. This Christological mystery can only be preached and therefore Bonhoeffer again points to the sacraments, where this proclamation finds its expression.[47] Bonhoeffer summarizes his understanding of Christ as the mediator (*Mittler*) as follows:

> [T]o call Christ the center of human existence, of history, and of nature – these are never abstract matters and are never to be distinguished from one another. It is a fact that human existence is both history and nature. Christ as the center means that Christ, as the mediator for the creation in its servitude, is the fulfillment of this law, the liberation from this servitude for the whole human being. Christ is all this only because he is the one who stands in my place, in my behalf before God, *pro-me*. Christ as the mediator is precisely the end of the old, fallen world and the beginning of the new world of God.[48]

---

42. Ibid., 308.
43. Ibid., 309.
44. DBWE 12, 326.
45. Ibid.
46. DBW 12, 310–11.
47. Ibid., 310.
48. DBWE 12, 327.

The theme of the mystery of Christ will not be pursued further here, as this theme in Bonhoeffer has been analysed in depth elsewhere.[49] Suffice it to mention that Bonhoeffer also reflects on this issue in his sermon on Paul's first letter to the Corinthians,[50] where he argues that the lost sense of mystery in modern life is an expression of our decay and poverty. Bonhoeffer contends that there is a deep mystery in life that evades any kind of access and that it is the foundation of life and all our concepts and understanding.[51] This mystery is fundamentally a divine mystery to which the world is hostile. The world does not accept the hiddenness of the mystery of God, just as the cross of Jesus Christ is the unmistakable sign of the world's blindness to this divine mystery. The unknown mystery is revealed in Jesus Christ as the divine love and proximity.[52] In these passages, Bonhoeffer also expresses a parallel between the two natures of Christ and the mystery of reality. Just as God and the world are reconciled in Christ, humankind is brought into proximity with God in Christ. With regard to the Chalcedonian motif, it is worth noting that Bonhoeffer actually says that God became human so that we could become divine. Hereby, he expresses an exchange between the human and divine properties that holds significant resemblance to the *communicatio idiomatum*. 'That is the unrecognized mystery of God in this world: Jesus Christ ... because God became a human being like us, so that we might become divine; because God came to us, so that we might come to God. God who becomes lowly for our sake, *God in Jesus of Nazareth – that is the secret and hidden wisdom ...*'[53]

In his sermon on Paul's letter to the Colossians,[54] Bonhoeffer also ponders the mystery of Christ. He reflects on the passage from Col. 3.1–4, where it says that the Christians are raised with Christ. Bonhoeffer discusses to what degree this makes sense for a contemporary mind, and argues that the problems in understanding such a passage comprise an expression of our having turned away from God.

---

49. Abromeit, *Das Geheimnis Christi*, 35–63; Feil, *Die Theologie Dietrich Bonhoeffers*, 28f., 81ff.; Kirsten Busch Nielsen, Ulrik Nissen and Christiane Tietz, eds, *Mysteries in the Theology of Dietrich Bonhoeffer: A Copenhagen Bonhoeffer Symposium* (Forschungen zur systematischen und ökumenischen Theologie; vol. 119; Göttingen: Vandenhoeck & Ruprecht, 2007).

50. Dietrich Bonhoeffer, *London. 1933–1935* (herausgegeben von Hans Goedeking, Martin Heimbucher und Hans-Walther Schleicher; Dietrich Bonhoeffer Werke; band 13; Gütersloh: Chr. Kaiser, 1994) (DBW 13), 359–63.

51. Ibid., 360.

52. Ibid., 362.

53. Dietrich Bonhoeffer, *London, 1933–1935* (ed. Keith Clements; trans. Isabel Best; Dietrich Bonhoeffer Works; vol. 13; Minneapolis, MN: Fortress Press, 2007) (DBWE 13), 362.

54. Dietrich Bonhoeffer, *Ökumene, Universität, Pfarramt. 1931–1932* (herausgegeben von Eberhard Amelung und Christoph Strohm; Dietrich Bonhoeffer Werke; band 11; Gütersloh: Chr. Kaiser, 1994) (DBW 11), 435–43.

The passage from the letter to the Colossians expresses God's thought (*Gottes Gedanken*)[55] and therefore will be revealed as the ultimate reality. This divine truth (*Gotteswahrheit*) will bind all humans together as humans and serve as the source from which true love is possible.[56]

> [I]f we come together as the crucified and risen ones of Jesus Christ, as those who have lost their prideful human life in order to win it anew in Christ, as those who were sentenced to death but pardoned – then we will find one another, then we would look into one another's eyes and would recognize one another completely anew, as we are recognized by God.[57]

God revealed in flesh as the holy mystery of Christmas

In the circular Christmas letter from 1939, Bonhoeffer writes powerfully on the importance of the incarnation for a Christian theology: 'No priest, no theologian stood at the cradle of Bethlehem. And yet all Christian theology finds its origin in the miracle of miracles, that God became human … Without that holy night, there is no theology. "God revealed in flesh," the God-human Jesus Christ, that is the holy mystery, which theology was instituted to preserve and protect.'[58] Bonhoeffer continues his reflections by pondering the early Christian dogmas (including the formula of Chalcedon). He points to three significant observations. First, Jesus Christ assumed human nature. Hereby, the universality of the Christmas miracle is signified. Second, the paradoxical understanding of the simultaneity of the two natures and one person is formulated in Chalcedon.

> Nowhere else but in and through the person of Jesus Christ are Godhead and humankind united with each other, '[which] can never more be separated nor mixed together with each other, nor can one be transformed into the other', as stated in Chalcedon, as the utmost paradox and at the same time most reverently preserving the mystery of the person of the mediator.[59]

---

55. Ibid., 443.

56. Ibid.

57. Dietrich Bonhoeffer, *Ecumenical, Academic, and Pastoral Work: 1931–1932* (ed. Victoria J. Barnett, Mark S. Brocker and Michael B. Lukens; trans. Anne Schmidt-Lange, Isabel Best, Nicolas Humphrey and Marion Pauck; Dietrich Bonhoeffer Works; vol. 11; Minneapolis, MN: Fortress Press, 2012 (DBWE 11), 457.

58. Dietrich Bonhoeffer, *Theological Education Underground, 1937–1940* (ed. Victoria J. Barnett; trans. Victoria J. Barnett, Claudia D. Bergmann, Peter Frick and Scott A. Moore; Dietrich Bonhoeffer Works; vol. 15; Minneapolis, MN: Fortress Press, 2012) (DBWE 15), 528–29.

59. Ibid., 532.

Finally, third, he ponders the Lutheran *genus majestaticum*, i.e. the communication of the properties (*communicatio idiomatum*) of the divine nature to the human nature. Bonhoeffer acknowledges the centrality of this concept for Lutheran theology – as we saw, in his lectures on Christology, he even refers to this as the core of Lutheran theology[60] – and argues that, even if this may be difficult to understand, it is testified in Scripture and therefore to be seen as an expression of God's unity with mankind. 'While it certainly remains incomprehensible how human nature, which is our nature, could partake in the attributes of the divine majesty, the Scripture teaches it, and with this teaching the deepest and ultimate union of God with the human being is expressed ...'[61]

The cantus firmus *and polyphony of the Christian life*

In addition to the Chalcedonian Christology found in Bonhoeffer's lectures on Christology and his sermons, he also returns to this idea in his later theology. In his *Letters and Papers from Prison* we find this motif in a metaphorical use of the musical polyphony. In a letter to his friend, Eberhard Bethge, Bonhoeffer writes about worldly love and compares this with polyphonic music.[62] The love for God is like the *cantus firmus* in relation to which all other kinds of love (as counterpoints) are at play. Therefore, Bonhoeffer also praises earthly love – not least how it is expressed in the *Song of Solomon*. When the *cantus firmus* is clear and distinct, all other counterpoints can unfold themselves powerfully. This is where Bonhoeffer reverts to the formula of Chalcedon and its expression of the relation between Christ's divine and human nature. Just as these two natures are 'undivided and yet distinct', the Christian life is differentiated and yet never separated from its relation to love for God.

> Where the *cantus firmus* is clear and distinct, a counterpoint can develop as mightily as it wants. The two are 'undivided and yet distinct', as the Definition of Chalcedon says, like the divine and human natures in Christ. Is that perhaps why we are so at home with polyphony in music, why it is important to us, because it is the musical image of this Christological fact and thus also our *vita christiana*?[63]

Three things are important to note in this letter: (1) Bonhoeffer acknowledges the understanding of the relation between the divine and human nature of Jesus Christ as stated in the formula of Chalcedon; (2) he broadens this understanding and interprets it figuratively using the metaphor from polyphonic music to express the

---

60. DBW 12, 330.
61. DBWE 15, 532–33.
62. DBW 8, 440–41.
63. DBWE 8, 394.

same kind of reality; and (3) he explicitly relates his Chalcedonian understanding to his ethics by contending that the Christian life is shaped by this reality. These observations will all play an important role when we turn our investigation to central concepts in Bonhoeffer's ethics in order to see how they are shaped by this Chalcedonian Christology.

Conclusion

We can now conclude our findings on the Chalcedonian Christology in Bonhoeffer's ethics. In this chapter we have seen how the Chalcedonian Christology was affirmed in his lectures on Christology and his Christmas letter from 1939. Here Bonhoeffer acknowledges this classical formulation of the relation between the two natures of Christ as a core expression of Lutheran theology. Yet, we also saw how Bonhoeffer affirmed the strength of Chalcedon in its transgression of itself (and thereby the more implicit affirmation), whereby he pointed to the church as the place of the revelation of Christ. Bonhoeffer maintained as central the question, *who* Jesus Christ is. The transgression of the Chalcedonian formulations was also seen both in his understanding of the Christological mystery of reality, and in the figurative expression of Chalcedon in polyphonic music. We saw this more figurative or metaphoric interpretation of the Chalcedonian Christology in one of his prison letters, where he writes about the love for God as a *cantus firmus* behind all other kinds of worldly love, and how this is an expression of a Christological mystery of reality.

Chapter 4

THE CHRISTOLOGICAL SHAPING OF CENTRAL
CONCEPTS IN BONHOEFFER'S ETHICS

As we have seen in the previous chapter, Bonhoeffer holds an affirmative view of the Chalcedonian Christology. In the present chapter we will turn to an analysis of the implications of Bonhoeffer's Christology for select central concepts in his ethic – his understanding of reality, the secular, Christonomy, reason and responsibility. It is not the aim of the book to undertake a complete analysis of each of these concepts. Rather, the aim is to ponder these concepts in light of the book's thesis and thereby to see if they may be read in light of the Chalcedonian Christology – and if this reading substantiates an understanding of Bonhoeffer's ethics between universality and specificity.

In this chapter the primary focus will be on his *Ethics*. However, this is not understood exclusively, but other Bonhoeffer texts are included with *Ethics* as the hermeneutical starting point. The focus on Bonhoeffer's *Ethics* – as far as Bonhoeffer's thought is concerned – has both an external and an internal reason. Externally, the focus is motivated by the book's interest in Bonhoeffer's ethical thought, of which *Ethics* is, undoubtedly, an absolutely central element. Internally, the research among Bonhoeffer scholars has shown lesser interest in *Ethics* than in the other of Bonhoeffer's major works – e.g. his *Sanctorum Communio, Act and Being* and *Letters and Papers from Prison*. This has to do with its posthumous and partly fragmentary nature, which has prevented *Ethics* from receiving the attention it rightly deserves. This lack of attention seems unjust, as *Ethics* can also be seen as the culmination of Bonhoeffer's theology.[1] Bonhoeffer even refers to it as the task of his life, '*Lebensaufgabe*'.[2] In this book I have therefore sought to engage with this work

---

1. Clifford J. Green, 'Ethical Theology and Contextual Ethics. New Perspectives on Bonhoeffer's Ethics', in *Religion im Erbe. Dietrich Bonhoeffer und die Zukunftsfähigkeit des Christentums* (ed. Christian Gremmels and Wolfgang Huber; Gütersloh: Chr. Kaiser, 2002), 255–69 (269).

2. Eberhard Bethge, *Dietrich Bonhoeffer. Theologe – Christ – Zeitgenosse. Eine Biographie* (8; Gütersloh: Gütersloher Verlagshaus, rev. edn, 2004), 804–05. See also Dietrich Bonhoeffer, *Widerstand und Ergebung. Briefe und Aufzeichnungen aus der Haft* (herausgegeben von Christian Gremmels, Eberhard Bethge und Renate Bethge in zusammenarbeit mit Ilse Tödt; Dietrich Bonhoeffer Werke; band 8; Gütersloh: Chr. Kaiser, 1998) (DBW 8), 237.

in greater depth. The analysis of *Ethics* is, however, primarily concerned with its *theology*, rather than the philological concerns arising from its posthumous nature.

Reality as the contradictory Christ-reality

The concept of reality is read as equivalent to the German *Wirklichkeit* (rendered into 'reality' in the English translation of Bonhoeffer's *Ethics*.[3] This is the concept which Bonhoeffer uses in the first section of his *Ethics*.[4] Bonhoeffer does not analyse the concept in detail in his *Ethics*, but uses it in his theological reflections, taking the understanding of it for granted. However, as the literature on his concept of reality shows, his use and understanding of it holds implications for several of his core concepts. One of the most recent contributions to this theme is by Ann Nickson.[5] Nickson focuses on the motif of freedom in Bonhoeffer's writings. Her primary concern is, therefore, not the concept of reality. Also, her concern lies not primarily with *Ethics*. In Jürgen Boomgaarden, the explicit focus is Bonhoeffer's understanding of reality.[6] But again this is not viewed in light of his *Ethics*. Instead the concern lies with the early *Act and Being*. In some of the older contributions to Bonhoeffer's understanding of reality, we find a similar approach – *Ethics* is included, but is not the main focus.[7]

When we are dealing with the concept of reality, it is important to differentiate between the different meanings associated with this concept. With regard to the *philosophical* use, the concept has its origins in the Aristotelian concept of ενέργεια.

---

3. The following section is a revised summary of the main findings in Ulrik Nissen, 'Letting Reality Become Real: On Mystery and Reality in Dietrich Bonhoeffer's Ethics', *Journal of Religious Ethics* 39, no. 2 (2011), 321–43.

4. Dietrich Bonhoeffer, *Ethik* (herausgegeben von Ilse Tödt, Heinz Eduard Tödt, Ernst Feil und Clifford Green; Dietrich Bonhoeffer Werke; band 6; Gütersloh: Chr. Kaiser, 2nd rev. edn, 1998) (DBW 6), 31–61.

5. Ann L. Nickson, *Bonhoeffer on Freedom: Courageously Grasping Reality* (Oxford: Ashgate, 2002).

6. Jürgen Boomgaarden, *Das Verständnis der Wirklichkeit: Dietrich Bonhoeffers systematische Theologie und ihr philosophischer Hintergrund in 'Akt und Sein'* (Gütersloh: Chr. Kaiser/Gütersloher Verlagshaus, 1999).

7. Jürgen Moltmann, *Herrschaft Christi und soziale Wirklichkeit nach Dietrich Bonhoeffer* (Theologische Existenz heute; vol. 71; München: Chr. Kaiser, 1959), 71; Heinrich Ott, *Wirklichkeit und Glaube* (Zum theologischen Erbe Dietrich Bonhoeffers; band 1; Zürich: Vandenhoeck & Ruprecht, 1966); André Dumas, *Une théologie de la réalité: Dietrich Bonhoeffer* (Geneva: Labor et Fides, 1968); Rainer Mayer, *Christuswirklichkeit. Grundlagen, Entwicklung und Konsequenzen der Theologie Dietrich Bonhoeffers* (Arbeiten zur Theologie, 2nd series; vol. 15; Stuttgart: Calwer, 1969); Larry L. Rasmussen, *Dietrich Bonhoeffer: Reality and Resistance* (Studies in Christian Ethics; Nashville, TN: Abingdon, 1972).

Here the concept denotes an ontologically prior status to being, as it determines the forms of being and thereby is present in all spheres of being. This lies behind its double meaning in a contemporary context, where it signifies both (1) issues of being vs. non-being; and (2) the question about the dimension of reality which is beyond the empirically verifiable. In *philosophy of religion* the phenomenological side of reality implies both that the worldly, human and religious phaenomena may be understood as pointing toward a transcendent reality. For philosophy of religion it is part of its aim critically to reflect on these religious phaenomena and assess their justification. With regard to its more *dogmatic* use, the concept of reality also refers to the believed reality. In this sense, there is a parallel to its use in aesthetics, e.g. in poetry and arts. Here we can also speak of a reality that is not 'real' in a perceivable sense of the term. Rather, it is a reality that is mediated through these forms of communication and where reality may be believed and taken for real. This does not necessarily entail that reality is 'only' a believed reality, but it does mean that there is another dimension to reality than its concrete and immediate sense and that reality in this sense is 'believed'. From this perspective, reality may also be understood as a relational concept, where reality is understood in relation to God. Therefore, just as the reality of God may be believed, so too may the reality of the world's inseparable relation to God as a believed reality. It is this dogmatic understanding of reality that plays a primary role in Bonhoeffer.[8]

When we turn to Bonhoeffer's concept of reality in his *Ethics*, it is immediately apparent that this is a concept of pivotal importance. Therefore, it is with good reason that his section on the concept of reality is placed as the first part in his *Ethics* (the editors of *Ethik* focus on the historical ordering of the various sections,[9] but from a more theological perspective the primacy of the section on reality also sheds an important hermeneutical light on the rest of *Ethics*). Bonhoeffer has at least three interlocking meanings of reality – a spatial, a temporal and an ontological. As regards the *spatial* understanding of reality, Bonhoeffer uses the German *Raum*, which has more explicit spatial connotations than the rendering into 'realm' in the standard English edition of his *Ethics*. Using this term, Bonhoeffer contends that there are not two 'realms', but only one Christ-reality.[10]

---

8. For a more elaborate overview of this concept, see e.g. Wolfgang Janke, 'Wirklichkeit. I. Philosophisch', in *Theologische Realenzyklopädie* (ed. James K. Cameron Horst Balz et al.; Berlin/New York: W. de Gruyter, 2004), 114–20; Joachim Kunstmann, 'Wirklichkeit II. Praktisch-theologisch', in *Theologische Realenzyklopädie* (Wiedergeburt-Zypern; band XXXVI; ed. James K. Cameron Horst Balz et al.; Berlin/New York: W. de Gruyter, 2004), 120–23; Wolf Krötke, 'Wirklichkeit', in *Religion in Geschichte und Gegenwart. Handwörterbuch für Theologie und Religionswissenschaft* (ed. Hans Dieter Betz, Don S. Browning, Bernd Janowski and Eberhard Jüngel; Tübingen: Mohr Siebeck, 2005), 1594–96.

9. DBW 6, 447–56.

10. Ibid., 43.

> There are not two realities, but *only one reality*, and that is God's reality revealed in Christ in the reality of the world. Partaking in Christ, we stand at the same time in the reality of God and in the reality of the world. The reality of Christ embraces the reality of the world in itself. The world has no reality of its own independent of God's revelation in Christ. It is a denial of God's revelation in Jesus Christ to wish to be 'Christian' without being 'worldly' or [to] wish to be worldly without seeing and recognizing the world in Christ. Hence there are not two realms, but only *the one realm of the Christ-reality* [*Christuswirklichkeit*], in which the reality of God and the reality of the world are united.[11]

To think in two separate 'rooms' or compartments of reality – according to Bonhoeffer – is to deny the unity of the one Christ-reality in which we stand. In this Christ-reality, any attempt to think in different *Räume* is rejected. Rather, the reality of God and the reality of the world are one in the Christ-reality. Consequently, Bonhoeffer also rejects the theme of two realms, stating that this contradicts both biblical and Reformation thought. On the contrary, everything is to be seen from the worldly reality as drawn into and held together in Christ.[12]

The *temporal* notion of reality is reflected in Bonhoeffer's understanding of a certain historical reality, namely the continuity between the unity of the west and its historical foundation in the history of the Jewish people. According to Bonhoeffer, this is a historical reality founded in Christ. 'The unity of the West is not an idea, but a historical reality whose only foundation is Christ.'[13] The Christological understanding of reality's temporal dimension is also seen when Bonhoeffer reflects on what it means that the '[g]ood is the action that is in accordance with the reality of Jesus Christ.'[14] As this must neither be understood as contrasting nor as accommodating historical reality, both of these potential misinterpretations are to be remedied in light of the incarnation of Christ.[15] The 'ethic of Jesus' risks an overemphasis on the specific characteristics of Christian ethics and thereby a negation of the concrete historical responsibilities.[16] The second misinterpretation runs the risk of separating reality from its Christological foundation and turning it into a universal and empty abstraction. Instead of these two misinterpretations, Bonhoeffer argues for the temporal understanding of reality founded in Christ.

> [W]hat is overlooked here is the decisive fact from which alone the structure of what is real can be understood, namely, God's becoming human, God's

---

11. Dietrich Bonhoeffer, *Ethics* (ed. Clifford J. Green; trans. Reinhard Krauss, Charles C. West and Douglas W. Stott; Dietrich Bonhoeffer Works; vol. 6; Minneapolis, MN: Fortress Press, 2005) (DBWE 6), 58.
12. DBW 6, 44.
13. DBWE 6, 109.
14. Ibid., 228–29.
15. DBW 6, 229–30.
16. Ibid., 229.

entering history, taking on *historical reality in the reality of Jesus Christ*. What is overlooked here is the fact that the Sermon on the Mount is the word of the one who did not relate to reality as a foreigner, a reformer, a fanatic, the founder of a religion, but as the one who bore and experienced the nature of reality in his own body, who spoke out of the depth of reality as no other human being on earth ever before. The Sermon on the Mount is the word of the very one who is the lord and law of reality. The Sermon on the Mount is to be understood and interpreted as the word of the God who became human. *That is the issue at stake when the question of historical action is raised, and here it must prove true that action in accord with Christ is action in accord with reality.*[17]

Lastly, the *ontological* dimension in Bonhoeffer's understanding of reality is closely linked to his distinction between ultimate and penultimate things.[18] As Bonhoeffer sees it, the relation between the ultimate and penultimate things in Christian life can be resolved as either a radical or a compromising solution.[19] However, both of these positions separate the ultimate from the penultimate, and thereby fundamentally negate the unity of the reality of God and the human reality in the Christ-reality.[20] Therefore, Bonhoeffer warns against both the radical and the compromising solution. 'To advocates of the radical solution it must be said that Christ is not radical in their sense; to followers of the compromise solution it must likewise be said that Christ does not make compromises. Accordingly, Christian life is a matter neither of radicalism nor compromise.'[21] This is the point where Bonhoeffer moves into an ontological understanding of reality. In his rejection of both the radical and compromising positions, he argues that there is no human being as such. Such an understanding would imply an exclusion of God. Rather, '[t]here is only the God-man Jesus Christ who is real, through whom the world will be preserved until it's ripe for its end.'[22] Also, Bonhoeffer's understanding of the ontological perspective is evident when he reflects on the subject matter of a Christian ethic. Because a Christian ethic is concerned with the realization of God's reality revealed in Christ among God's creatures,[23] the good is not separate from that which exists. The central concern in Christian ethics becomes the realization of reality understood as participation in God's reality revealed in Christ.

For the purposes of this book it is important to note that, even if we can demonstrate these different layers of meaning in Bonhoeffer's concept of reality, there is still a unifying theme in the underlying Chalcedonian Christology. This is

---

17. DBWE 6, 230–31 (my emphasis).
18. DBW 6, 137–62.
19. Ibid., 144.
20. Ibid., 146.
21. DBWE 6, 154.
22. Ibid., 155.
23. DBW 6, 34.

apparent when Bonhoeffer simultaneously maintains the unity and differentiation between the reality of God and the reality of the world in the Christ-reality.[24] For Bonhoeffer, the Christ-reality is a differentiated unity of the reality of God and the reality of the world. Neither is understood separately from the other, nor is either identified with the other. Rather, it is an appreciation and affirmation of both realities existing in one and the same reality, at the same time. Bonhoeffer therefore argues that one cannot be 'Christian' without also being 'worldly' at the same time. As the reality of Christ embraces the reality of the world, the Christian is never separated from the world, nor is the world separated from Christ. The reality of the world and the reality of God are held together as a polemical unity in the Christ-reality[25] or contradictory unity (*Widerspruchsvolle Einheit*).[26] However, even if the term 'polemical' indicates an unresolved contradiction in this relatedness, it is important for Bonhoeffer still to maintain that this unity is derived from the reconciliation between God and the world in the incarnation of Christ. Therefore, Bonhoeffer argues that the incarnation is the source of this differentiated unity:

> Because in Jesus Christ God and humanity became one, so through Christ what is 'Christian' and what is 'worldly' become one in the action of the Christian. They are not opposed to each other like two eternally hostile principles. Instead, the action of the Christian springs from the unity between God and the world, and the unity of life that have been created in Christ. In Christ life regains its unity.[27]

In this sense, one can point to a certain 'mystery' (*Geheimnis*) in Bonhoeffer's notion of reality.[28] However, for a Christian ethic it is not sufficient to point to this mystery of reality. The Christian ethic must also ask how the reality of Christ becomes concrete in human experience and how life should be lived in this reality. For Bonhoeffer it is important that this Christ-reality is not just an abstract idea, but rather has concrete, formative implications for human life and reality. With this concrete formation of the Christ-reality in the world, Bonhoeffer once again stresses that the reality of God and the reality of the world are affirmed at the same time:

---

24. Ibid., 43.
25. Ibid., 45.
26. Ibid., 251–53. The English translation renders this as 'a living unity full of unresolved contradictions' (DBWE 6, 252). I prefer to speak of a 'contradictory unity', as this comes closer to the dynamic in Bonhoeffer's original expression.
27. DBWE 6, 253.
28. DBW 6, 40. See also Kirsten Busch Nielsen, Ulrik Nissen and Christiane Tietz, eds, *Mysteries in the Theology of Dietrich Bonhoeffer: A Copenhagen Bonhoeffer Symposium* (Forschungen zur systematischen und ökumenischen Theologie; vol. 119; Göttingen: Vandenhoeck & Ruprecht, 2007).

The Christian ethic asks, then, how this reality of God and of the world that is given in Christ becomes real in our world… [T]he question is how the reality in Christ – which has long embraced us and our world within itself – works here and now or, in other words, how life is to be lived in it. What matters is *participating in the reality of God and the world in Jesus Christ today*, and doing so in such a way that I never experience the reality of God without the reality of the world, nor the reality of the world without the reality of God.[29]

This challenge to Christian ethics also points forward to the social-ethical implications of Bonhoeffer's understanding of reality, which we will return to in the next chapter.

The secular as saeculum

When we turn to Bonhoeffer's concept of the secular, it is evident how his understanding of reality implies that he holds a positive concept of the secular.[30] This concept is fundamental to the book for two reasons. First, the understanding of the secular plays a central role in the contemporary debate on the relation between religion and politics. For a plurality of worldviews to coexist in the public, we need to maintain some kind of secularity to maintain a common realm.[31] However, if the public sphere is understood as a secular realm devoid of any Christian qualification, the book's thesis is problematized. Therefore in 'Dietrich Bonhoeffer and the Ethics of Plenitude' I ponder the concept of the secular and argue for a theological qualification of this concept. Second, in Bonhoeffer, the concept of the secular plays a crucial role. This is particularly true of his later years of which both *Ethics* and *Letters and Papers from Prison* bear witness. The latter work has been influential in the reading of Bonhoeffer as a forerunner of the secular theology of the 1960s, and in contemporary theology he is often quoted to

---

29. DBWE 6, 55.

30. The following section is a revised summary of the main findings in Ulrik Nissen, 'Dietrich Bonhoeffer and the Ethics of Plenitude', *Journal of the Society of Christian Ethics* 26, no. 1 (2006), 97–114. This article has also been published in a revised Danish and German version: 'Saeculum og fyldens etik. en radikal læsning af Dietrich Bonhoeffer', *Dansk teologisk tidsskrift* 68, no. 4 (2005), 285–304; 'Dietrich Bonhoeffer's Ethik in einer säkularen Welt des Terrors', in *Bonhoeffer weiterdenken…* (ed. Andreas Klein and Matthias Geist; Münster: LIT, 2006), 17–32. It is the original English version that I draw upon for this book.

31. See also Nigel Biggar, 'Saving the "Secular": The Public Vocation of Moral Theology', *Journal of Religious Ethics* 37, no. 1 (2009), 159–78; Luke Bretherton, *Christ and the Common Life. Political Theology and the Case for Democracy* (Grand Rapids, MI: W. B. Eerdmans, 2019), chapter 8 (227–58).

sustain the idea that today we have to speak post-metaphysically about God. The question about the role of Bonhoeffer's theology with regard to these issues is a highly debated theme – usually in light of his prison letters.[32]

Bonhoeffer's understanding of the secular and the world having come of age grows out of an interplay between his theological deliberations and his concrete experiences of the political and theological turmoil he witnessed. Nielsen gives a systematic theological overview of five different interpretative approaches to the relation between the underlying Christology and the historical analysis: (1) the understanding of godlessness is driven by a *theologia crucis* motif (Eberhard Jüngel and Regin Prenter); (2) the first approach is supplemented by a critique of metaphysics (Andreas Klein); (3) the cultural-historical and theological deliberations are focused on the concept of religion (Ernst Feil and Ralf K. Wüstenberg); (4) Bonhoeffer's concept of secularization, autonomy and the world having come of age are read in light of each other (Klaus Bartl and Trygve Wyller); (5) Bonhoeffer's late writings are read from a hermeneutical perspective (Gerhard Ebeling).[33]

If the current book were to place itself in this scheme, it would come closest to the fourth of these approaches. However, it has not been the aim of this book to engage in this debate. Rather, it has been the intention to see if Bonhoeffer's concept of the secular could also be understood in light of a Chalcedonian Christology and, subsequently, be seen as supportive of the book's general thesis. In pursuing this reading it proved fruitful to establish a discussion between Bonhoeffer and

---

32. See e.g. Edward D. Schneider, 'Bonhoeffer and a Secular Theology', *Lutheran Quarterly* 15, no. 2 (1963), 151–57; Ralf K. Wüstenberg, *Glauben als Leben: Dietrich Bonhoeffer und die nichtreligiöse Interpretation biblischer Begriffe* (Kontexte; Frankfurt am Main: Peter Lang, 1996); Ralf K. Wüstenberg, 'Religionless Christianity: Dietrich Bonhoeffer's Tegel Theology', in *Bonhoeffer for a New Day* (Grand Rapids, MI: W. B. Eerdmans, 1997), 57–71; Tom Greggs, 'Religionless Christianity in a Complexly Religious and Secular World: Thinking Through and Beyond Bonhoeffer', in *Religion, Religionlessness and Contemporary Western Culture* (Frankfurt am Main: Peter Lang, 2008), 111–25; Barry Harvey, 'Preserving the World for Christ: Toward a Theological Engagement with the "Secular"', *Scottish Journal of Theology* 61, no. 1 (2008), 64–82; Kirsten Busch Nielsen, 'Critique of Church and Critique of Religion in Bonhoeffer's Late Writings', in *Dietrich Bonhoeffers Theologie heute* (Gütersloh: Gütersloher Verlagshaus, 2009), 319–34.

33. Kirsten Busch Nielsen, *Syndens brudte magt: en undersøgelse af Dietrich Bonhoeffers syndsforståelse* (Publikationer fra Det Teologiske Fakultet, 1; Københavns: Det Teologiske Fakultet, Københavns Universitet, 2008), 128 (footnote 54). In this book I refer to the Danish original version. It also exists in a German translation: *Die gebrochene Macht der Sünde: der Beitrag Dietrich Bonhoeffers zur Hamartologie* (Arbeiten zur systematischen Theologie; vol. 2; Leipzig: Evangelische Verlagsanstalt, 2010).

John Milbank on the concept of the secular.³⁴ Hereby, the book has ascertained a Christological interpretation of Bonhoeffer's concept of the secular that implies a fullness of the secular understood as *saeculum*.³⁵

Secularization is usually understood as the reduced influence of religion with regard to convictions, science, social and political institutions. As such it is to be differentiated from 'secularism', which is an ideology consciously contending non- and/or antireligious principles and beliefs. Understood in this way, secularization is a long process primarily to be found in Western democracies, where it may also be seen as an integral part of religion itself, not least Lutheranism. The Lutheran understanding of the justification by faith has been read as supporting the process of secularization in its emphasis on the individual's relation to God. However, as we have seen in the book's reading of Luther, this interpretation does not take Luther's understanding of the real presence of God in his political theology sufficiently into consideration. When we turn to Bonhoeffer, the current book contends that the concept of the secular is understood in a theologically affirmative sense. This is understood both in the sense that (1) the reality of God cannot be neglected without the highest degree of absurdity and that even the secular claim, therefore, is made before God; and (2) the *saeculum* is understood as the penultimate (*vorletzte*) being before God which is never separate from the ultimate (*letzte*) reality (both qualitatively and temporarily).³⁶

The most important reference to Bonhoeffer's view on the secular is in his prison letters. It is here that we find the famous phrases declaring that we are moving towards a religionless period, and where Bonhoeffer also has a critique of the individualistic, particularistic and metaphysical sides of religion.³⁷ We will have to speak of Christianity in religionless terms if Christianity is to have any appeal. The

---

34. Here I have particularly focused on two works of Milbank: John Milbank, *Theology and Social Theory: Beyond Secular Reason* (Signposts in Theology; repr.; Oxford: Blackwell, 1997); *Being Reconciled: Ontology and Pardon* (Radical Orthodoxy Series; London: Routledge, 2003).

35. In a relatively recent book, Barry Harvey takes a similar approach where he argues for a faithful and profound this-worldliness in light of Bonhoeffer's prison letters, see Barry Harvey, *Taking Hold of the Real: Dietrich Bonhoeffer and the Profound Worldliness of Christianity* (Eugene, OR: Cascade Books, 2015).

36. For an overview of the concept of secularization, see e.g. S. Reicke, 'Säkularisation', in *Die Religion in Geschichte und Gegenwart. Handwörterbuch für Theologie und Religionswissenschaft* (ed. Wilfrid Werbeck; Tübingen: J. C. B. Mohr (Siebeck), 1961), 1280–88; Hans-Otto Binder, 'Säkularisation', in *Theologische Realenzyklopädie* (Religionspsychologie – Samaritaner; band XXIX; ed. James K. Cameron Horst Balz et al.; Berlin/New York: W. de Gruyter, 1998), 597–602; Bryan Wilson, 'Secularization', in *Encyclopedia of Religion* (ed. Lindsay Jones; Detroit, MI: Macmillan Reference USA, 2005), 8214–20.

37. Kirsten Busch Nielsen, 'Überlegungen zum Religionsverständnis Dietrich Bonhoeffers: Zwischen Kritik und Konstruktion', *Dietrich Bonhoeffer Jahrbuch* 1 (2003), 93–106.

world has come of age, as Bonhoeffer asserts. The world, as such, no longer needs religion, which sets new preconditions for how to speak about Christianity.[38]

It is important to note that in Bonhoeffer's understanding of the world having come of age, his assertion is both a result of an analysis of Christianity within his own lifetime and a theological thesis. With regard to the former, Bonhoeffer argues that various areas – science, political life, art, ethics, religion and so on – have become autonomous and no longer need God as a working hypothesis.[39] As regards the latter, the assertion as a theological thesis, Bonhoeffer employs certain characteristic dialectical phrases. In continuation of his historical analysis, Bonhoeffer submits that it is part of intellectual decency to let go of God as a 'working hypothesis'. However, at the same time he argues that the impossibility of hypothesizing God's being is made before God. The world that has come of age is closer to God than the world that has not come of age.[40] It is also here that we find the famous phrase: 'Before God, and with God, we live without God.'[41]

It is in connection with this paradoxical understanding that Bonhoeffer's theological normative understanding of the secular becomes apparent. Here, I follow Busch Nielsen's reading of Bonhoeffer, when she argues that Bonhoeffer's religionless Christianity implies the Christian faith's responsibility for the world.[42] This follows from an understanding of religionless Christianity as being deeply embedded in Christianity itself. Bonhoeffer aims to argue the case for a worldly understanding of Christianity, where there is no division between the world and the Christian. Christ is not only to be endorsed as the Lord within narrow ecclesial borders; Christ is – radically speaking – the lord of the world.[43] All being before one's neighbour is, therefore, also a being in Christ; a participation in Christ's being-for-others. In being for the other, one partakes in the being of Christ.[44] Bonhoeffer takes this view to its limits when, as a consequence of this theology of the cross, he argues that God is most significantly present when he is most absent. It is in our living in the world as if God were not there that God is with us. God who is with us is God who forsakes us. It is before and with God that we live without God. In the light of the cross, it is as weak and powerless that God is with us and helps us.[45]

---

38. DBW 8, 402.

39. Ibid., 476–77, 529–35.

40. Ibid., 537.

41. Dietrich Bonhoeffer, *Letters and Papers from Prison* (ed. John W. De Gruchy; trans. Isabel Best, Lisa E. Dahill, Reinhard Krauss and Nancy Lukens; Dietrich Bonhoeffer Works; vol. 8; Minneapolis, MN: Fortress Press, 2010) (DBWE 8), 479.

42. Nielsen, 'Überlegungen zum Religionsverständnis Dietrich Bonhoeffers', 101.

43. DBW 8, 405.

44. Ibid., 558.

45. Ibid., 533.

For the concept of the secular, this implies that the worldly in Bonhoeffer is by no means separate from the 'Christian'. Rather, the worldly and the Christian cannot be understood apart from one another, and Christianity should place itself at the very heart of life.⁴⁶ This also reflects Bonhoeffer's understanding of reality. From Bonhoeffer's point of view it therefore makes no sense to see the secular as that which is separate from the sacred. The secular and the sacred may be differentiated, but not separated. Hereby, the secular in Bonhoeffer holds a Christological motif of significant pertinence to the book. This also brings Bonhoeffer and Milbank into conversation with each other. Both Bonhoeffer and Milbank find it meaningless to argue that there is a being separate from God. Every being partakes in the divine being. Therefore, any attempt to ignore this being in God ends up as a formal abstraction, which is a reduction of the fullness of human life. This is the point at which Bonhoeffer and Milbank come together, and both could play a role in endorsing a plenitude (or fullness) of reality that can serve as an ontological foundation for an ethic of plenitude that moves beyond the traditional antagonism of the sacred and the secular.⁴⁷

Even if Milbank and Bonhoeffer argue quite differently, they both end up endorsing the secular as a temporal and a theological idea. One could say that in both senses the secular in Bonhoeffer and in Milbank is another word for the *humanum*, human reality. The secular – understood as *saeculum* – is a way of describing human reality, which can never be separate from God. In this sense the secular is understood as depicting the worldly reality expressed in the Greek αιων, rendered into *saeculum* in the *Vulgata* (cf. e.g. 1 Cor. 1.20, 2.6, 3.19).⁴⁸ Therefore, the *saeculum* is understood as the period of time before the *eschaton* and in that sense the present is qualified in light of the eschatological. This means that the present time, the *saeculum*, is a temporal concept and yet also theologically can never be understood separate from the *eschaton* (neither temporarily nor theologically). The book contends that this is a fundamental insight in Bonhoeffer's reflections on the relation between the ultimate and penultimate,⁴⁹ and that this may be endorsed in light of Bonhoeffer's understanding of the Christ-reality. In Milbank, a comparable position is found in his Thomistic understanding of participation. Their views lead both authors to affirm the universal, and yet Bonhoeffer and Milbank both derive an affirmation of the universal from a very particular basis. Bonhoeffer's theological course actually brings him to the very roots (*radix*) of theology and makes anything but a profound theological argument an empty abstraction. That is why his view of the secular remains a profound theological concept (see also

46. Kirsten Busch Nielsen, 'The Concept of Religion and Christian Doctrine: The Theology of Dietrich Bonhoeffer Reconsidered', *Studia theologica* 57, no. 1 (2003), 4–19 (8f.).
47. See Nissen, 'Dietrich Bonhoeffer and the Ethics of Plenitude', 108–10.
48. G. Lanczkowski, 'Saeculum', in *Die Religion in Geschichte und Gegenwart. Handwörterbuch für Theologie und Religionswissenschaft* (ed. Wilfrid Werbeck; Tübingen: J. C. B. Mohr (Siebeck), 1961), 1279–80.
49. DBW 6, 137–62.

Chapter 7 for a brief pondering of the Augustinian background of the concept of *saeculum* and how this is understood along the lines mentioned here).

The implications of this concept of the secular, and of a plenitude of reality, are pertinent to the book's thesis. What is implied is that the secular no longer divides reality into separate spheres. On the contrary, there is one reality in which the secular – understood as *saeculum* – is merely a period of time before the *eschaton*. It is the same understanding of *saeculum* that we find in e.g. Robert A. Markus: 'The secular is that which belongs to this age and will have no part in the age to come, when Christ's kingship will hold universal sway. Political authority and institutions, with all the agencies of compulsion and enforcement, are destined for abrogation when the rule of God in Christ is finally revealed.'[50] Such a reassessed understanding of the secular also has implications for the discussion of the relation between religion and politics. In this respect, too, reality is no longer divided into separate spheres.

Christonomy as the foundation of the human condition

Closely associated with the secular is the understanding of autonomy.[51] This concept can be understood both individually and in more social categories, as we can speak of both the autonomy of individuals, science, politics and areas of life such as art, music and literature. As such the concept of autonomy is often seen in close connection with the concept of secularization. Cf. also Nielsen who defines Bonhoeffer's concept of autonomy by viewing it in close connection with his concept of the '*Mündigkeit*' in his late writings. She shows how this concept is particularly inspired by Wilhelm Dilthey.[52] We find all these aspects in Bonhoeffer's reflections on this concept. Historically, the concept is closely associated with the idea of freedom. This concept has its roots in the ancient understanding of ελευθερία, where it is seen in connection with the law constituting the πόλις. In the New Testament, freedom is understood as a divine gift and understood in light of the obedience of faith. The understanding of the Christian freedom, *libertas christiana*, becomes important for the Lutheran theology, where it is

---

50. Robert A. Markus, *Christianity and the Secular* (Notre Dame, IN: University of Notre Dame Press, 2006), 14. See also Oliver O'Donovan, *The Desire of the Nations: Rediscovering the Roots of Political Theology* (Cambridge: Cambridge University Press, 1996), 211–12; Luke Bretherton, *Christianity and Contemporary Politics: The Conditions and Possibilities of Faithful Witness* (Chichester: Wiley, 2010), 81–88; Bretherton, *Christ and the Common Life*, chapter 8 (227–57).

51. The following section is a revised summary of the main findings of Ulrik Nissen, 'Disbelief and Christonomy of the World', *Studia theologica* 60, no. 1 (2006), 91–110.

52. Nielsen, *Syndens brudte magt*, 126 (footnote 51).

understood as service for the neighbour grounded in faith.[53] This is part of the reason why Bonhoeffer speaks affirmatively of freedom instead of autonomy – and why he understands freedom as passivity surrendering to God's guidance[54] or obedience to the will of God.[55] 'Obedience without freedom is slavery, freedom without obedience is arbitrariness. Obedience binds freedom, freedom enobles obedience.'[56] Bonhoeffer's affirmative understanding of freedom is derived from its relationality. This is already apparent in his *Creation and Fall*, where he explains the interconnectedness between being free *from* and free *for* something.[57] 'The "for" and "from" give the basic fabric for all other thoughts and deliberations concerning freedom and forms of freedom within the liberating Christ relation which forms Bonhoeffer's life and thought.'[58]

After the Enlightenment the concept of autonomy becomes an almost indisputable standpoint for philosophical and theological ethics. This is not least due to the influence from Immanuel Kant's moral philosophy. Kant emphasizes the individual as its own lawgiver,[59] whereby autonomy is understood in contrast to heteronomy.[60] However, this autonomy is not understood in contrast to universality, as the test of universalization implies that the individual must act as if the categorical imperative could be a universal law.[61] Even if the concept of autonomy after Kant almost becomes a *conditio sine qua non* for a reasonable

---

53. Eberhard Amelung, 'Autonomie', in *Theologische Realenzyklopädie* (Autokephalie-Biandrata; band V; ed. James K. Cameron Horst Balz et al.; Berlin/New York: W. de Gruyter, 1980), 4–17.

54. DBW 6, 225.

55. Ibid., 288.

56. DBWE 6, 287. See also Wolfgang Huber, 'Freiheit als Form der Liebe. Die Aktualität christlicher Freiheit in den gesellschaftlichen Herausforderungen unserer Zeit', in *Religion im Erbe. Dietrich Bonhoeffer und die Zukunftsfähigkeit des Christentums* (ed. Christian Gremmels and Wolfgang Huber; Gütersloh: Chr. Kaiser/Gütersloher Verlagshaus, 2002), 17–36, who argues convincingly for the connection between freedom, responsibility and love in Bonhoeffer's ethic.

57. Dietrich Bonhoeffer, *Schöpfung und Fall* (herausgegeben von Martin Rüter und Ilse Tödt; Dietrich Bonhoeffer Werke; band 3; Gütersloh: Chr. Kaiser, 2nd rev. edn, 2002) (DBW 3, 58–59, 62–63).

58. Eberhard Bethge, 'Freiheit und Gehorsam bei Bonhoeffer', in *Schöpferische Nachfolge* (Heidelberg: FEST, 1978), 342–43 (author's translation). See Bethge also for an account of the different contexts of Bonhoeffer's concept of freedom, i.e. the social, psychological, theological, ecclesial and political.

59. Immanuel Kant, *Grundlegung zur Metaphysik der Sitten* (ed. Karl Vorländer; Philosophische Bibliothek; vol. 41; Hamburg: Felix Meiner, 1994), 56, 65.

60. Ibid., 65ff.

61. Ibid., 42. See also Roger J. Sullivan, *Immanuel Kant's Moral Theory* (Cambridge: Cambridge University Press, 1989), 46–47.

understanding of ethics in general, and therefore also Christian ethics, the concept is not unchallenged. The concept of human autonomy remains the continuous source of an ongoing debate in Christian ethics. For quite a few theologians and Christian ethicists, this concept is not quite as self-evident as one is often led to believe. Bonhoeffer is such a theologian, who criticizes the concept of human autonomy as the source of ethics. Rather, it is the relation to Christ which is the foundation of moral life.

> Where Christ, true God and true human being, has become the unifying center of my existence, conscience in the formal sense still remains the call, coming from my true self, into unity with myself. However, this unity can now no longer be realized by returning to my autonomy that lives out of the law, but instead in community with Jesus Christ… The origin and goal of my conscience is not a law but the living God and the living human being as I encounter them in Jesus Christ.[62]

This leads Bonhoeffer to his concept of Christonomy in light of the Christological foundation of his ethics. We can ascertain Bonhoeffer's understanding of Christonomy from looking at his *Ethics*. The concept itself is central to that work as a whole, even if it is mentioned explicitly only once, where Bonhoeffer speaks of it as a concept whereby the antagonism between heteronomy and autonomy is overcome.[63] So far, Bonhoeffer's understanding of Christonomy has not been studied in any great detail. No studies have been found dealing explicitly with this concept. To analyse this concept, the study by Trygve Wyller becomes an immediate interlocutor, as his thesis points in the opposite direction.[64] Wyller argues that Bonhoeffer holds a positive concept of autonomy,[65] and is careful to argue that autonomy and faith are not understood in antagonistic terms. Therefore, the contention of autonomy is not conceived in contrast to the claim of God's presence in the world. I admit that this sounds quite Bonhoefferian. The problem, however, is that Wyller takes the step to argue affirmatively for the concept of autonomy itself, which repeatedly is repudiated in Bonhoeffer's own writings either in the concept of *Autonomie* or *Eigengesetzlichkeit*. In this critique I concur with Wannenwetsch, who also points to the deficit in Wyller's concept of autonomy and how this implies that he does not sufficiently take into account Bonhoeffer's critique of modernity.[66]

---

62. DBWE 6, 278.
63. DBW 6, 406.
64. Trygve Wyller, *Glaube und autonome Welt: Diskussion eines Grundproblems der neueren systematischen Theologie mit Blick auf Dietrich Bonhoeffer, Oswald Bayer und K. E. Løgstrup* (Theologische Bibliothek Töpelmann; 91; Berlin: W. de Gruyter, 1998).
65. Ibid., 216.
66. Bernd Wannenwetsch, 'Trygve Wyller: Glaube und Autonome Welt. Rezension', *Theologische Literaturzeitung* 124 (1999), 799–803.

4. The Christological Shaping of Central Concepts in Bonhoeffer's Ethics

Finally, Bonhoeffer's Christonomy is significant for his socio-political thought, and may serve as a resource for contemporary Christian social ethics. Linking in with his understanding of the Christ-reality, Bonhoeffer argues that just as one cannot separate the orders of creation from the reality of Christ, or make a separation between worldly and Christian, profane and sacred spaces, one cannot separate the non-believer from Christ. Arguing that all of reality is included in Christ, he makes the point that the non-believer, too, is in Christ. This is exemplified in Bonhoeffer's understanding of the unconscious Christian.[67] Bonhoeffer encourages the Christian to regard as Christians those people who cannot call themselves Christian, and to help them to a confession of Christ.[68] This inclusive understanding of the relation between belief and non-belief follows from Bonhoeffer's understanding of reconciliation; a reconciliation that concerns all of humanity, as it is reconciled with God in the incarnation of Christ. 'There is no human being as such, just as there is no God as such; both are empty abstractions. Human beings are accepted in God's becoming human and are loved, judged, and reconciled in Christ, and God is the God who became human.'[69] In relation to this reading of Bonhoeffer, Nielsen rightly makes the point that one should be careful not to downplay the cross and resurrection in the attempt to appropriate Bonhoeffer's Christology for the affirmation of human and worldly life. Nielsen argues that Bonhoeffer's distinction between the ultimate and the penultimate implies the connectedness between the life, death and resurrection of Christ.[70] Bonhoeffer understands the incarnation, the cross and the resurrection in close connection to each other.[71]

The community with Jesus Christ is understood inclusively. Reflecting upon the ethical implications of Jesus Christ as the crucified redeemer, Bonhoeffer argues – with the terminology Luther used in the debate on the Holy Communion – that true worldliness is only possible 'in, with, and under' the preaching of Christ. With the analogy to the Holy Communion, Bonhoeffer underlines that the world does not cease to be world – just as the bread and wine do not cease to be bread and wine – in the preaching of Christ; rather, true worldliness depends upon the preaching of the cross of Christ.[72] When reflecting on the implications of Jesus Christ as risen and all earthly powers as subjected to him, Bonhoeffer points out that the preaching of Christ is now a calling to all creatures to the lordship of Jesus Christ. But for Bonhoeffer this does not imply a law, which is different from the law of creation. Rather, the law of Christ liberates creation to fulfilment of its own law.[73] The law of Christ does not constitute a lordship of the church over

---

67. DBW 6, 83, 162, 344.
68. Ibid., 162.
69. DBWE 6, 253.
70. Nielsen, *Syndens brudte magt*, 145 (footnote 69).
71. DBW 6, 148–50.
72. Ibid., 404–5.
73. Ibid., 406.

other authorities in public life, family or culture. Bonhoeffer maintains the law of Christ, but underlines that it is a law that confirms the divine mandates in their own fulfilling. Family, culture and political authority are all liberated to their own being – which has its source in Jesus Christ.

It is in connection with these reflections that Bonhoeffer introduces the concept of Christonomy in order to overcome the contrast between heteronomy and autonomy. At one and the same time, Bonhoeffer affirms human reality (and in this sense maintains autonomy) and points to its foundation beyond itself (endorsing heteronomy). In so doing, he argues for a third concept (Christonomy) as the possible way to overcome the apparent contradiction implied in the relation between the two former concepts. This approach implies that Bonhoeffer can endorse both the particularity (given in the specific qualification of Christonomy) and the universality (given in the recognition of autonomy and the implied affirmation of human reality) in his concept of the normative foundation (*nomos*) of human reality, irrespective of belief and non-belief.

It is central to Bonhoeffer's understanding of Christonomy that he wishes to counter the tendency in some versions of Lutheran social ethics to endorse a separation between the worldly realm and the spiritual realm. He criticizes a pseudo-Lutheran tendency to see the two kingdoms doctrine as an argument for two separate spheres.[74] This is also found e.g. in his essay 'State and Church',[75] where he differentiates between grounding the political authority in the nature of the human being,[76] seeing it as a protection against human sinfulness[77] and grounding it in Jesus Christ.[78] It is in the last understanding of the foundation of political authority that we find Bonhoeffer's consent. Therefore, it makes no sense to speak of worldly authority independently of Jesus Christ, i.e. the church. '[I]t is therefore under no circumstances possible to speak theologically of government apart from Jesus Christ nor, since he is indeed the head of his church, apart from the *church of Jesus Christ*.'[79]

Tearing apart the Christological relation between the worldly and the spiritual realm opens up the risk of seeing certain areas of life as secular and autonomous, i.e. independent from God. According to Bonhoeffer, the claim of the autonomous spheres of life tears apart the unity of life given in Christ.[80] Fundamentally, this

---

74. Ibid., 41–43.

75. Dietrich Bonhoeffer, *Konspiration und Haft. 1940–1945* (herausgegeben von Jørgen Glenthøj, Ulrich Kabitz und Wolf Krötke; Dietrich Bonhoeffer Werke; band 16; Gütersloh: Chr. Kaiser, 1996) (DBW 16), 506-35.

76. Ibid., 509–12.

77. Ibid., 512–14.

78. Ibid., 514–17.

79. Dietrich Bonhoeffer, *Conspiracy and Imprisonment* (ed. Mark S. Brocker; trans. Lisa E. Dahill; Dietrich Bonhoeffer Works; vol. 16; Minneapolis, MN: Fortress Press, 2006) (DBWE 16), 510–11.

80. DBW 6, 251.

is a negation of a Trinitarian understanding of Christ, as the lordship of Christ is the lordship of the Creator, Reconciler and Redeemer. Any attempt to separate the worldly from the proclamation of Christ leads to a deification of the worldly.[81] Claiming the autonomy of the worldly realm, therefore, fundamentally may be regarded as rejecting Jesus Christ as the lord of reality.[82] In Bonhoeffer, this is what has happened in the secularist misunderstanding of the worldly realm as autonomous.[83]

The implications of Bonhoeffer's endorsement of Christonomy are quite central for a contemporary debate on the identity of a Christian social ethic in a public discourse. The significance of Bonhoeffer's understanding is to be found in his continuous insistence on a specifically Christological foundation that underlies a common source of ethics. He holds an identity-specific understanding of the common basis of worldly, human life. This implies that he can affirm worldly, human life and yet maintain a specific understanding of its conditions of being. Bonhoeffer thereby finds the *aurea mediocritas* between what he calls, respectively, 'the radical solution' and 'the compromise'[84] and refers to elsewhere as 'sectarianism' and 'secularism'.[85]

The Christological ontology of reason

When we turn to his concept of reason, we see a similar double-sidedness reflecting the underlying Chalcedonian Christology.[86] As we have seen in Bonhoeffer's 'Lectures on Christology', he understands Christ as the centre of human existence. In these lectures, he also argues for Christ as the centre of all knowledge, even if this is only seen in faith.[87] This understanding is furthered in his *Ethics*, where he argues that reason comes to itself in Christ, meaning that reason is affirmed in Christ, as he is seen as the true origin (*Ursprung*) of reason. Christ is the centre and the power (*Kraft*) of reason. In his section on 'Church and World I' in *Ethics*,[88] Bonhoeffer ponders the surprising experience of several concepts, e.g. reason, culture, humanity and tolerance, returning to their origins in Christianity when threatened. At a point

---

81. Ibid., 404–5.
82. Ibid., 263–64.
83. Ibid., 236, 263.
84. Ibid., 144–45.
85. Ibid., 235–36, 263–64.
86. The following section is a revised summary of the main findings of Ulrik Nissen, 'The Christological Ontology of Reason', *Neue Zeitschrift für systematische Theologie und Religionsphilosophie* 48, no. 4 (2006), 460–78.
87. Dietrich Bonhoeffer, *Berlin. 1932–1933* (ed. Carsten Nikolaisen and Ernst-Albert Scharffenorth; Dietrich Bonhoeffer Werke; band 12; Gütersloh: Chr. Kaiser, 1997) (DBW 12), 280–81.
88. DBWE 6, 339–51.

in time where Christianity was under severe pressure and therefore replied in an uncompromising manner to reason, culture, humanity and tolerance, these concepts themselves took refuge in the shadow of the church.[89] Bonhoeffer describes this with the metaphor of the child returning to its mother. 'Even though their appearance and language had changed a great deal during the time of their alienation, at the decisive moment mother and children recognized one another. Reason, justice, culture, humanity, and other concepts like these sought and found new meaning and new strength in their origin.'[90] Bonhoeffer understands Jesus Christ as the origin of these concepts – i.e. also reason. As Christ is the origin of these concepts, it is only with a participation in Christ and a protection under Christ that these concepts can live.

> This origin is Jesus Christ [i.e. the origin to which the concepts have returned (my note)] … Only that which participates in Christ can endure and overcome. Christ is the center and power of the Bible, of the church, of theology, but also of humanity, *reason*, justice, and culture. To Christ everything must return; only under Christ's protection can it live.[91]

As we have seen with other concepts in the book, Bonhoeffer holds a characteristically paradoxical understanding. Concepts that have often played an adverse role with regard to Christianity are understood as having their origin in Christ and thereby being affirmed in Christ in their most true sense. This is also the case for his understanding of reason. Reason is understood best when it is seen as having its origin in Christ.

As is characteristic of other central concepts in Bonhoeffer,[92] he does not elaborate on his understanding of reason in analytical detail. Therefore, he does not e.g. draw a sharp distinction between theoretical and practical reason. Rather, it is a point that the two are not separated. Reason has a knowledge of the natural – i.e. in a general and common sense[93] – but this is also a knowledge of the individual's rights of nature.[94] In contemporary theological ethics a very nuanced and precise definition of reason has proven necessary. Stefan Grotefeld gives a comprehensive overview of this background and discourse. He differentiates between seven types of reason in contemporary ethics: (1) rationality as pursuit of self-interest (e.g. Ernst Tugendhat); (2) rationality supplemented with reason (e.g. John Rawls); (3) communicative rationality and discourse ethics (e.g. Jürgen Habermas);

---

89. DBW 6, 343.
90. DBWE 6, 341.
91. Ibid. (my italics).
92. Christiane Tietz-Steiding, 'Verkrümmte Vernunft und intellektuelle Redlichkeit. Dietrich Bonhoeffers Erkenntnistheorie', in *Religion im Erbe. Dietrich Bonhoeffer und die Zukunftsfähigkeit des Christentums* (ed. Christian Gremmels and Wolfgang Huber; Gütersloh: Chr. Kaiser, 2002), 293–307 (302, footnote 45).
93. DBW 6, 166–71.
94. Ibid., 177.

(4) morality as rationality (e.g. Richard M. Hare); (5) moral justification through insight into universal purposes (e.g. Nicholas Rescher); (6) contextual rationality (e.g. Alasdair MacIntyre); (7) rational deliberation of aims and wishes (e.g. Stefan Gosepath).[95] Placing Bonhoeffer in this typological scheme would, however, appear somewhat anachronistic. As a definition of the concept of reason analysed in the present book, it must suffice, therefore, to say that focus is on Bonhoeffer's view of *Vernunft* as it is deployed in *Ethik*. His notion of *Verstand* is not excluded, but it is not clear from the apparently four times it is used in *Ethik*[96] that this term describes something different from *Vernunft*. These two terms are, therefore, both included in the book's use of the term 'reason'.[97]

Bonhoeffer ponders the Christological foundation of reason when he reflects on 'Natural Life'.[98] He finds it important that 'the natural' is understood in a relation between the original created shape of life and its redemption and renewal in Christ.[99] It is only in Christ that natural life is affirmed. This does not mean, however, that it is a preliminary stage towards life with Christ. Rather, the confirmation of natural life through Christ is derived from Christ's having entered into natural life. It is by the incarnation of Christ that natural life becomes the penultimate directed towards the ultimate. 'Only by Christ's becoming human does natural life become the penultimate that is directed toward the ultimate. Only through Christ's becoming human do we have the right to call people to natural life and to live it ourselves.'[100] This leads Bonhoeffer to distinguish between the natural as determined formally and according to content. The formal determination can only be understood in light of the preserving will of God and the orientation of the natural toward Christ. Formally, the natural, therefore, can only be determined by looking at Jesus Christ.[101] With regard to the content, Bonhoeffer affirms reason as 'the organ for recognizing the natural'.[102] Reason is not understood as a divine principle of cognition superior to the natural. Rather, it is understood as the conscious perception of the natural in its givenness. Hereby, the natural and reason are related to each other as the form of being and the form of consciousness of preserved life. This also means that reason recognizes the natural in its fallenness into which reason has been drawn. But nonetheless, it recognizes the natural as the given and it recognizes the content of the natural.[103]

---

95. Stefan Grotefeld, 'Rationalität, Vernunft und Moralbegründung', in *Ethik, Vernunft und Rationalität/Ethics, Reason and Rationality* (ed. Alberto Bondolfi, Stefan Grotefeld and Rudi Neuberth; Münster: LIT, 1997), 55–89.

96. DBW 6, 106, 324, 326, 400.

97. See also Nissen, 'The Christological Ontology of Reason', 462 (footnote 14).

98. DBWE 6, 171–218.

99. DBW 6, 166.

100. DBWE 6, 174.

101. DBW 6, 166.

102. DBWE 6, 174.

103. DBW 6, 167.

The recognition of the content of the natural also implies for Bonhoeffer that he argues for natural rights.[104] Reflecting on the rights of the community ('die Rechte der Gemeinschaft'), he argues that these cannot be understood without recognizing the individual's right ('das Recht des Einzelnen'). This individual right is given as a consequence of God's will to create the individual being and to give him or her eternal life. This condition of human life is known from natural life, and failing to recognize it will have grave consequences. It is therefore the concern of reason to acknowledge this right of the individual – without referring to the will of God.[105] 'God's having created individuals and called them to eternal life is a reality that is effective in natural life. To disregard it has ominous consequences. It is therefore *the business of reason* within natural life to take account of the right of the individual, even when the divine background of this right is not recognized.'[106] The parallel to the Grotian impious hypothesis is quite astonishing, even if Bonhoeffer does not refer to Grotius.[107] Reason recognizes (even without recurring to the divine background) – as fallen reason – the natural rights given with the fallen world.

Still, even if Bonhoeffer does recognize the abilities of reason, he consistently maintains the Christological origin. Reason cannot be separated from the Christological reality. As such one could say that Bonhoeffer endorses an unlimited recognition of the abilities of reason – as long as reason is understood in light of reality, and its true source is maintained. The understanding of reason as coming to itself in Christ implies that reason as such is recognized – in Christ. As such we can speak of a Christological ontology of reason. Here, ontology is not understood in the sense of the Danish theologian K. E. Løgstrup, when he understands it as the fundamental human conditions of life, where human lives are interwoven with each other.[108] Rather, ontology is understood in an ontological-theological sense in light of the contention of Jesus Christ as the centre of human existence. In Bonhoeffer's use of the concept of '*Mitte*' (which is translated as 'center' in the English edition), it is not completely clear what he means by this concept. However, it does not suffice to regard it merely as a metaphor. Rather, it should be seen as a term describing Christ as the centre of human existence which essentially cannot be disregarded. Hereby, he understands Christ as the centre of human existence, which implies that he is both the judgement over and the justification of human life.[109] This brings him close

---

104. Ibid., 173–217. See also Chapter 5, the section entitled 'Natural Law Christologically Reshaped'.

105. DBW 6, 177.

106. DBWE 6, 184 (my italics).

107. This is, however, done elsewhere. See e.g. DBW 8, 530. See also Chapter 1.

108. K. E. Løgstrup, *Etiske begreber og problemer* (Løgstrup biblioteket; Aarhus: Klim, 3rd edn, 2014), 12.

109. See also Chapter 3, particularly the section 'The Who, How and Where in the "Lectures on Christology"'.

4. The Christological Shaping of Central Concepts in Bonhoeffer's Ethics

to the passages in *Ethics* where he ponders the Christ-reality as the simultaneity of the life, death and resurrection of Christ.[110]

Philosophically, ontology can be understood in various ways. Analytically, it is taken to refer to the 'philosophical investigation of existence, or being' (where it asks what 'being' means), or the 'ontology of a theory', whereby it signifies that which has to exist for a theory to be true.[111] Theologically, it is not least Bonhoeffer's own work *Act and Being* that is essential for an elaboration of the concept of ontology. Referring to Hartmann, Bonhoeffer defines real ontology accordingly: 'It is the concern of *true* ontology to demonstrate the primacy of being over against consciousness and to uncover this being. Ontology initially wishes to say no more than that there is "a real being outside consciousness, outside the sphere of logic and the limits of ratio" …'[112]

I understand the concept of ontology along the lines of Rainer Mayer, when he points to both the Christological ontology in Bonhoeffer's early writings[113] and the Christological ontology in *Ethics*.[114] Mayer understands Christological ontology in the sense of being in Christ (*Sein in Christus*).[115] Hereby, ontology comes close to the concept of reality and Bonhoeffer's claim that there is no being apart from Christ. When ontology is understood in this sense, there is an immediate inseparability of the Christ-reality for Bonhoeffer's concept of reason. Mayer's understanding of ontology in Bonhoeffer is paralleled in Heinrich Ott, when he argues that Bonhoeffer's understanding in *Ethics* (i.e. that all concepts of reality must be understood in relation to the Christ-reality) implies 'that Bonhoeffer structures the ontology of reality Christologically, or in other words: the Christology

---

110. See e.g. DBW 6, 60, 148–50, 249–50.

111. Edward Craig, *Ontology* (London: Routledge, 1998). For an historical overview of philosophical approaches to the concept of ontology with an account of this concept from the sixteenth and seventeenth centuries until the twentieth century with e.g. Edmund Husserl, Nicolai Hartmann and Martin Heidegger, see K. Kremer, 'Ontologie', in *Historisches Wörterbuch der Philosophie* (ed. Joachim Ritter and Karlfried Gründer Basel/Stuttgart: Schwabe & Co., 1984), 1189–98.

112. Dietrich Bonhoeffer, *Act and Being: Transcendental Philosophy and Ontology in Systematic Theology* (ed. Wayne Whitson Floyd, Jr; trans. Martin Rumscheidt; Dietrich Bonhoeffer Works; vol. 2; Minneapolis, MN: Fortress Press, 1996) (DBWE 2), 59. I will not go further here into Bonhoeffer's concept of ontology in *Akt und Sein*, but instead refer to Nissen, 'The Christological Ontology of Reason', where I raise a discussion with Christiane Tietz-Steiding, *Bonhoeffers Kritik der verkrümmten Vernunft: Eine erkenntnistheoretische Untersuchung* (Beiträge zur historischen Theologie; 112; Tübingen: Mohr Siebeck, 1999); Tietz-Steiding, 'Verkrümmte Vernunft und intellektuelle Redlichkeit'.

113. Mayer, *Christuswirklichkeit*, 15, 84ff.

114. Ibid., 193–94.

115. Ibid., 194.

becomes the ontology of all of reality'.[116] Hereby, Ott also emphasizes (alluding to Bonhoeffer's famous Christological question from *Letters and Papers*) that the aim of Bonhoeffer is to ponder who Jesus Christ is for us today.[117] This reading implies that reason understood separately from the Christ-reality is a distorted reason, taken apart from its true foundations. Reason is true reason in Christ. It is not a limited reason, but a reason that has come to itself.[118]

The Christological understanding of reason in *Ethics* implies a tension between reason in its own right and reason as coming to itself in Christ. When this is understood in connection with the Chalcedonian Christology in Bonhoeffer's Christology lectures, it opens the door to understanding the affirmation of reason as a consequence of the affirmation of humanity in Christ's incarnation. This understanding of reason thus follows from the understanding of Christ as the true human being. Just as humanity is confirmed and restored in Christ, so is reason, as the constitutive ability of the human being. However, at the same time, Bonhoeffer maintains his critical view on reason when it is separate from Christ. Christ is seen as the source of reason, and apart from Christ reason is viewed as deceived. This does not, however, seem to lead Bonhoeffer to reject the abilities of reason. Rather, it is based on a presupposition of faith. It is only because Christ is this centre that it makes any sense to endorse the soundness of reason. But to view Christ as the centre of reason, and as the core that is the very source of the soundness of reason, also means that the true source of reason can only be revealed. The true source of reason is not apparent to reason in itself. Reason thereby comes to itself in giving itself up. This paradoxical affirmation of reason points to the responsive dimension in Bonhoeffer's ethics, to which we now turn with regard to his concept of responsibility.

Responsibility and Christological responsiveness

The last concept in Bonhoeffer's ethic, where we will seek to find the Chalcedonian Christology as an underlying and formative thought structure, is his understanding of responsibility.[119] The concept of responsibility plays a central role in Bonhoeffer's

---

116. Ott, *Wirklichkeit und Glaube*, 149 (my translation).

117. Ibid. For a critique of this ontological reading of Bonhoeffer, see Ernst Feil, *Die Theologie Dietrich Bonhoeffers: Hermeneutik, Christologie, Weltverständnis* (Studien zur systematischen Theologie und Ethik; band 45; Berlin: LIT, 5th ext. edn, 2005), 162 (footnote 19).

118. DBW 6, 252–53, 342–44.

119. The following section is a revised summary of the main findings of Ulrik Nissen, 'Responding to Human Reality: Responsibility and Responsiveness in Bonhoeffer's Ethics', in *Being Human, Becoming Human: Dietrich Bonhoeffer and Social Thought* (ed. Brian Gregor and Jens Zimmerman; Eugene, OR: Wipf & Stock, 2010), 203–25.

ethic. Several studies have been dedicated to an analysis of this concept.[120] Even if many of these studies concentrate on the interplay between responsibility and political issues, the concept of reality or Christological motifs, none of these are reading his concept of responsibility with the aim of seeking an underlying Chalcedonian mode of thought. In Christine Schliesser's work the focus is on a very particular side of this concept, i.e. the concept of taking on guilt as part of the Christian's responsibility.[121] Even if this is closely associated with the underlying Christological presuppositions, Schliesser does not look for the implicit Chalcedonian Christology. A similar picture emerges in another recent major work by Gunter Prüller-Jagenteufel.[122] The central concern in Prüller-Jagenteufel's habilitation is the relation between justification and sin in Bonhoeffer's ethics. This leads him to an analysis of responsibility as the core of a Christian ethic.[123] Prüller-Jagenteufel argues that Bonhoeffer's concept of responsibility is deeply rooted in both his Christology[124] and ecclesiology.[125] This is due to Bonhoeffer's concept of responsibility as derived from the justification of the sinner. Sin and guilt are fundamentally understood as irresponsibility.[126] Even if Prüller-Jagenteufel

---

120. See e.g. Tiemo Rainer Peters, 'Jenseits von Radikalismus und Kompromiss: die politische Verantwortung der Christen nach Dietrich Bonhoeffer', in *Verspieltes Erbe* (Munich: Chr Kaiser, 1979), 94–115; Larry Rasmussen, 'The Ethics of Responsible Action', in *The Cambridge Companion to Dietrich Bonhoeffer* (ed. John W. De Gruchy; Cambridge: Cambridge University Press, 1999), 206–25; Bernd Wannenwetsch, '"Responsible Living" or "Responsible Self"? Bonhoefferian Reflections on a Vexed Moral Notion', *Studies in Christian Ethics* 18, no. 3 (2005), 125–40; Peter Dabrock, 'Wirklichkeit verantworten: der responsive Ansatz theologischer Ethik bei Dietrich Bonhoeffer', in *Verantwortungsethik als Theologie des Wirklichen* (ed. Wolfgang Nethöfel, Peter Dabrock and Siegfried Keil; Göttingen: Vandenhoeck & Ruprecht, 2009), 117–58; Wolfgang Huber, 'Sozialethik als Verantwortungsethik', in *Verantwortungsethik als Theologie des Wirklichen* (ed. Wolfgang Nethöfel, Peter Dabrock and Siegfried Keil; Göttingen: Vandenhoeck & Ruprecht, 2009), 74–100. Even if this list is far from exhaustive, it gives an impression of important readings of Bonhoeffer's concept of responsibility. Also, two influential anthologies have centred around this theme: John D. Godsey and Geffrey B. Kelly, *Ethical Responsibility: Bonhoeffer's Legacy to the Churches* (Toronto Studies in Theology; New York/Toronto: Edwin Mellen Press, 1981); Wayne Whitson Floyd and Charles Marsh, *Theology and the Practice of Responsibility: Essays on Dietrich Bonhoeffer* (Valley Forge, PA: Trinity Press International, 1994).

121. Christine Schliesser, *Everyone Who Acts Responsibly Becomes Guilty: Bonhoeffer's Concept of Accepting Guilt* (Louisville, KY: Westminster John Knox, 2008).

122. Gunter M. Prüller-Jagenteufel, *Befreit zur Verantwortung: Sünde und Versöhnung in der Ethik Dietrich Bonhoeffers* (Ethik im Theologischen Diskurs; Münster: LIT, 2004).

123. Ibid., 484–510.

124. Ibid., 272–79, 490–92.

125. Ibid., 492–97.

126. Ibid., 499–511.

does recognize the relation between the incarnational ethic and responsibility in Bonhoeffer, as it is derived from his understanding of the Christ-reality,[127] his reading of Bonhoeffer's concept of responsibility tends to pull it too strongly in the direction of relating it to Bonhoeffer's understanding of the justification of the sinner. Prüller-Jagenteufel does admit that responsibility is also made possible for all human beings due to the universality of the Christ-event.[128] But, at the same time, Prüller-Jagenteufel links responsibility so closely to the church as the place of the discipleship and responsibility, it makes it difficult to see how he can maintain Bonhoeffer's paradoxical affirmation of the reality of the world and the reality of God in the Christ-reality as the place of responsibility. The most recent study is by Esther Reed.[129] Reed shows how the concept of responsibility has become problematic in the modern approaches to this concept. The central problem for many of these approaches is that the complexity of today's systemic and structural relations of responsibility makes it very difficult to talk of agency in a direct individual sense. Here, we reach the limits of responsibility. With the background of her encounters with the mining industries in South Africa, Chile and Peru, Reed argues that our understanding of responsibility today needs to take its starting point in 'the other'. We need to develop an understanding of a 'You-I-You' of ethical responsibility, which opens the way for a responsibility for our global neighbour. Bonhoeffer's Christological and responsive understanding of responsibility plays a central role in this new understanding of responsibility.

In Bonhoeffer, the universality of responsibility is derived from his understanding of the one Christ-reality. As we have seen with other concepts central to Bonhoeffer's ethics, the one Christ-reality implies an affirmation of the whole of human reality. As regards his understanding of responsibility, Bonhoeffer establishes a crucial link between being human and being responsible towards the other. This is an understanding that we already find in his early *Sanctorum Communion*.[130] 'The I comes into being only in relation to the You; only in response to a demand does *responsibility* arise. "You" says nothing about its own being, only about its demand.'[131] Bonhoeffer fundamentally understands the human being

---

127. Ibid., 490–92.

128. Ibid., 509.

129. Esther D. Reed, *The Limit of Responsibility: Engaging Dietrich Bonhoeffer in a Globalizing Era* (ed. Brian Brock and Susan F. Parsons; T&T Clark Enquiries in Theological Ethics; London: T&T Clark, 2018).

130. Dietrich Bonhoeffer, *Sanctorum Communio. Eine dogmatische Untersuchung zur Soziologie der Kirche* (herausgegeben von Joachim von Soosten; Dietrich Bonhoeffer Werke; band 1; Gütersloh: Chr. Kaiser, 1986) (DBW 1).

131. Dietrich Bonhoeffer, *Sanctorum Communio: A Theological Study of the Sociology of the Church* (ed. Clifford J. Green; trans. Reinhard Krauss and Nancy Lukens; Dietrich Bonhoeffer Works; vol. 1; Minneapolis, MN: Fortress Press, 1998) (DBWE 1), 54.

as a relational being set within bonds of sociality.[132] However, Bonhoeffer takes this a step further than e.g. Martin Buber, when he (i.e. Bonhoeffer) integrates the understanding of God as creator into his understanding of the You, the other, as a real, concrete You. The real relation to the other is determined by my relation to God and, therefore, the relation to the other is determined by the revelation of God's love.[133] Hereby, he argues against the idea of the individual as an isolated being who has an absolute criterion by which to determine good and evil. This is fundamentally an abstraction and a reduction of the human condition's ethical dimension.[134] Parallel to this is the temptation to pull back from the ethical responsibilities of historical existence, safeguarding oneself by using certain general principles that are applied to any situation, regardless of the consequences. Both of these types of isolation of the individual negate the historicity of human existence.[135] In response to these approaches, Bonhoeffer argues in favour of understanding the human being in the immediate encounter with the other – the encounter out of which responsibility arises. Furthermore, it is not simply a responsibility for the individual, but a responsibility for entire communities and groups of communities.[136]

Bonhoeffer stresses this point, going on to argue that the ethical dimension is not something that exists as a static norm. Rather, the ethical dimension is given in the concrete encounter with the other, and in the acceptance of responsibility for the other.[137]

> The moment a person accepts responsibility for other people – and only in so doing does the person live in reality – the genuine ethical situation arises. This is really something different from the abstract way in which people usually seek to come to terms with the ethical problem. The subject of the action is no longer the isolated individual, but the one who is responsible for other people. The action's norm is not a universal principle, but the concrete neighbour, as given to me by God.[138]

But this also means that the ethical individual acts in freedom in this concrete situation. As there are no universal principles that define, beforehand, the ethical

---

132. Clifford J. Green, *Bonhoeffer. A Theology of Sociality* (Grand Rapids, MI: W. B. Eerdmans, rev. edn, 1999). See also the recent study on Bonhoeffer's early ecclesiology, where it is demonstrated how Bonhoeffer understands the church both as an empirical reality and as a community in Christ and the work of the Holy Spirit: Michael Mawson, *Christ Existing as Community: Bonhoeffer's Ecclesiology* (Oxford: Oxford University Press, 2018).
133. DBW 1, 32–35.
134. DBW 6, 218–19, 246–48.
135. Ibid., 219.
136. Ibid., 219–20.
137. Ibid., 220, 260.
138. DBWE 6, 221.

situation and no norm that guides the ethical discernment independently of the immediate encounter, the ethical individual acts freely. Responsibility presupposes freedom.[139] 'Responsibility is human freedom that exists only by being bound to God and neighbor.'[140] The individual is left to judge the situation on his or her own, and to answer for the consequences of the action without any support from other people or principles.[141]

This understanding of responsibility implies a universal dimension in Bonhoeffer's understanding of the foundation of ethics. Ethics understood as responsibility is given with being human and in the immediate encounter between one another. However, this universal dimension cannot be separated from its specific foundation. Bonhoeffer already makes this clear in the beginning of his *Ethics* by referring to the foundation of Christian ethics in the will of God.[142] For Bonhoeffer, this has to do with the very concept of reality, which leads him to assert that the main concern in Christian ethics is the question of how the reality of God everywhere can show itself to be 'the ultimate reality'. However, Bonhoeffer also stresses that this phrase is not meant to disparage the actual world. Rather, it is to be seen as an affirmation of the world as it is known in the revelation of God in Jesus Christ. Therefore, the source of a Christian ethic is not the reality of one's own self, but the reality of God as it is revealed in Jesus Christ.[143]

As far as responsibility is concerned, this implies that the responsible person does not impose a foreign law on reality, but acts in accordance with reality.[144] However, this is not just meant to be understood as a servile attitude towards the 'facts of reality'. In Bonhoeffer, it is important that worldly reality is both affirmed and negated at the same time.[145] This double-sidedness is closely related to Bonhoeffer's underlying Chalcedonian Christology. It is in this Christologically shaped understanding of the 'Yes' and 'No' to reality that reality finds its true foundation and source of responsibility.[146] Bonhoeffer explicitly relates this to Jesus Christ as *the* real one, i.e. God incarnate, the God who became human.[147] 'Because in Jesus Christ God and humanity became one, so through Christ what is "Christian" and what is "worldly" become one in the action of the Christian.'[148] 'God became human, taking on human being in bodily form, thus reconciling humanity's world with God. The affirmation of human beings and their reality

---

139. DBW 6, 283.
140. DBWE 6, 283.
141. DBW 6, 220–21, 268.
142. Ibid., 31.
143. Ibid., 33.
144. Ibid., 260.
145. Ibid., 148–52, 249–53.
146. Ibid., 250–51.
147. Ibid., 252, 261.
148. DBWE 6, 253.

was based on God's taking on humanity, not vice versa.'[149] The affirmation and negation of reality at the same time is closely linked to Bonhoeffer's understanding of life itself – in its entirety – as a response to the word of God addressed to us in Jesus Christ.[150] This 'responsive life is what Bonhoeffer calls 'responsibility'.

> This life, lived in answer to the life of Jesus Christ (as the Yes and No to our life), we call *'responsibility'* [*Verantwortung*]. This concept responsibility denotes the complete wholeness and unity of the answer to the reality that is given to us in Jesus Christ, as opposed to the partial answers that we might be able to give, for example, from considerations of usefulness, or with reference to certain principles.[151]

This also means that the notion of responsibility is given an ontological plenitude,[152] which implies that the fullness of responsibility is derived from its Christological foundation. The biblical sense of responsibility fundamentally means taking responsibility for Jesus Christ. Bonhoeffer refers to passages in the New Testament, where Paul speaks about his defence of the gospel, whereby responsibility and witness come close to each other. The Christian is called to answer, and take responsibility, for what has happened through Jesus Christ.[153] In this responsibility the Christian bears witness of Christ before human beings, but at the same time the Christian represents human beings before Christ, as he or she takes responsibility for human beings before Christ (as the human being is never an isolated individual). The Christian is thereby held responsible before God and before human beings at the same time.

> My answering [*Verantwortung*] for Christ before human ears simultaneously reaches the ears of Christ as my answering for human beings. Being accountable [*Verantwortung*] *for* Jesus Christ before human beings at the same time means being accountable for human beings before Christ; only thus can I take responsibility for myself before God and before human beings.[154]

This Christological foundation of responsibility also carries with it certain specific Christological traits, such as vicarious representation, willingness to bear guilt and willingness to suffer for the other. Common to these traits is the understanding that, as responsibility is fundamentally rooted in Christ, true responsibility shows itself in a conformation to Christ. It is in the likeness with Christ that responsibility affirms both the universal dimension and the specific dimension of responsibility at the same time. The *vicarious representation* is derived from the vicarious representation of Jesus Christ. True human responsibility is rooted in God's becoming human, and in the manner in which this brought about

---

149. Ibid., 262.
150. DBW 6, 253.
151. DBWE 6, 254.
152. See Nissen, 'Dietrich Bonhoeffer and the Ethics of Plenitude'.
153. DBW 6, 255.
154. DBWE 6, 256.

the vicarious representation of Jesus Christ on behalf of all human beings. For Bonhoeffer it is only possible to speak of true responsibility from this source:

> Jesus Christ is the very embodiment of the person who lives responsibly... he lives only as the one who in himself has taken on and bears the selves of all human beings. His entire life, action, and suffering is vicarious representative action... In this real vicarious representative action in which his human existence consists, he is the responsible human being par excellence. *All human responsibility is rooted in the real vicarious representative action of Jesus Christ on behalf of all human beings. Responsible action is vicarious representative action.* Vicarious representative action is not presumptuous and overbearing only insofar as it is grounded in God's becoming human, which brought about the real vicarious representative action of Jesus Christ on behalf of all human beings. It is only on this ground that there is genuine vicarious representative action and thus responsible action.[155]

This responsibility has love as its content, and freedom as its form.[156] Hereby, Bonhoeffer emphasizes that the Christian is called into a life lived in God's love, which Bonhoeffer understands as equivalent with reality. This follows from God's love being fulfilled in the world. Therefore, the call to live lives in concrete, responsible action is not seen in contrast to the fulfilment of God's law in Jesus Christ, but rather as an expression of the Christ-reality taking on form in the world. 'The commandments of God's righteousness are fulfilled in vicarious representative action, which means in concrete, responsible action of love for all human beings.'[157]

The specific Christological shape of responsibility is also seen in his understanding of *the willingness to bear guilt*. As mentioned, Schliesser has analysed this side of Bonhoeffer's ethical thought in detail. She analyses the motif of bearing guilt in Bonhoeffer's major writings from his early works to his prison letters and concludes her work by a systematic reconstruction of this motif. With regard to *Ethics*, Schliesser argues that the specific contribution of this work pertaining to this motif is the active incurring of guilt for the sake of the other.[158] Further, Schliesser argues that Bonhoeffer's insistence on the Christian's willingness to bear guilt is an expression of the disciple's call to be formed into the image of Christ. At the same time, however, she demonstrates how this side of Bonhoeffer's ethical thought suffers from an inconsistency, as he does not provide a satisfactory argument for the Christological source of the active incurring of guilt.[159] I concur with Schliesser and others who point to the historical and political context as

---

155. Ibid., 231–32 (my italics).

156. DBW 6, 231.

157. DBWE 6, 232.

158. Schliesser, *Everyone Who Acts Responsibly Becomes Guilty*, 171.

159. Christine Schliesser, 'Accepting Guilt for the Sake of Germany: An Analysis of Bonhoeffer's Concept of Accepting Guilt and Its Implications for Bonhoeffer's Political Resistance', *Union Seminary Quarterly Review* 60, no. 1–2 (2006), 56–68.

an important background for understanding this side of Bonhoeffer's ethics,[160] even if I will also maintain that this historical background should not prevent us from reading this side of Bonhoeffer's ethic with an eye to its implications for our current understanding of the Christologically rooted call to bear guilt for the sake of others.

Finally, *the willingness to suffer for the other* is important. This follows from the Christian's fellowship with Jesus Christ as the one who has suffered.[161] The willingness to suffer becomes a witness of discipleship. The Christian is called to bear the cross of Christ and thereby take part in the suffering which is part of partaking in the Christ-reality. 'Just as Christ is only Christ as one who suffers and is rejected, so a disciple is a disciple only in suffering and being rejected, thereby participating in crucifixion. Discipleship as allegiance to the person of Jesus Christ places the follower under the law of Christ, that is, under the cross.'[162] The call to bear the cross is not given up in his *Ethics*, but Bonhoeffer does give it a different accentuation with a more affirmative view on worldly norms and ideals. Christians are called to live responsive and responsible lives in the world under the cross of Christ.

Conclusion

In this chapter we have found the foundation of the Chalcedon returning in several of the core concepts in Bonhoeffer's ethic – reality, the secular, Christonomy, reason and responsibility. With regard to his concept of *reality*, we saw how he understands this concept in both a spatial, temporal and ontological sense. The spatial dimension implies for Bonhoeffer that we cannot think in 'rooms' or compartments of reality, as this would contradict the one Christ-reality. The temporal entails e.g. that when the good is understood in accord with the Christ-reality, this can never be understood as contrasting or accommodating historical reality. These two misunderstandings are avoided in the incarnation of Christ. Ontologically, reality is understood in light of the relation between the ultimate and penultimate. All three dimensions of reality are understood as expressions of

---

160. See e.g. Heinz Eduard Tödt, 'Conscientious Resistance: Ethical Responsibility of the Individual, the Group, and the Church', in *Ethical Responsibility: Bonhoeffer's Legacy to the Churches* (ed. John D. Godsey and Geffrey B. Kelly; New York/Toronto: Edwin Mellen Press, 1981), 17–42; Rasmussen, 'The Ethics of Responsible Action'. See also my essay on Bonhoeffer's move from pacifism to resistance, where some of these themes are elaborated upon: Ulrik Nissen, 'Dietrich Bonhoeffer: A Journey from Pacifism to Resistance', in *Christianity and Resistance in the 20th Century* (Leiden/Boston, MA: Brill, 2009), 147–74.

161. DBW 6, 345–53.

162. Dietrich Bonhoeffer, *Discipleship* (ed. Geffrey B. Kelly and John D. Godsey; trans. Barbara Green and Reinhard Krauss; Dietrich Bonhoeffer Works; vol. 4; Minneapolis, MN: Fortress Press, 2003) (DBWE 4), 85.

the polemical, contradictory Christ-reality. The concept of reality also implies a positive understanding of the *secular*. In the analysis of this concept we saw how Bonhoeffer understands it as a fundamentally theological concept in the sense of *saeculum*. This concept implies that there is no being apart from God, and that the secular becomes a term for the period of time before the eschaton. The secular is therefore understood in close affinity to an understanding of a fullness of reality, where the godlessness or religionlessness is always stated before God. Bonhoeffer's concept of the secular hereby holds the same paradoxical characteristic that we have also seen in his contradictory understanding of the Christ-reality.

When we turned to his understanding of *Christonomy*, we saw how this concept is also shaped by Bonhoeffer's view of the Christ-reality. In Bonhoeffer, it is freedom rather than autonomy understood as law of reason that is central. Freedom is closely connected to relationality, understood as being in relation to Christ and 'the other'. This also implies that, when Bonhoeffer speaks about Christonomy, he is concerned with being in Christ and living out this reality. Hereby, Bonhoeffer holds an identity-specific understanding of the common basis of worldly, human life. In Bonhoeffer's concept of *reason* we saw a similar picture emerging. Bonhoeffer's Chalcedonian Christology implied an affirmation of reason and yet this is understood as reason coming to itself in giving itself up. Jesus Christ is understood as the centre of all knowledge, even if this is only grasped in faith. This also implies that, just as natural life is affirmed in Christ, reason is affirmed in Christ. Therefore, Bonhoeffer has an unlimited recognition of the abilities of reason, as long as it is understood in light of reality, and its true source in Christ is maintained.

In Bonhoeffer's concept of *responsibility* we saw how his relational anthropology and theology came to the fore. Responsibility is derived from the human being living in relation to other human beings and God. It is out of this relationality and the corresponding response to the other that responsibility arises. Therefore Bonhoeffer also rejects any principles or laws that beforehand determine what is right. Rather, the individual acts freely in the concrete encounter with the other. At the same time, however, Bonhoeffer qualifies this responsibility Christologically. When the human being acts in accord with reality this is understood as the Christ-reality, which is why true responsibility shows itself in a participation in and conformation to Christ.

Chapter 5

BONHOEFFER'S SOCIAL ETHICS BETWEEN UNIVERSALITY AND SPECIFICITY

The broadly conceived Chalcedonian Christology underlying Bonhoeffer's ethics substantiates a reading of Bonhoeffer whereby he can be understood in support of a differentiated unity of universality and specificity. The central concepts in Bonhoeffer's ethics that we have investigated in Chapter 4 hold essential implications for a social ethic in which these two dimensions are understood in a polemical unity with each other. This differentiated unity in Bonhoeffer's political thought implies an understanding whereby he may be read as holding a position between, on the one hand, a radical emphasis on the identity-specific nature of Christian ethics, and, on the other hand, a compromising accommodation of Christian ethics to a universalist understanding of the foundation of Christian political thought. This was seen in several of the concepts we have just analysed, but especially in his understanding of the relation between the ultimate and penultimate, where we saw how Bonhoeffer argues for a position between radicalism and compromise.[1]

> Radicalism always arises from a conscious or unconscious hatred of what exists. Christian radicalism, whether it would flee the world or improve it, comes from the hatred of creation. The radical cannot forgive God for having created what is… Compromise always arises from hatred of the ultimate. The Christian spirit of compromise comes from this animosity against the justification of the sinner by grace alone. The world, and life in it, must be protected from this invasion into its domain.[2]

An anthology from 2009 on Bonhoeffer's theology approaches this theme with various contributions to the question of whether Bonhoeffer's theology can be

---

1. Dietrich Bonhoeffer, *Ethik* (herausgegeben von Ilse Tödt, Heinz Eduard Tödt, Ernst Feil und Clifford Green; Dietrich Bonhoeffer Werke; band 6; Gütersloh: Chr. Kaiser, 2nd rev. edn, 1998) (DBW 6), 144–48.

2. Dietrich Bonhoeffer, *Ethics* (ed. Clifford J. Green; trans. Reinhard Krauss, Charles C. West and Douglas W. Stott; Dietrich Bonhoeffer Works; vol. 6; Minneapolis, MN: Fortress Press, 2005) (DBWE 6), 155–56.

regarded as placing itself between fundamentalism and secularism.³ Even if this terminology is not identical with 'radicalism' and 'compromise', the concern is quite similar. Bonhoeffer is determined to argue for such a position, where he understands his ethics between radicalism and compromise, and where he sees them reconciled in Jesus Christ. In this mediating position, we find Bonhoeffer arguing for a position that comes close to the aim in the present book of establishing a position between universality and specificity. Even if universality and compromise cannot be completely identified with each other, they come close, which is also the case for radicalism and specificity. For Bonhoeffer it is important to maintain the insights of both radicalism and compromise; the problem is the absolutization of both of these positions. 'Both solutions are extreme in the same respect, and likewise both contain truths and falsehoods ... Both wrongly absolutize ideas that are necessary and right in themselves.'⁴ The reconciliation of these two positions is not to be found in giving up on either of them. Rather, they are to be seen as reconciled in Christ. Here, we find Bonhoeffer's concept of the Christ-reality returning. As we saw in the analysis of Bonhoeffer's concept of reality, Bonhoeffer also argues here that God's reality and human reality become one in Jesus Christ. In other words, we find the incarnational Christology as the interpretative scheme, where the present book contends that this can be read as the expression of an underlying Chalcedonian Christology. 'Neither the idea of a pure Christianity as such nor the idea of the human being as such is serious, but only God's reality and human reality as they have become one in Jesus Christ.'⁵ Contrasting radicalism and compromise as polar opposites that cannot be reconciled is in opposition to Christ, where these concepts are one.

> To contrast radicalism and compromise like this makes clear enough that both attitudes are equally opposed to Christ; for the concepts that are here set up against each another [sic.] are one in Jesus Christ. The question about the Christian life, therefore, will be answered neither by radicalism nor by compromise; Jesus Christ himself decides and answers it. The relationship between the ultimate and the penultimate is resolved only in Christ.⁶

In this chapter of the book the focus is on some of the implications of this understanding for Bonhoeffer's political thought. However, due to (1) his ethic of responsibility; and (2) the historical and political context in which he writes his *Ethics*, the implications of his ethics for his political thought are often stated

---

3. John W. De Gruchy, Stephen Plant and Christiane Tietz, *Dietrich Bonhoeffers Theologie heute: Ein Weg zwischen Fundamentalismus und Säkularismus?/Dietrich Bonhoeffer's Theology Today: A Way Between Fundamentalism and Secularism?* (Gütersloh: Gütersloher Verlagshaus, 2009).
4. DBWE 6, 154.
5. Ibid., 155.
6. Ibid., 157.

implicitly or indirectly. Therefore, when he ponders these issues it often has the character of fundamental theological deliberations, rather than explicit political implications of this ethic. The present part of the book will not engage in the comprehensive literature on Bonhoeffer's political thought. This literature is often focused on the historical context of Bonhoeffer's theology and is often interested in what motives led him to an active participation in the plot against Hitler.[7]

In one of the relatively recent contributions to Bonhoeffer's political thought, it is shown how one can point to different emphases in Bonhoeffer's earlier and later writings. In his earlier writings, the church has a threefold duty: (1) indirect and direct political word: the church both reminds the state of its limits (the indirect word) and at times may have to speak out against injustices (the direct word); (2) social action: the church is called to help victims of the state; and (3) direct political action: certain situations may arise where the church not only helps the victims under the wheel, but even has to put a spoke in the wheel. In his later writings, we can identify four political tasks: (1) indirect political word: the church's political task is to proclaim Christ's dominion, whereby the government is called to realize its essence as a mandate of God; (2) direct critical word: the church does not proclaim a concrete earthly order, but it does define the boundaries of an order, where obedience to Christ is possible; the church, therefore, directly criticizes economic attitudes and conditions that hinder faith in Jesus Christ; (3) direct constructive word: constructive suggestions for a new order can be developed only by 'Christian experts', where their contribution is derived from their expert knowledge; and (4) resistance in responsibility: in extraordinary situations the Christian may be called to act in free responsibility with an active resistance as the *ultima ratio*.[8] Rather than engaging with Bonhoeffer's political thought in general, the aim here is to point to and briefly discuss Bonhoeffer's thought in light of the findings of the current book.

---

7. See my article on Bonhoeffer's move from pacifism to resistance, where I also give an overview of the literature related to this theme: Ulrik Nissen, 'Dietrich Bonhoeffer: A Journey from Pacifism to Resistance', in *Christianity and Resistance in the 20th Century* (Leiden/Boston, MA: Brill, 2009), 147–74. In this focus on the theological implications of Bonhoeffer's thought for contemporary theology, I am also following the turn in Bonhoeffer scholarship, which Jennifer McBride has coined as 'going beyond Bonhoeffer with Bonhoeffer'. Jennifer M. McBride, *The Church for the World: A Theology of Public Witness* (Oxford: Oxford University Press, 2012), 11–12. McBride's is a significant contribution to more recent attempts to develop a public theology or political theology in light of Bonhoeffer. For a broader collection of essays on his political theology, see Kirsten Busch Nielsen, Ralf Karolus Wüstenberg and Jens Zimmermann, eds, *Dem Rad in die Speichen fallen: Das Politische in der Theologie Dietrich Bonhoeffers/A Spoke in the Wheel: The Political in the Theology of Dietrich Bonhoeffer* (Gütersloh: Gütersloher Verlagshaus, 2013).

8. Christiane Tietz, '"The Church is the Limit of Politics": Bonhoeffer on the Political Task of the Church', *Union Seminary Quarterly Review* 60, no. 1–2 (2006), 23–36.

Christian political thought as a contradictory affirmation of reality

The three dimensions of Bonhoeffer's concept of reality – the spatial, temporal and ontological[9] – also hold implications for his social ethics. However, here we are immediately challenged by his understanding of 'social ethics'. Bonhoeffer is quite critical of this concept, regarding it as an ethical aporia.[10] He criticizes the concept for implicitly dissolving the unity between the good and the real, or the person and his or her works. Bonhoeffer finds it important that the question of what is 'good' is derived from the very concept of reality, and that this encompasses all of God's creation – including the human being and his or her motives and works.[11] A further reason for Bonhoeffer's critique of the term 'social ethics' is his notion of sociality, which can be seen as a unifying theme throughout his theology.[12] According to Bonhoeffer, all of humanity is united by bonds of sociality. This also influences, for instance, his understanding of responsibility as arising from the encounter with the other.[13] However, in his work this affirmative view on reality as the source of the moral norm is understood Christologically. It is the incarnation of Christ that enables people to act in accordance with reality. Only through Christ's incarnation is it possible for the world to remain world, as God has taken care of the world and declared it under His rule. Action in accordance with reality is only possible in Christ. It is in the reconciliation given with the incarnation of Christ that one finds the source of action in accord with reality.[14]

> In Christ, all human reality is taken on. That is why it is ultimately only in and from Christ that it is possible to act in a way that is in accord with reality. The origin of action that is in accord with reality is neither the pseudo-Lutheran Christ whose only purpose is to sanction the status quo, nor the radical, revolutionary Christ of all religious enthusiasts who is supposed to bless every revolution, but rather the God who became human, Jesus Christ, who loved human beings, judged them, and reconciled them with God.[15]

In this understanding of the Christologically founded concept of reality and its implication for the immediate encounter with the other as the place where the ethical situation arises, we find the Chalcedonian theme returning. Bonhoeffer

---

9. See Chapter 4, the section entitled 'Reality as the Contradictory Christ-Reality'.
10. DBW 6, 36.
11. Ibid., 37.
12. See Clifford Green's book on the concept of sociality in Bonhoeffer's theology. Clifford J. Green, *Bonhoeffer: A Theology of Sociality* (Grand Rapids, MI: W. B. Eerdmans, rev. edn, 1999).
13. See Chapter 4, the section entitled 'Responsibility and Christological Responsiveness'.
14. DBW 6, 223.
15. DBWE 6, 224.

emphasizes that it is in God who became human that human beings are loved, judged and reconciled – and that this Christ reality is the 'origin of action'.

Even if Bonhoeffer is critical of the concept itself, the implications that his understanding of reality has on social ethics are evident, at least when we simply take the term 'social ethics' to connote the ethical issues related to the political and social dimensions of human existence.[16] Returning to the above-mentioned three perspectives on reality, we also detect the presence of the Chalcedonian motif. With regard to the *spatial* understanding, Bonhoeffer employs ecclesiological deliberations. First, he argues that the church takes up space in the world. This is understood as closely associated with the revelation of God in Jesus Christ. Bonhoeffer understands this as an act of God's embracing the whole reality of the world in this narrow space and revealing its ultimate foundation in Jesus Christ. The Church is not competing with the world, but rather testifying to the world that it is still world, loved and reconciled by God.[17] Bonhoeffer is here in line with his earlier reflections in *Discipleship*, where he ponders the visible congregation[18] and his later *Letters and Papers from Prison*, where he speaks about the church being placed in the middle of the village.[19] 'I'd like to speak of God not at the boundaries but in the center, not in weakness, but in strength, thus not in death and guilt but in human life and human goodness … God is the beyond in the midst of our lives. The church stands not at the point where human powers fail, at the boundaries, but in the center of the village.'[20] Just as the body of Jesus Christ is visible and takes up space in the world, the Christian congregation is visible and takes up space as the body of Jesus Christ.[21] The church's social-ethical task is, therefore, to bear witness to the world about the source of the bonds of sociality in the reconciliation with God in Jesus Christ. Consequently, any attempt to operate with separate rooms of reality is broken down in the reconciliation in Christ.[22] This witness also applies with regard to the state, where the church reminds the state of the limits of its authority (even if Bonhoeffer does not forget that this reminder also goes the other way, from the state to the church). Therefore, in

---

16. See also Chapter 1, the section entitled 'Is There a Third Position?'

17. DBW 6, 48–49.

18. Dietrich Bonhoeffer, *Nachfolge* (herausgegeben von Martin Kuske und Ilse Tödt; Dietrich Bonhoeffer Werke; band 4; Gütersloh: Chr. Kaiser, 1994) (DBW 4), 241–68.

19. Dietrich Bonhoeffer, *Widerstand und Ergebung. Briefe und Aufzeichnungen aus der Haft* (herausgegeben von Christian Gremmels, Eberhard Bethge und Renate Bethge in zusammenarbeit mit Ilse Tödt; Dietrich Bonhoeffer Werke; band 8; Gütersloh: Chr. Kaiser, 1998) (DBW 8), 407–08.

20. Dietrich Bonhoeffer, *Letters and Papers from Prison* (ed. John W. De Gruchy; trans. Isabel Best, Lisa E. Dahill, Reinhard Krauss and Nancy Lukens; Dietrich Bonhoeffer Works; vol. 8; Minneapolis, MN: Fortress Press, 2010) (DBWE 8), 366–67.

21. DBW 4, 241–68.

22. DBW 6, 50.

his essay on the state and the church,[23] Bonhoeffer speaks both of the political authority's responsibility for the church, and the church's responsibility for the political authority. The political authority's responsibility is primarily to protect the pious and provide safe conditions for the religious communities. In doing so, the political authority remains religiously neutral.[24] The church's political responsibility is to remind the political authority of its limits ... but also frankly to name sin as sin.[25] It is the church's responsibility publicly to warn about sin and in its preaching call to belief in Christ and witness of his Lordship.[26]

Concerning the *temporal* perspective on reality, Bonhoeffer is careful that this should not entail any political conservatism. This becomes apparent when he reflects upon the concept of guilt.[27] Both individual guilt and corporate guilt are to be confessed in church. In the proclamation of the grace of Christ, guilt is not only acknowledged, but also forgiven. The church thereby becomes the place for personal and corporate rebirth and renewal,[28] and the place where Jesus makes His form real in the midst of the world. The formative aspect of the proclamation of forgiveness counters political conservatism, in that the historically acknowledged guilt – the Western world's falling away from Christ – serves to argue for the formative role of the church in the realization of Christ in the world.

Lastly, the *ontological* motif underscores the social-ethical implications of Bonhoeffer's understanding of reality. Bonhoeffer argues that 'the good' is reality itself, as it is seen and recognized in God. It is created reality as a whole, as it is held in the hands of God.[29] For this meaning of reality, Bonhoeffer accentuates the concrete implications of his own concept of reality and his effort to avoid severing reality into separate parts, preferring human beings to be seen as indivisible wholes in both person and work, and as members of the human and created community.[30] The Christological underpinnings of this understanding of reality become apparent when Bonhoeffer maintains the close link between this notion of reality and the understanding of Christ as 'the Real One'.[31] Reality is not impersonal, but is revealed in Jesus Christ. Hence, the ontological dimension of reality holds fundamental social-ethical implications, since it claims that all of reality is one in Christ.

---

23. Dietrich Bonhoeffer, *Konspiration und Haft. 1940–1945* (herausgegeben von Jørgen Glenthøj, Ulrich Kabitz und Wolf Krötke; Dietrich Bonhoeffer Werke; band 16; Gütersloh: Chr. Kaiser, 1996) (DBW 16), 506–35.

24. Ibid., 529–31.

25. Ibid., 531–33.

26. Ibid.

27. DBW 6, 125–36.

28. Ibid., 126.

29. Ibid., 37.

30. Ibid., 38.

31. Ibid., 261.

The spatial, temporal and ontological dimensions of reality are closely associated with the paradoxical affirmation of reality found in Bonhoeffer's Chalcedonian Christology. The world, the natural, the profane, reason – all are included in God. The worldly has its reality in God's reality in Christ.[32] The reality of the world rests in a polemical unity with the reality of Christ. The worldly and the Christian can neither be understood rightly in terms of identity, nor in terms of separation.[33] Bonhoeffer is therefore critical of any attempt to speak of orders of creation as separate from the reality of Christ.[34] This is seen, for example, in his reflections on the Johanine notion that Jesus Christ is 'the life' (Jn 14.6).[35] Jesus Christ being 'the life' means that our life lies beyond ourselves – in Jesus Christ. This leads to a denial and an affirmation of our life at the same time. It is a denial of our fallen life without Christ, but also an affirmation of our life as created and reconciled in Christ.[36]

Christian ethics between participation and witness

In addition to the contradictory affirmation of reality, we have also seen how Bonhoeffer understands the Christian's role in a political context as situated between participation and witness.[37] This is found e.g. in his understanding of responsibility as a concept of responsivity, where the ecclesiological theme becomes more pronounced. This theme is articulated through discussions about the church's visibility and role in the public realm.

---

32. Ibid., 44.
33. Ibid., 47.
34. Ibid., 54–61.
35. Ibid., 248–56.
36. Ibid., 250. There is a future question to be studied here – whether Bonhoeffer's understanding of Jesus Christ as 'the life' with reference to the Johanine understanding is comparable with the French phenomenologist, Michel Henry, who in his later writings focuses his phenomenology of life on the words of Christ being the life. Michel Henry, *I Am the Truth: Toward a Philosophy of Christianity* [*C'est moi la vérité*] (Cultural Memory in the Present; Stanford, CA: Stanford University Press, 2003). I take up this question in parts of my next book with reference to the implications for a theological anthropology and current theological bioethics, Ulrik Nissen, *The Responsive Body. Beginning, Altering, and Fulfilling Human Life* (forthcoming).
37. McBride's constructive project to develop a theology of public witness in light of Bonhoeffer's theology also can be read as a position between participation and witness. She argues for a position which is formed by a theology of the cross rather than a theology of glory in order to emphasize a repentant activity and engagement from the church with and for the concrete community of which it is part. In this 'nontriumphal witness in a pluralistic society' the church bears witness to Christ. McBride's book also includes ethnographic explorations of concrete communities, where such a life is exemplified. See McBride, *The Church for the World*.

We have already seen a markedly ecclesiological outlook in the analysis of the Chalcedonian traits in Bonhoeffer's understanding of reality and the implied spatial motif. The same outlook was also apparent in the social-ethical implications of this position. Besides the central characteristic in Bonhoeffer – that ethics, anthropology and ecclesiology cannot be understood as separate from each other[38] – this dimension is also a consequence of the church's witnessing nature in Bonhoeffer, since the church can never give up on its truthful proclamation of the gospel.[39] Hauerwas describes this visibility as 'the heart of Bonhoeffer's theological politics'.[40] Even if Hauer was is right to emphasize this side of Bonhoeffer's political thought, he is stretching the resemblances to his own theology too far when he turns Bonhoeffer's Lutheran background against himself: 'Bonhoeffer's attempt to rethink the Lutheran two-kingdom theology in light of his Christological recovery of the significance of the visible church, I think, failed to escape from the limits of the Lutheran position.'[41] Bonhoeffer's aim is not to escape from Lutheran theology. Rather, as we have seen throughout this book, in challenging the political theology of his Lutheran contemporaries, Bonhoeffer is pondering the ecclesial and political implications of the Christological assertion of the one Christ-reality. These implications are apparent in the outlined understanding of the church as the body of Jesus Christ, and its implied visibility and taking up space in the world.

The church is called to be in the world and bear witness to the world of its reconciliation with God in Jesus Christ.[42] The fulfilment of this role of the church grows out of the Holy Spirit's work in the church,[43] and yet it is a bearing witness that calls the world into a community of the body of Christ to which the world already belongs.[44] Obviously, Bonhoeffer does not think in categories of separation when pondering the relation between the church and the world. It is rather a question of the church's role in letting the reality of the world become real.[45] This understanding is paralleled by Bonhoeffer's concept of the mandates, where the church's mandate is understood in relation to its role in affirming reality. Bonhoeffer distinguishes between four mandates – the church, marriage,

---

38. Larry L. Rasmussen, *Dietrich Bonhoeffer: Reality and Resistance* (Studies in Christian Ethics; Nashville, TN: Abingdon, 1972), 20.

39. Stanley Hauerwas, *Performing the Faith: Bonhoeffer and the Practice of Nonviolence* (London: SPCK, 2004), 55–72.

40. Stanley Hauerwas, 'Dietrich Bonhoeffer', in *The Blackwell Companion to Political Theology* (ed. Peter Scott and William T. Cavanaugh; Malden, MA: Blackwell Publishing, 2004), 136–49 (139).

41. Ibid., 145.

42. DBW 6, 49.

43. Ibid., 50.

44. Ibid., 54.

45. See Ulrik Nissen, 'Letting Reality Become Real: On Mystery and Reality in Dietrich Bonhoeffer's Ethics', *Journal of Religious Ethics* 39, no. 2 (2011), 321–43.

culture (or work) and authority (*Obrigkeit*).⁴⁶ He understands these mandates in relation to Luther's three estates,⁴⁷ but in doing so Bonhoeffer emphasizes two important adjustments. First, the orders are not to be understood as orders of creation. Rather, they are to be seen as 'God's orders of preservation that uphold and preserve us for Christ'.⁴⁸ Hereby, Bonhoeffer wants to emphasize that they are not given as static and conservative orders. The orders of creation could be used to sanction anything given and thereby become static. In contrast, Bonhoeffer wants to emphasize that the orders of preservation are given to preserve life and that they are oriented towards Christ and therefore should be open for the preaching of the gospel.⁴⁹ Second, he emphasizes their commissioned character. They rest on a commission upon which they are also conditioned.⁵⁰ The theological aim here is to argue for the same – i.e. that this commission safeguards these orders from becoming autonomous, and that they can only be understood rightly in light of God's commission.

With regard to the church, Bonhoeffer argues that its commission is to allow 'the reality of Jesus Christ to become real in proclamation [*Verkündigung*], church order, and Christian life – in short, its concern is the eternal salvation of the whole world'.⁵¹ The mandate of the church thereby reaches into the other mandates – work, marriage and government – because all of the mandates overlap one another. The mandate of the church hereby affirms the other mandates as being included in the one Christ-reality.⁵² For Bonhoeffer this does not merely apply to the church in the abstract sense, but is to be seen as affirming the calling of the human being. Rather than seeing the human being as the place where the

---

46. DBW 6, 54–61, 392–412; DBW 16, 523–27. For a more elaborate analysis of the mandates, see also Ulrik Nissen, 'Responding to Human Reality: Responsibility and Responsiveness in Bonhoeffer's Ethics', in *Being Human, Becoming Human: Dietrich Bonhoeffer and Social Thought* (ed. Brian Gregor and Jens Zimmerman; Eugene, OR: Wipf & Stock, 2010), 203–25.

47. DBW 6, 60–61; DBW 16, 558–63. See also Chapter 2 and Michael Richard Laffin, *The Promise of Martin Luther's Political Theology: Freeing Luther from the Modern Political Narrative* (ed. Brian Brock and Susan F. Parsons; T&T Clark Enquiries in Theological Ethics; London: T&T Clark, 2016), 153–94.

48. Dietrich Bonhoeffer, *Creation and Fall: A Theological Exposition of Genesis 1–3* (ed. John W. De Gruchy; trans. Douglas Stephen Bax; Dietrich Bonhoeffer Works; vol. 3; Minneapolis, MN: Fortress Press, 1997) (DBWE 3, 140).

49. Dietrich Bonhoeffer, *Schöpfung und Fall* (herausgegeben von Martin Rüter und Ilse Tödt; Dietrich Bonhoeffer Werke; band 3; Gütersloh: Chr. Kaiser, 2nd rev. edn, 2002) (DBW 3), 129–30; Dietrich Bonhoeffer, *Ökumene, Universität, Pfarramt. 1931–1932* (herausgegeben von Eberhard Amelung und Christoph Strohm; Dietrich Bonhoeffer Werke; band 11; Gütersloh: Chr. Kaiser, 1994) (DBW 11), 312, 324–25, 335–38.

50. DBW 6, 393; DBW 16, 525.

51. DBWE 6, 73.

52. DBW 6, 59–60.

mandates are in mutual conflict with one another, Bonhoeffer understands the mandates as aiming at the whole person, standing in reality before God. It is in the human being, in concrete human life and action, that the mandates are united. It is in reality in all its manifold aspects that the church bears witness that all the mandates are one in the incarnation of Christ. 'This is the witness the church has to give to the world, that all the other mandates are not there to divide people and tear them apart but to deal with them as whole people before God the Creator, Reconciler, and Redeemer – that reality in all its manifold aspects is ultimately *one* in God who became human, Jesus Christ.'[53] Hereby, Bonhoeffer again affirms his incarnational approach to his concept of reality. Reality, the mandates and reality's political implications all point to the body of Christ as the reconciliation of God and man. 'So here again everything finally flows into the reality of the body of Jesus Christ, in whom God and human being became one.'[54]

Bonhoeffer consistently maintains the mandates' double-sidedness, arguing that they are both 'divine' and 'worldly' at the same time. They are divine due to their original and final relation to Christ and their origin in God's commandments. They are worldly in the affirmation of worldly life in Jesus Christ. The mandates' worldliness is seen, for instance, in Bonhoeffer's understanding of the cross. In his reflections on the mandate of the church, Bonhoeffer argues that the worldliness of the world is given its identifying mark in the cross. This follows from the cross being the sign of the godlessness of the world in its rejection of Christ. However, the cross is also the reconciliation of the godless world with God. Therefore, the cross of Christ sets the world free to live in genuine worldliness before God. This also implies that the cross of Christ 'sets us free to live before God in the midst of the godless world, sets us free to live before God in genuine worldliness [*weltlichkeit*]'.[55] In the cross of Christ true worldliness is made possible, as it proclaims the lordship of Christ over all of creation.

The understanding of the lordship of Christ links Bonhoeffer's understanding of the mandates with his concept of responsibility. This follows from the German word *Berufung* (vocation), which implies that someone is being 'called upon'. In Bonhoeffer, this is a calling to a life in community with Christ; a calling that meets and claims the human being in the worldly conditions as they are. The human being is called in the world and to live as justified before God, regardless of the state he or she is living under. In this Christological foundation of the calling, where the world is affirmed as it is, we once again find the same recurring theme from Chalcedonian Christology. And this is closely linked to responsibility. As Bonhoeffer says: 'From Christ's perspective this life is now my vocation; from my own perspective it is my responsibility.'[56] In his double-sided understanding of the vocation, Bonhoeffer wants to emphasize both the call that transcends the

---

53. DBWE 6, 73.
54. Ibid., 74.
55. Ibid., 400.
56. Ibid., 290.

earthly obligations, and the worldly character of these obligations.[57] It is only in this double-sided understanding of the calling of Jesus Christ to live responsibly within the world that the calling simultaneously maintains its worldly realization and its Christological foundation.

The incarnational affirmation of the worldly life – and the subsequent call to bear witness in the world – is also found in Bonhoeffer's understanding of the two kingdoms doctrine.[58] Bonhoeffer does not reject Luther's two kingdoms doctrine, but he is critical of his contemporaries' interpretation of it.[59] For Bonhoeffer it is important that it is read in close connection with his Christological starting point. As we have seen, the world, the natural, the profane and reason are all confirmed in Christ. Yet this is not simply a unity. Rather, they are to be differentiated, as the Christian is not simply identified with the worldly, or the natural with the supernatural, or revelation with reason.[60] Rather, they are to be understood in a polemical relation to each other, where each is confirmed and yet contradicted at the same time. 'This unity is preserved by the fact that the worldly and the Christian, etc., mutually prohibit every static independence of the one over against the other, that they behave toward each other polemically, and precisely therein witness to their common reality, their unity in the Christ-reality.'[61] Bonhoeffer understands this as being in accord with Luther's intention concerning the relation between the sacred and the worldly. It is important to note that, when Bonhoeffer points to the theological argument for this polemical unity, he explicitly refers to the reconciliation of the reality of God and the reality of the world in Jesus Christ: 'The issue in both cases is precisely the same, namely referring to the reality of God and the reality of the world in Jesus Christ.'[62] In other words, it is Bonhoeffer's Chalcedonian Christology that serves as the hermeneutical background for understanding this differentiated unity between the reality of the world and the reality of God. 'Only in this sense of a polemical unity may Luther's doctrine of the two kingdoms [*zwei Reiche*] be used. That was probably its original meaning.'[63] Put differently, Bonhoeffer feels confident that Luther's original intention was the same as his own – i.e. to claim a polemical unity between the reality of God and the reality of the world. It is this polemical affirmation of worldly life which makes it possible for Bonhoeffer both to maintain the affirmation of worldly life and, at the same time, to remind the church and the Christians of their call to bear witness in the world.

---

57. DBW 6, 290–91.
58. See also Chapter 2.
59. DBW 6, 45, 102, 118.
60. Ibid., 45.
61. DBWE 6, 59.
62. Ibid., 60.
63. Ibid.

Natural law Christologically reshaped

'We secure firm ground under our feet only by the biblical grounding of government in Jesus Christ. If and to what extent then from this standpoint a new natural law can be found is a theological question that remains open.'[64] These are the concluding lines in Bonhoeffer's deliberations concerning the Christological foundation of authority (*Obrigkeit*) in his essay on state and church.[65] In the immediately preceding passage, however, Bonhoeffer is critical of natural law as the foundation of the state. '[B]ecause the concept and content of natural law are ambiguous... it does not suffice as the grounding of the state.'[66] This follows from the Christological foundation (i.e. Jesus Christ as the source of all authority) and eschatological fulfilment of the state, where church and state ultimately will be one. 'In the heavenly polis, state and church will be one.'[67] Having voiced this critique of natural law, it is striking that Bonhoeffer in this same essay can recognize a central idea in natural law, i.e. that the content of natural law as the second table of the Decalogue is also known among the gentiles. This is important for Luther's understanding of natural law.[68] But what is more striking is that we find this classical natural law idea recurring in Bonhoeffer: 'Government exists also among non-Christians'.[69] And as he continues a few pages later: 'In the case of a godless government, however, a providential correspondence exists between the content of the second table and the law inherent in historical life itself. The failure to observe the second table destroys the very life that government is supposed to protect.'[70] This also leads Bonhoeffer to ponder the question of whether the state hereby has its foundation in natural law. Bonhoeffer rejects this, as he differentiates between authority and state. It is only the former which as a sign of God's providence comes to the knowledge of natural law, a knowledge which is immediate (*offenbar*) in Christ. This is derived from his understanding of natural law as 'grounded in Jesus

---

64. Dietrich Bonhoeffer, *Conspiracy and Imprisonment* (ed. Mark S. Brocker; trans. Lisa E. Dahill; Dietrich Bonhoeffer Works; vol. 16; Minneapolis, MN: Fortress Press, 2006) (DBWE 16), 512–13.

65. DBW 16, 506–35.

66. DBWE 16, 512.

67. Ibid.

68. See e.g. Ulrik Nissen, 'Martin Luthers und Philipp Melanchthons Verständnis vom natürlichen Gesetz', in *Luther Between Present and Past. Studies in Luther and Lutheranism* (ed. Ulrik Nissen, Anna Vind, Bo Holm and Olli-Pekka Vainio; Helsinki: Luther-Agricola-Society, 2004), 208–34 (214).

69. DBWE 16, 510.

70. Ibid., 515. In the German original Bonhoeffer writes about the government 'bei den Heiden' (DBW 16, 514) and the 'heidnische Obrigkeit' (DBW 16, 520). This parallel is less clear in the English translation.

Christ'.[71] In other words, Bonhoeffer holds an ambivalent attitude to natural law. He recognizes natural law thought (and this is often overlooked in research on Bonhoeffer), but at the same time he maintains that it has its foundation in Christ and therefore is known fully in Christ.

Throughout this book the theme of natural law has been an underlying topic. It has been dealt with most explicitly in Chapter 2 and is taken up again in Chapter 6. Several of the papers underlying the book are pivotal for a Christological reassessment of natural law. In this sense, the book may be seen as a contribution to the open question concerning a new natural law that Bonhoeffer formulated in the quoted passage. Hereby, the current book contributes to the research into Bonhoeffer's view on natural law and natural rights, which is only emerging.[72] For example, Barth analyses the Christological background of Bonhoeffer's concept of natural law and its relation to the classical Thomistic understanding.[73] Further, she shows how Bonhoeffer is influenced by the *Lebensphilosophie* from the early twentieth century,[74] but places this within his own Christological ethic.

Bonhoeffer's most elaborate treatment of natural law is in the section on 'Natural Life' in *Ethics*.[75] The dating of the essay quoted above is uncertain, but there are indications that it was written after April 1941.[76] If this is the case, it may have been written around the same time as he wrote the section on natural life, as he

---

71. DBWE 16, 515.

72. Roger Mehl, 'La notion du naturel dans l'éthique de Bonhoeffer', in *Evangile hier et aujourd'hui; melanges offerts au Franz J. Leenhardt* (Geneva: Editions Labor et Fides, 1968), 205–16; William F. Conner, 'Laws of Life: A Bonhoeffer Theme with Variations', *Andover Newton Quarterly* 18, no. 2 (1977), 101–10; Hiroki Funamoto, 'Penultimate and Ultimate in Dietrich Bonhoeffer's Ethics', in *Being and Truth* (London: SCM Press, 1986), 376–92; Friederike Barth, *Die Wirklichkeit des Guten: Dietrich Bonhoeffers 'Ethik' und ihr philosophischer Hintergrund* (Beiträge zur historischen Theologie; 156; Tübingen: Mohr Siebeck, 2011), 367–90; Christine Schliesser, '"The First Theological-Ethical Doctrine of Basic Human Rights Developed by a Twentieth-Century German Protestant Theologian" – Dietrich Bonhoeffer and Human Rights', in *Dem Rad in die Speichen fallen. Das Politische in der Theologie Dietrich Bonhoeffers/A Spoke in the Wheel. The Political in the Theology of Dietrich Bonhoeffer* (ed. Kirsten Busch Nielsen, Ralf K. Wüstenberg and Jens Zimmermann; Gütersloh: Gütersloher Verlagshaus, 2013), 369–84; Jens Zimmermann, 'Bonhoeffer's "Realistic Responsibility": Religion as the Foundation for Liberal Democratic Societies', in *Dem Rad in die Speichen fallen. Das Politische in der Theologie Dietrich Bonhoeffers/A Spoke in the Wheel. The Political in the Theology of Dietrich Bonhoeffer* (ed. Kirsten Busch Nielsen, Ralf K. Wüstenberg and Jens Zimmermann; Gütersloh: Gütersloher Verlagshaus, 2013), 395–414.

73. Barth, *Die Wirklichkeit des Guten*, 372–74.

74. Ibid., 381.

75. DBW 6, 163–217.

76. DBW 16, 506 (footnote 1).

was beginning to write on this in December 1940.[77] The section on natural life is of central importance to Bonhoeffer, as he here tries to develop a concept of natural rights on the basis of his Christological ethic that can protect the individual from totalitarian injustices from the state.[78] Bonhoeffer's understanding of the natural can be conceived of with respect to both its foundation and its content. With regard to its *foundation*, Bonhoeffer contends that the concept of the natural has fallen into disrepute, as it has been understood either 'in the darkness of general sinfulness' or in 'the brightness of the primal creation'.[79] As a consequence, it has been left to Catholic ethics. This, however, means that protestant thought has lost its orientation with regard to many practical questions in natural life. Therefore, Bonhoeffer argues for the necessity of rehabilitating the natural in light of the gospel.[80] Such a rehabilitation also implies that the natural is understood within the categories of the ultimate and penultimate.[81] 'The natural is that which, after the fall, is directed toward the coming of Jesus Christ. The unnatural is that which, after the fall, closes itself off from the coming of Jesus Christ.'[82] In other words, the natural is that which is aimed at its fulfilment in Christ. Hereby, the natural holds the same dialectical affirmation as we have also seen in his concept of reality and the secular.[83]

With regard to its *content*, Bonhoeffer is careful to differentiate his understanding of 'natural reason' from both a Catholic understanding and the one found in the Enlightenment. Whereas the former understands reason as having maintained a fundamental integrity (divinity of reason), the latter understands reason as spontaneous. In contrast to these concepts of reason, Bonhoeffer understands reason as recognizing the natural as objectively given and yet holding this ability precisely as fallen reason.[84] The content of the natural Bonhoeffer finds closely associated with 'the "basic will" of preserved life'.[85] The natural, in other words, is that which is life-affirmative, just as the unnatural is the enemy of life.[86] When Bonhoeffer turns to a more specific account of the content of the natural, he ponders e.g. the principle of justice from Roman law, *suum cuique*, as an expression of 'the diversity of the natural and the multiplicity of its rights, as

77. DBW 6, 163 (footnote 1).
78. Barth, *Die Wirklichkeit des Guten*, 369.
79. DBWE 6, 171.
80. DBW 6, 165.
81. Bonhoeffer was writing on these topics at the same time as he wrote the section on natural life, see DBW 6, 137 (footnote 1).
82. DBWE 6, 173.
83. See also DBW 16, 558–59.
84. DBW 6, 167. See also Ulrik Nissen, 'The Christological Ontology of Reason', *Neue Zeitschrift für systematische Theologie und Religionsphilosophie* 48, no. 4 (2006), 460–78.
85. DBWE 6, 176.
86. DBW 6, 169.

well as the unity of justice that is granted within this multiplicity'.[87] I will not go into detail regarding Bonhoeffer's understanding of this principle,[88] but only point to a central concern for Bonhoeffer, i.e. the relation between the individual and the collective. It is surely a consequence of the political context of Bonhoeffer's writings, but nonetheless, he emphasizes the recognition of the rights of the individual and that this is a right that supports the rights of the community.[89] That the individual holds this right is an expression of the individual being created by God and it is a right that holds validity irrespective of its divine background.[90]

> It follows from the will of God, who creates individuals to give them eternal life, that there is a natural right of the individual. It is this fact that, recognized or unrecognized, is expressed repeatedly in natural life and successfully resists social eudaemonism as unnatural. God's having created individuals and called them to eternal life is a reality that is effective in natural life. To disregard it has ominous consequences. It is therefore the business of reason within natural life to take account of the right of the individual, even when the divine background of this right is not recognized.[91]

In the following sections Bonhoeffer ponders the right to bodily life, what this implies with regard to warfare, euthanasia, the incurably ill and the value of life beyond its social utility.[92] He also turns to the classical question about the right to suicide[93] and reproductive issues (marriage, abortion and sterilization).[94] It would lead too far for the present book to go into detail regarding these implications of Bonhoeffer's Christologically conceived natural rights. Suffice it to state that this side of Bonhoeffer's ethics holds significant implications for a variety of issues currently being debated in Christian (bio)ethics. The awareness of the implications of Bonhoeffer's ethics for e.g. the bioethical debate has only recently been acknowledged.[95]

---

87. DBWE 6, 181–85.
88. See instead Barth's analysis in *Die Wirklichkeit des Guten*, 384–87.
89. DBW 6, 177.
90. Ibid.
91. DBWE 6, 183–84.
92. DBW 6, 179–91.
93. Ibid., 192–99.
94. Ibid., 199–212.
95. Ralf K. Wüstenberg, Stefan Heuser and Esther Hornung, *Bonhoeffer and the Biosciences: An Initial Exploration* (Frankfurt: Peter Lang, 2010). See also Neil Messer, *Respecting Life: Theology and Bioethics* (London: SCM Press, 2011); Neil Messer, *Theological Neuroethics: Christian Ethics Meets the Science of the Human Brain* (ed. Brian Brock and Susan F. Parsons; Enquiries in Theological Ethics; London: T&T Clark, 2017).

Conclusion

In this chapter we have investigated the implications of the differentiated unity of universality and specificity for Bonhoeffer's social ethics. We have particularly focused on the contradictory affirmation of reality, Christian ethics between participation and witness, and his Christological reshaping of natural law. Common to these themes, on the one hand, was the continuous affirmation of worldly life and human reality. On the other hand, this affirmation was never separate from its specific foundation and qualification in Christ. It is in Christ that the reality of God and the reality of the world continuously are held together in a polemical unity giving rise to both the foundation and the implications of his social ethics and political thought. In other words, Bonhoeffer's incarnational Christology reappears in his political thought as the interpretative scheme, making it possible for him to endorse a position between radicalism and compromise.

Chapter 6

POLITICAL THOUGHT IN THE POLITY OF CHRIST

The universal side of Christian social ethics has repeatedly been affirmed throughout the book. From the very outset the book's theme was set in the context of the classical natural law tradition. It was contended that '[t]he natural law tradition is an essential and necessary part of a Lutheran social ethic [and that this] ... provides this tradition with an inevitable universal dimension.'[1] This universal dimension has been reaffirmed in the various chapters and sections of the book, most notably in Bonhoeffer's concept of reality, the secular and responsibility. Likewise, the specific side has repeatedly been affirmed. It has been shown that Bonhoeffer's concept of reality is understood as a Christ-reality, his understanding of autonomy is inseparable from its Christological foundation, reason is fundamentally understood as reason in Christ, and the responsibility toward the other is shaped by the inseparability from the Christ-reality. In other words, universality and specificity have been found to be different and yet inseparable throughout the book – just as both sides have been found to be essential and necessary for a Christian ethic. In this chapter of the book, we will turn to the contemporary implications of this simultaneity of universality and specificity. We will do this by turning to three conceptual challenges in Christian political thought: the understanding of law and justice, Christian humanism and responsibility.

Law and justice between universality and specificity

In a Danish context the debate continues unabated regarding whether there is a Christian ethic. This book partially reflects that discussion and contends that the persistence of this debate is to some extent due to influences from the Danish theologian and philosopher K. E. Løgstrup.[2] Løgstrup argues in his work *The*

---

1. See Chapter 1.
2. The following section is a summary of the main findings in Ulrik Nissen, 'Reconciliation and Public Law. Christian Reflections about the Sources of Public Law', *Studia theologica* 58, no. 1 (2004), 27–44.

Ethical Demand that there is no Christian ethic.[3] This view has been seen as an attempt to reformulate a classical Lutheran understanding of natural law on a philosophical basis.[4] The link to Luther raises the question of whether Luther's understanding of natural law implies that there is no Christian ethic, and especially whether his notion of natural law entails that there is no Christian *social* ethic.[5] The challenges in the Lutheran tradition have been seen throughout the book, but especially in Chapter 2. As we saw in that chapter, the Lutheran tradition not only poses some particular challenges regarding the unity and differentiation between the worldly and spiritual realms in Luther's two kingdoms doctrine, but also may be key to the solution. Part of the way forward seems to be a Christological ethic with Chalcedonian traits. From this viewpoint, it seems possible to argue for a differentiated unity of what this book has called 'universality' and 'specificity'. This differentiated unity also holds a significant potential with regard to the relation between religion and politics in a contemporary context. As we have also seen implied in the readings of Bonhoeffer, the differentiated unity between universality and specificity also points to an understanding of the relation between state and church, or politics and religion, where they are not seen as separate spheres, but rather are to be seen in a dynamic and differentiated unity.

These reflections may be tested with relation to the question about the sources of public law. When we ponder the question of 'public law', we can differentiate between a narrow and a broader understanding of this concept. In a narrow sense, 'public law' pertains to a theory of law concerning the public under which various subdisciplines such as e.g. administrative law and criminal law are central. In this understanding, public law is often differentiated from private law concerning the relations between individuals or individuals and various organizations. In a broader sense, 'public law' may be understood as the law holding public validity.

---

3. K. E. Løgstrup, *Den etiske fordring* (Løgstrup biblioteket; Aarhus: Klim, 4th edn, 2010), 122–32. Løgstrup was professor of theology at Aarhus University and has been influential in Scandinavian theology (particularly in Denmark and Norway). The referenced work is also published in an English translation: Knud Ejler Løgstrup, *The Ethical Demand* [Den etiske fordring] (Revisions; Notre Dame, IN: University of Notre Dame Press, 1997). In the current book I refer to the Danish original. Two recent books engage thoroughly with his thought: Hans Fink and Robert Stern, eds, *What Is Ethically Demanded? K. E. Løgstrup's Philosophy of Moral Life* (Notre Dame, IN: University of Notre Dame Press, 2017); Robert Stern, *The Radical Demand in Løgstrup's Ethics* (Oxford: Oxford University Press, 2019). As an Aarhus theologian, I am influenced by Løgstrup's position. But the current book is (also) an attempt to move a step beyond Løgstrup and argue that there is a Christian ethic – both in a normative sense and in the sense of an account of the Christian life as a living response to the word of God, as it is revealed in Christ's call to discipleship.

4. Svend Andersen, *Løgstrup* (Frederiksberg: Anis, 2nd edn, 2005), 54–59.

5. I particularly focus on this question (and here primarily in light of Lutheran ethics) in Nissen, 'Reconciliation and Public Law'.

Here 'public' basically refers to the conditions that law must fulfil in order to hold justification in a public realm. In this understanding, 'public law' is differentiated from e.g. 'religious law'. The 'public law' is therefore the law which we (in a democracy) are subject to as citizens, irrespective of our various religious or other forms of worldview. Hereby, public law is understood in light of the debate on the criteria for the just and stable liberal democracies found in e.g. John Rawls.[6] However, this also raises the question of how this public law (understood in light of a shared concept of political justice) can be affirmed from the perspective of various worldviews. I hereby seek to place myself between liberalism and communitarianism.[7] In line with the argument of this book, I connect this to a specific Christian understanding of justice, which may serve as the source of public law. This specific perspective on public law implies affirmation of the universal dimension, understood here as the public law that also holds a common validity. Consequently, the unity and differentiation between universality and specificity is understood as implied in the specific Christian understanding of law and justice.[8]

The affirmative view on the universal dimension of Christian social ethics is the part of the book where, to a certain extent, it concurs with the understanding of Lutheran social ethics found in a reformulation of Luther's political thought in light of his understanding of the relation between power and love.[9] Previously, Svend Andersen argued that the Lutheran natural law position implies a dualism that unites particularistic and universalistic claims.[10] However, more recently

6. John Rawls, *Political Liberalism* (Columbia Classics in Philosophy; New York: Columbia University Press, paperback edn, 1996); John Rawls, 'The Idea of Public Reason Revisited', *The University of Chicago Law Review* 64, no. 3 (1997), 765–807.

7. This is a position that holds many similarities to the one found in e.g. David Fergusson, *Community, Liberalism and Christian Ethics* (New Studies in Christian Ethics; Cambridge: Cambridge University Press, 1998). Fergusson also places his understanding in an appreciation of Jeffrey Stout, even if Stout is more inclined to maintain a Hauerwasian inspiration. See also David Fergusson, 'Beyond Theologies of Resentment: An Appreciation of Jeffrey Stout's Democracy and Tradition', *Scottish Journal of Theology* 59, no. 2 (2006), 183–97.

8. For a rich discussion on authority and law in light of the legacy of Christendom, see Oliver O'Donovan, *The Desire of the Nations: Rediscovering the Roots of Political Theology* (Cambridge: Cambridge University Press, 1996), 226–42.

9. See Svend Andersen, *Macht aus Liebe. Zur Rekonstruktion einer lutherischen politischen Ethik* (Berlin/New York: W. de Gruyter, 2010). Andersen is right in placing his emphasis on the universal side of Luther's political thought due to his emphasis on natural law and his understanding of the necessity for a strong political authority motivated by love. But Andersen's attempt to read Luther's political thought in light of John Rawls' political philosophy is not convincing and leads to a Kantian reading of Luther, which makes him too much of a theologian of modernity.

10. Svend Andersen, 'Theological Ethics, Moral Philosophy, and Natural Law', *Ethical Theory and Moral Practice* 4 (2001), 349–64.

he has placed himself explicitly in the tradition of Løgstrup and, in this light, contends that the Christian must argue on the same premises as anybody else in the public realm.[11] This understanding also shapes Andersen's reconstruction of Luther's political thought.[12] I cannot do justice to this work here, but instead refer to other detailed readings.[13] In the present context it is Andersen's Rawlsian reading of Luther that is of interest.

Andersen's main thesis is that Luther's political thought can be subsumed into Rawlsian liberalism: 'A certain affinity is argued between Lutheran ethics and John Rawls' political liberalism. In particular I see his concept of the "overlapping consensus" as a secular equivalent to the Lutheran two kingdoms doctrine.'[14] Andersen's detailed readings of Luther's political thought, the shaping of Lutheran ethics in modernity, and the contribution to a reformulation of Lutheran political ethics in the twenty-first century leads him to contend that there is a fundamental agreement between Rawls' concept of the overlapping consensus in the political sphere and the Lutheran distinction between the two kingdoms. Andersen claims that the Lutheran two kingdoms doctrine implies that there is a duality in the Christian's worldview (*Lebensdeutung*) and that the Christian therefore must be able to distinguish between concerns related to faith

---

11. Svend Andersen, 'Die Rolle theologischer Argumentation im öffentlichen Leben', in *Religion und Theologie im öffentlichen Diskurs. Hermeneutische und ethische Perspektiven* (ed. G. Ulshöfer; Frankfurt am Main: Haag, 2005), 9–23; Svend Andersen, 'Christliche Bioethik in Europa', in *Religion in bioethischen Diskursen* (ed. Friedemann Voigt; Berlin/New York: W. de Gruyter, 2010), 293–311. See also Nigel Biggar's discussion of Andersen on this point: Nigel Biggar, *Behaving in Public. How to Do Christian Ethics* (Grand Rapids, MI/Cambridge: W. B. Eerdmans, 2011), 31–36.

12. This is not least the case in the monograph on Luther's political thought: Andersen, *Macht aus Liebe*. Unfortunately, Laffin does not engage with this work in his recent study on Luther's political thought. See Michael Richard Laffin, *The Promise of Martin Luther's Political Theology: Freeing Luther from the Modern Political Narrative* (ed. Brian Brock and Susan F. Parsons; T&T Clark Enquiries in Theological Ethics; London: T&T Clark, 2016). Laffin and Andersen go in very different directions in their attempts to reformulate Luther for contemporary theology. Laffin could have used Andersen's position as an example of a Lutheran interpretation that seeks to place Luther in the context of a Rawlsian liberalism.

13. Heinrich Assel, 'Er luthersk politisk teologi valgbeslægtet med liberalisme og republikanisme?', *Dansk Teologisk Tidsskrift* 74 (2011), 313–18. Andersen's study has the strength of raising a genuine theological discussion of political liberalism and how Luther's theology can contribute to this. But, at the same time, we are left with a reading of Luther that seems to block the fruitful contributions at the heart of Luther's theology. A similar critique can also be found in Michael Coors, 'Macht aus Liebe: zur Rekonstruktion einer lutherischen politischen Ethik', *Theologische Literaturzeitung* 136, no. 2 (2011), 198–200.

14. Andersen, *Macht aus Liebe*, 4 (my translation).

and those related to the common political life.[15] Even if this implies an affirmation of political liberalism from a Lutheran standpoint, this does not mean that the ethic of neighbourly love is simply identical to a universalistic ethic. The Kantian attempt to subsume neighbourly love in an ethic of common, practical reason is, therefore, also criticized.[16] At this point, Andersen also criticizes Løgstrup's position and contends that there is something more than just this universalistic ethic, even if it does not become completely clear how he understands this "'more" of a Christian ethic'.[17] Andersen's hesitant recognition of the specific dimension of a Christian ethic is also seen in his general understanding of his own work, where he sees it as an alternative[18] or even contrast[19] to what he calls 'Christian political self-overestimation' – or what in the present book is read as a more specific (or distinct) line of thought in contemporary theological ethics (e.g. Milbank, Hauerwas and O'Donovan) – in this reading Andersen seems to have moved away from his earlier partial recognition of Hauerwas.[20] A critical reading of the more specific line in theological ethics also seems to lie behind his rejection of Bonhoeffer as a possible source of inspiration for a constructive approach to contemporary Protestant Christianity.[21]

The present book takes a different course in its aim to argue for the differentiated unity of universality and specificity. Hereby, it acknowledges the insights from both the universalist and particularist approaches to Christian ethics, contending that both need to be maintained and yet neither is sufficient in itself. Therefore, the book turns to the more identity-specific tradition in contemporary Christian social ethics and ponders the question of how this can be maintained without letting go of the universalist approach. In a Danish context, this specific identity of a Christian ethic is found in a contemporary of Løgstrup, i.e. N. H. Søe. Completely opposite to Løgstrup, Søe argues that the good can only be known in light of God's revelation: 'all our knowledge about God is mediated through the revelation in the Holy Scripture. This also pertains to our knowledge about God's will and our knowledge of the good. Christian

---

15. Ibid., 299.

16. Ibid., 302.

17. Ibid., 302-3 (my translation).

18. Svend Andersen, 'Democracy and Modernity – A Lutheran Perspective', in *Religion and Normativity* (ed. Peter Lodberg; Religion, Politics, and Law; vol. 3; Aarhus: Aarhus University Press, 2009), 14–29.

19. Svend Andersen, 'Lutheran Political Theology in the Twenty-First Century', in *Transformations in Luther's Theology. Historical and Contemporary Reflections* (ed. Christine Helmer and Bo Kristian Holm; Arbeiten zur Kirchen- und Theologiegeschichte; Leipzig: Evangelische Verlagsanstalt, 2011), 245–63.

20. Andersen, 'Theological Ethics, Moral Philosophy, and Natural Law', 356.

21. Andersen, 'Democracy and Modernity', 19–20.

ethics is tied to Scripture.'[22] In a contemporary context, this distinctive approach to Christian ethics is, however, often found in representatives of the ecclesial turn of Christian ethics which we have witnessed since the early 1980s, not least with Stanley Hauerwas as a leading figure.

In a Lutheran context, such a representative of an ecclesial ethic may be found in e.g. Bernd Wannenwetsch. For Wannenwetsch, worship is the origin of Christian ethics: '*Ethics begins in worship and in the moral rationality proper to it*; not, as it might be, only later, when the "moral implications" are worked out. It begins *in* worship, at the very moment it takes place and among the people who engage in it together.'[23] In other words, he is interested in an ethic that grows out of worship.[24] This leads Wannenwetsch to an understanding of worship constituting a polis of its own, where Christians are conceived of as Christian citizens.[25] Worship is understood as a context that critically[26] empowers[27] Christian citizens. Hereby, he both emphasizes that Christian ethics grows out of this transformative praxis and that this implies a rejection of the foundation of Christian ethics.[28] Rather than seeking a foundation, Christian ethics is about living out the life form which is an expression of worship in the Christian congregation.

This approach to his understanding of Christian ethics holds several (problematic) implications for the present book. First, Wannenwetsch's rejection of a foundation of Christian ethics is fundamentally at odds with the present project, where it has been the continuous aim to establish a foundation between universality and specificity grounded in a Christological ethic. Second, due to his emphasis on the ecclesial origin of Christian ethics, Wannenwetsch ends up hardly giving space to Luther's understanding of natural law, when he is giving an outline

---

22. N. H. Søe, *Kristelig etik* (København: G. E. C. Gads, 2nd edn, 1946), 23 (author's translation). Søe was a contemporary of Bonhoeffer, and they shared being Lutheran theologians and having a Barthian inspiration. The influence from Barth on Søe's theological ethic has been demonstrated in e.g. Carsten Elmelund Petersen, 'Etik mellem Luther og Barth: en analyse af N.H. Søes teologiske etik', *Dansk teologisk tidsskrift* 59, no. 2 (1996), 106–24.

23. Bernd Wannenwetsch, *Political Worship: Ethics for Christian Citizens* (trans. Margaret Kohl; Oxford/New York: Oxford University Press, 2004), 19. The quoted passage is from the translation of Wannenwetsch's 'Habilitationsschrift'. In the following I refer to the original text: Bernd Wannenwetsch, *Gottesdienst als Lebensform: Ethik für Christenbürger* (Stuttgart: W. Kohlhammer, 1997). More recently, such an approach is also the focus in Gifford A. Grobien, *Christian Character Formation: Lutheran Studies of the Law, Anthropology, Worship and Virtue* (Oxford Studies in Theological Ethics; Oxford: Oxford University Press, 2019). Grobien also analyses Wannenwetsch's position among others.

24. Wannenwetsch, *Gottesdienst als Lebensform*, 19.

25. Ibid.

26. Ibid., 109–274.

27. Ibid., 275–338.

28. Ibid., 19.

of Luther's moral theology.²⁹ Instead, when he analyses Luther's understanding of the Decalogue, he argues that, according to Luther, 'the content of God's law in its original purpose and scope is only really intelligible in Jesus Christ'.³⁰ So instead of recognizing the role that natural law plays in Luther's political thought, Wannenwetsch hardly has any place for this concept in his reading of Luther.³¹ Third, Wannenwetsch argues for an understanding of the public, where the church is understood as the one public: 'There is good evidence that "public" is from the outset not merely a matter of reference for Christian worship, determined by outer conditions of access; rather worship provides its own particular public due to its adoration of a *cosmocrator*'.³² One of the critical questions that must be raised with regard to Wannenwetsch's position is: is this not too enthusiastic concerning the church? A similar question has also been raised by other readers of Wannenwetsch.³³ Does this really hold true of the church that it is such a radically transformative and critically empowering praxis? Surely it is a beautiful vision of the church as a Christian community living out the story by which it is itself narrated and, in this sense, it *is* a social ethic – here Wannenwetsch refers to Hauerwas³⁴ – but is this not an eschatological hope rather than a political reality here and now?

Just as I have pointed to some significant points of discussion between Wannenwetsch and the position I am arguing for, it is also important to bear in mind where our two positions hold significant similarities. This is particularly the case regarding two ideas. First, we both aim to make use of the Lutheran understanding of the *communicatio idiomatum*. For the present book this has been apparent throughout as part of the Chalcedonian Christology for which I have been arguing. Wannenwetsch also elaborates on this theme and also ponders the simultaneity of the relation to God and the relation to one's fellow citizens.³⁵ However, in Wannenwetsch the focus is decidedly liturgical and sacramental: 'In

---

29. Bernd Wannenwetsch, 'Luther's Moral Theology', in *The Cambridge Companion to Martin Luther* (ed. Donald K. McKim; Cambridge: Cambridge University Press, 2003), 120–35.

30. Ibid., 121.

31. Ibid., 123–24.

32. Bernd Wannenwetsch, 'The Political Worship of the Church: A Critical and Empowering Practice', *Modern Theology* 12, no. 3 (1996), 269–99 (282). See also Wannenwetsch, *Gottesdienst als Lebensform*, 241–74.

33. Christofer Frey, 'Gottesdienst als Lebensform: Ethik für Christenbürger', *Zeitschrift für evangelische Ethik* 44, no. 1 (2000), 70–72.

34. Wannenwetsch, 'The Political Worship of the Church', 272.

35. Bernd Wannenwetsch, 'Communication as Transformation: Worship and the Media', *Studies in Christian Ethics* 13 (2000), 93–106; Wannenwetsch, 'Luther's Moral Theology', 135; Bernd Wannenwetsch, 'Liturgy', in *The Blackwell Companion to Political Theology* (ed. Peter Scott and William T. Cavanaugh; Malden, MA/Oxford: Blackwell Publishing, 2004), 76–90 (85).

order to capture the political character of relationships among Christians as a sacramental body, Luther employs the Christological logic of the *communicatio idiomatum*, which originally expresses the intimate relation of the two natures of Christ. In a similar intimate way, political worship *simultaneously* relates the believers to God and to their fellow citizens.'[36] However, even if Wannenwetsch makes use of the same concept in Lutheran theology, his liturgical emphasis leads him to play down the affirmation of the worldly and common human life also entailed in this idea. Second, we are both exploring the possibilities of establishing a sacramental ethic. Wannenwetsch explicitly pursues this aim in several of his writings.[37] However, whereas Wannenwetsch situates the reflections on the sacramental ethics in an ecclesial and liturgical approach, the present book explores this theme in light of a Christological understanding of Christ's real presence in reality.

When we ponder the relation between the universal and specific side of justice, it is important to differentiate between outer and inner perspectives. Whereas the former is concerned with the relation between the worldviews represented within society, the latter focuses on the understanding of justice from within these worldviews. Justice in a political society cannot claim validity until the challenge of attaining justice in light of this inner perspective has been adequately addressed – 'adequacy' in this context meaning an awareness and consideration of the particular qualification of justice determined by the multiplicity of worldviews. In other words, one cannot claim there is justice in a society until all implied parties in principle agree that it is actually just. This implies that political justice is not only qualified from a secular, non-religious perspective. Rather, political justice is only justice insofar as it is specifically qualified – for instance, by a religious worldview. This understanding of justice is in line with the book's overall theme.

The inner perspective of justice may be elaborated upon from communitarian ideas in a contemporary understanding of justice, as we find them in e.g. Alasdair MacIntyre and Michael Walzer.[38] MacIntyre argues that the notion of justice and the concept of rationality are qualified by their particular communities. One cannot define justice and rationality independently of these particular communities: 'theories of justice and practical rationality confront us as aspects of traditions, allegiance to which requires the living out of some more or less systematically embodied form of human life, each with its own specific modes of social relationship, each with its own canons of interpretation and explanation in respect of the behaviour of others, each with its own evaluative practices'.[39] Walzer

---

36. Wannenwetsch, 'Liturgy', 85.

37. Wannenwetsch, 'Communication as Transformation', 96–101; Wannenwetsch, 'Luther's Moral Theology', 133–35; Wannenwetsch, 'Liturgy', 84–86.

38. Particularly some of their main works: Michael Walzer, *Spheres of Justice: A Defense of Pluralism and Equality* (New York: Basic Books, 1983); Alasdair MacIntyre, *Whose Justice? Which Rationality?* (London: Duckworth, 1988).

39. MacIntyre, *Whose Justice?*, 391.

employs a similar argument when he makes the point that justice *per se* is a notion that requires acknowledgement of the diversity of worldviews among which it is to be found. Instead of a liberal concept of a simple equality, Walzer argues for a complex equality.[40] Hereby, Walzer understands the need for taking into consideration that justice must respect the various autonomous spheres within society. One must take into account the *spheres of justice*.[41] A proper theory of justice is, therefore, relative and sensitive to social meanings.

> Justice is relative to social meanings. Indeed, the relativity of justice follows from the classic non-relative definition, giving each person his due, as much as it does from my own proposal, distributing goods for 'internal' reasons. These are formal definitions that require, as I have tried to show, historical completion. We cannot say what is due to this person or that one until we know how these people relate to one another through the things they make and distribute. There cannot be a just society until there is a society; and the adjective *just* doesn't determine, it only modifies, the substantive life of the societies it describes. There are an infinite number of possible lives, shaped by an infinite number of possible cultures, religions, political arrangements, geographical conditions, and so on.[42]

Both MacIntyre and Walzer may be right in their endorsement of a communitarian understanding of justice. Certainly, the contextuality of justice and rationality is an important critique of a liberal theory of justice. However, it is also important to keep in mind that the recognition of these differences is also an awareness of sources of potential conflict within political society. Such conflicts may arise either when the differences are emphasized too strongly, or when the differences are not respected sufficiently. If the differences are emphasized too strongly, the common political sphere may suffer from fragmentation and disruption. It will no longer be possible to maintain a common, political space. This may be the result of absolutizing one specific worldview – be it secular or religious. It is important to keep in mind that this potential threat to political society is not only to be argued with reference to religious worldviews. It is also important for a secular notion of politics to keep in mind that such an understanding cannot be endorsed as a comprehensive view. Any attempt to endorse a secular understanding of politics and law as a comprehensive view would entail the neglect of religious worldviews, which is obviously incompatible with notions of justice such as equality and fairness. However, it would also be a wrong course if the differences were not taken sufficiently into consideration. Political justice is not attained satisfactorily if the political citizens are not authentically present in the political debate. It may be argued that the notion of authenticity implies that the political citizen should be able to draw upon his or her worldview in a manner

---

40. Walzer, *Spheres of Justice*, 17.
41. Ibid., 10.
42. Ibid., 312–13.

consistent with this worldview in the political debate.[43] This would be the only way to ensure a genuine and authentic participation as a political citizen. If the political citizen cannot integrate his or her religious worldview in this debate, he or she will always be left with a sense of *Entfremdung* in relation to the political society. Such a sense of difference – or maybe even indifference – with regard to the political society in which one participates carries with it a potential threat to this society.[44] Having argued for the necessity of including the authentic religious voice in the political or public debate, we can move on to the next vital step: finding ways to ensure this participation while maintaining the acknowledgement of the common discourse, in order to ensure the stability of the political, democratic society.[45]

As we have seen several times in this book, there is a particular challenge in Lutheran theology, as this tradition can be said to be particularly prone to the risk of understanding justification by faith individualistically, causing the justification to become isolated from its socio-political implications.[46] However, as we have also seen, the Lutheran tradition does not ignore the societal implications of the reconciliation in Christ. To phrase it more concisely, it makes no sense to ignore that religion plays a crucial and decisive role in the formation also of political societies that claim to be *a*religious or secular. One must, of course, distinguish between the analytic and the more normative question. Whereas the first asks, *if or if not* religion is present in public life, the normative question would ask *should or should not* religion be present. Admittedly, I find the normative question the more interesting – not withholding my position, where I would argue that of course it should be present in public life. The most interesting question, however, is *how* religion is (or should be) present in public life. Maybe we could call this the philosophical question – i.e. a question related to either political philosophy or philosophy of religion. On what kind of arguments is (or should) the role of religion in public life (be) endorsed?

---

43. See also Charles Taylor, *The Ethics of Authenticity* (Cambridge, MA: Harvard University Press, 1991). Taylor explores not only the challenges associated with the concept of authenticity in light of modernity, but also shows how this concept may be reformulated in ways that maintain what we have in common as human beings.

44. See also Kent Greenawalt for a similar standpoint in conclusion of his discussion on the relation between liberalism and religious diversity: Kent Greenawalt, *Religious Convictions and Political Choice* (New York: Oxford University Press, 1988), 258.

45. A similar aim is found in Bretherton's recent political theology: Luke Bretherton, *Christ and the Common Life. Political Theology and the Case for Democracy* (Grand Rapids, MI: W. B. Eerdmans, 2019). However, the different emphasis between our positions maybe lies in Bretherton's stronger accentuation of lived ethics, whereas I explore more the foundation of faithful Christian life in a diverse political reality. But I do not see these different emphases as more than different accentuations of a similar aim.

46. Duncan B. Forrester, 'Social Justice and Welfare', in *The Cambridge Companion to Christian Ethics* (ed. Robin Gill; Cambridge: Cambridge University Press, 2000), 195–208 (200).

Even if we may agree with Ronald Thiemann when he – in his *Religion in Public Life. A Dilemma for Democracy* – says that 'there is nothing inherent in religious belief or in communities of faith that should preclude them from participating fully in the persuasive forum of democratic politics',[47] we still have – just as Thiemann does – to discuss the conditions of publicity. We have to discuss under which conditions religion may take part in the public, democratic debate. From a Lutheran perspective, this will usually lead to an understanding of public discourse under the conditions of natural law, but even this may (as we have seen) be understood in a Christologically saturated sense or in light of a Christologically shaped understanding of natural law.

Consequently, it may be argued that (from the perspective of a Lutheran understanding of natural law) we can maintain both the universality given in the affirmation of the moral law in creation and the understanding that natural law cannot be separated from divine love. This entails that justice, as based upon a notion of natural law, is not confined to matters of power. The love of God is mysteriously present within the spheres of justice. This point has been made by Carl E. Braaten.[48] The work of Antti Raunio – where the focus explicitly is on Luther's writings – makes a similar point: that natural law is not separable from the love of God. Raunio argues that this does not imply disregard for the universal understanding of natural law. Rather, in Luther, all of physical nature serves the law of love. The whole of creation is embraced by the law of God and is, in this sense, necessarily interwoven with the love of God. In Luther – according to Raunio – the notion of the golden rule and natural law means that every human being's reason is full of natural law and love.[49] The idea of natural law as being in accord with a more specific qualification is also found in Tage Kurtén.[50] He concurs with Raunio's understanding of the golden rule in Luther (even if he is referring to another work of Raunio's),[51] whereby he emphasizes that the importance in Luther's understanding of natural law is not the notion of 'law' as a given set of moral norms known by reason. Rather, the important feature is that it is given

---

47. Ronald F. Thiemann, *Religion in Public Life: A Dilemma for Democracy* (A Twentieth Century Fund Book; Washington, DC: Georgetown University Press, 1996), 135.

48. Carl E. Braaten, 'Natural Law in Theology and Ethics', in *Two Cities of God* (ed. Carl E. Braaten and Robert W. Jenson; Grand Rapids, MI: W. B. Eerdmans, 1997), 42–58. See also Chapter 2 for the Chalcedonian affirmation of the real presence of God within the worldly order in Luther, and Chapter 4 for Bonhoeffer's understanding of the mystery of Christ's real presence in the worldly reality.

49. Antti Raunio, 'Natural Law and Faith: The Forgotten Foundations of Ethics in Luther's Theology', in *Union with Christ* (Grand Rapids, MI: W. B. Eerdmans, 1998), 96–124.

50. Tage Kurtén, 'Kärlekens lag eller den naturliga lagen? Biblisk moraltradition i dag', in *Bibeln och kyrkans tro i dag* (Synodalavhandling; ed. Maarit Hytönen; Tammerfors: Kyrkans forskningscentral, 2004), 178–95.

51. Ibid., 192.

with human existence.⁵² Therefore, Kurtén follows Løgstrup in his understanding of the ethical demand arising in the immediate encounter with the other.⁵³ Yet, at the same time, he understands this as being in accord with Hauerwas' ecclesial virtue ethics,⁵⁴ the central argument being that the formation of moral character supports an ethic arising in the immediate encounter with the other.⁵⁵

A Chalcedonian affirmation of Christian humanism

As we have seen how we can understand law and justice between universality and specificity in light of a Chalcedonian Christology, we can now turn to a concept that has received renewed attention within theology and theological ethics, and where we can also find the simultaneity of universality and specificity – i.e. Christian humanism.⁵⁶ Two of the more significant new contributions to this development are the books written by David E. Klemm and William Schweiker and John De Gruchy.⁵⁷ Since these contributions to Christian humanism, the works by Jens Zimmermann have also attracted attention. In a work from 2012 he argues for an understanding of how religion and humanism are not to be seen as opposites. Instead, we should see Western humanism as rooted in religious traditions and how it sustains a humanism of vital importance for our current societies and cultures. Bonhoeffer is included in this work as a source for a Christian humanism from a Protestant tradition, where it is also shown how Bonhoeffer's Christological humanism politically leads away from a fragmented

---

52. Ibid., 178.
53. Ibid., 181–83.
54. Ibid., 183–85.
55. Ibid., 192. See also Chapter 4, particularly the section entitled 'Responsibility and Christological Responsiveness' on the Christ formation in Bonhoeffer.
56. The following section is a summary of the main findings in Ulrik Nissen, 'Being Christ for the Other: A Lutheran Affirmation of Christian Humanism', *Studia theologica* 64, no. 2 (2010), 177–98. See the whole anthology for several contributions substantiating Bonhoeffer as a Christian humanist: Jens Zimmermann and Brian Gregor, *Being Human, Becoming Human: Dietrich Bonhoeffer and Social Thought* (ed. K. C. Hanson, Charles M. Collier and D. Christopher Spinks; Princeton Theological Monograph Series; Eugene, OR: Pickwick, 2010). For some of the reasons behind this resurgence of Christian humanism, see the mentioned article and William Schweiker, 'Freedom within Religion (with Response by John W. De Gruchy)', *Conversations in Religion and Theology* 6, no. 1 (2008), 100–19.
57. John W. De Gruchy, *Confessions of a Christian Humanist* (Minneapolis, MN: Fortress Press, 2006); David E. Klemm and William Schweiker, *Religion and the Human Future. An Essay on Theological Humanism* (Blackwell Manifestos; Malden, MA/Oxford: Wiley-Blackwell, 2008).

understanding of reality.[58] In a Nordic context, the book by Carl-Henric Grenholm also signals the attention that Christian humanism has lately been receiving, even if he holds a critical view of it.[59] One reason behind the resurgence of Christian humanism seems to be the debate in recent years about the role of religion in the public discourse and the subsequent search for a shared human morality without the exclusion of the religious traditions.[60] In this book, I argue that the concept of Christian humanism holds a double-sidedness of universality and specificity which is of particular pertinence to this debate. Further, the book seeks to contribute to a reshaped concept of Christian humanism in light of the book's findings.

Schweiker and De Gruchy may be read as the primary representatives of a contemporary attempt to revitalize and reformulate the classical tradition of Christian humanism and share many concerns in their common endeavour. One is the understanding of the interrelation between the life of the human being and that of other life forms. De Gruchy argues for an affirmation of 'the integrity of creation', recognizing that human life is rooted in and dependent on the earth'.[61] The Christian humanist is concerned with the well-being of the earth and recognizes that all of life is bound together in an evolutionary web of life. Relatively similar to this, Schweiker argues for the notion of human flourishing, which is derived from an ethical naturalism whereby 'the good' is linked with that which respects and enhances the integrity of life.[62] This idea of the integrity of life plays a central role in Schweiker's position.[63] It follows from reflections on natural life in a wider perspective, and on the interrelatedness of all life forms. Life is considered an

---

58. See Jens Zimmermann, *Humanism and Religion. A Call for the Renewal of Western Culture* (Oxford: Oxford University Press, 2012), chapter 7 (particularly 289–315). During the final stages of my work, Zimmermann's new book on Bonhoeffer's Christian humanism appeared: *Dietrich Bonhoeffer's Christian Humanism* (Oxford: Oxford University Press, 2019). It has not been possible for me to engage more substantially with this work. But we seem to have a common aim in tracing the roots of Bonhoeffer's Christology to the early church. One of the differences between our approaches seems to be that I am here pointing to Bonhoeffer's Lutheran heritage, as they share this Chalcedonian Christology.

59. Carl-Henric Grenholm, *Bortom humanismen. En studie i kristen etik* (Stockholm: Verbum, 2003).

60. Such an aim could also be said to be found in Bretherton's recent book, *Christ and the Common Life*. In chapter 2 on 'Humanitarianism' he shows how humanitarianism can be seen as a political theology, even if it has an ambiguous relation to the Christian tradition (ibid., 51–81). But in chapter 10 on 'Humanity' he argues that the notion of a shared humanity is urgent and holds important sources for sustaining and forming a common life which plays a central role in his understanding of political theology (ibid., 291–322).

61. De Gruchy, *Confessions of a Christian Humanist*, 30.

62. William Schweiker, 'Theological Ethics and the Question of Humanism', *Journal of Religion* 83, no. 4 (2003), 539–61 (539 footnote 1).

63. Klemm and Schweiker, *Religion and the Human Future*, chapter 5 (73–93).

integrated whole that goes beyond the human domain. The integrity of life implies 'goods' that are basic (derived from the human being as a finite being), social (derived from the social nature of the human being), reflective (derived from the human being's reflective capabilities) and natural – and human life is understood as situated within the complex interrelation of these levels of goods. In this respect, Schweiker also understands his position as being in 'some continuity with traditional Christian natural law ethics'.[64]

Schweiker uses this understanding of the integrity of life forms as the foundation for his ethic of responsibility. Arising from the interrelated levels of goods and the corresponding norms for right action, Schweiker's imperative of responsibility addresses the moral claim implied in the integrity of life. 'The imperative of responsibility at the heart of theological humanism is this: *in all actions and relations respect and enhance the integrity of life before God*.'[65] De Gruchy does not emphasize the notion of responsibility, but instead argues that the Christian humanist endorses the common humanity with all human beings, and that it is crucial for the future of the world that this common humanity is recognized.[66]

Both De Gruchy and Schweiker relate theological/Christian humanism to social and political issues that have implications for this book's thesis. In De Gruchy, the political and societal implications of Christian humanism are deeply embedded in Christian faith. There is an inextricable link between knowing God and acting justly.[67] At the same time, De Gruchy argues – following Bonhoeffer – that the incarnation of Christ holds fundamental implications for the relation between, on the one hand, the reconciliation of God and the human being and, on the other hand, the reconciliation in its societal and political dimension.[68] For the Christian humanist it is imperative to understand reconciliation from a wider perspective. Schweiker does not argue Christologically – e.g. with regard to Bonhoeffer's ethic of responsibility, he can argue that it holds, 'even if we bracket his ecclesial and Christological claims'.[69] As regards this book, however, it is important to note that Schweiker balances, on the one hand, affirming religious voices' rootedness in their particular traditions against, on the other, emphasizing the critical stance to one's own tradition. This implies an endorsement of the public character of theology[70] as well as a critical-appreciative reflection on the contractarian tradition so influential in contemporary politics. Schweiker affirms both the positive, formative role of

---

64. William Schweiker, *Responsibility and Christian Ethics* (New Studies in Christian Ethics; Cambridge: Cambridge University Press, 1995), 2; William Schweiker, *Theological Ethics and Global Dynamics in the Time of Many Worlds* (Oxford: Blackwell, 2006), 28.

65. Klemm and Schweiker, *Religion and the Human Future*, 82. See also Schweiker, *Responsibility and Christian Ethics*, 123–33.

66. De Gruchy, *Confessions of a Christian Humanist*, 30–32.

67. Ibid., 140–41.

68. Ibid., 153.

69. Schweiker, *Responsibility and Christian Ethics*, 57.

70. Schweiker, 'Freedom within Religion'.

religious traditions and the equality and justice inherent in the contractarian tradition. Therefore, the aim of Schweiker is to argue for a foundation of politics that neither suspends the role of religious traditions nor ignores truth and justice as derived from acts of freedom, reason and choice.

However, Schweiker and De Gruchy also represent different approaches, which is important to keep in mind. The most significant difference between them pertains to their understanding of the relation between Christian humanism and other worldviews. Whereas Schweiker emphasizes the necessity of the humanist commitment to make public arguments for its position – which is also seen as a central argument for his notion of a *theological* rather than a Christian humanism – De Gruchy maintains the idea of a critical humanism, which he sees as 'inclusive in character and holistic in extent', thereby endorsing the openness of this position even while affirming its rootedness in a confessional Christian faith tradition.[71] The difference between the two positions appears to be one of emphasis rather than strategy. For both positions it is important to maintain the openness as constitutive of the humanist approach. In this way the position shares the aim of the book, when I argue for the universal, common dimension of a Christian ethic and yet maintain that this is rooted in and qualified by a particular foundation – i.e. the implications of a broadly conceived Chalcedonian Christology.

Taking the cue from the contemporary understanding of Christian humanism, we can turn to the Lutheran tradition, more specifically to Luther and Bonhoeffer, and draw on their ethical thought as a source of Christian humanism. Despite the apparent ambivalent use of Luther's thought to sustain the idea of Christian humanism, I argue that it contains central notions that can be seen as supportive of this idea. Notable examples are his concepts of reason, natural law and political authority.[72] In Luther the law of nature shines as a light in every human being's reason. Therefore, natural law is understood as a universal law and thereby entails an affirmation of the moral potentials and abilities of all human beings – at least in terms of knowledge of the natural law. Natural law is not dependent upon a specific cultural or religious context. Its sole precondition is that the human being is created as a rational being. Consequently, Luther can also speak of the gentile knowing natural law just as well as anyone else. Hereby, Luther seems to come to an understanding of the moral reason of the human being which may be seen as an expression of a Christian humanism. The understanding of the universality of natural law and the derived moral capability of the human being is paralleled in Luther's view on political authority. Luther states that e.g. the gentiles have a finer and wiser understanding of political authority than the Christians, and the Turks have (according to Luther) one of the finest and most stable political regimes. As we have seen throughout the book, this emphasis on what we can call the universal side of moral life for Luther is not to be seen in contrast to the specific side.

---

71. Ibid.
72. See Chapter 2.

Turning to Bonhoeffer, in addition to the already mentioned readings of his theology, the findings of the book – most notably his concepts of reality, responsibility and autonomy – may be constructively appropriated in an affirmation of the Christian humanism in Bonhoeffer. These concepts are shaped by a Chalcedonian Christology and consequently become supportive of a Christian humanism.

If we turn to Bonhoeffer's understanding of *reality*, we have seen that this is fundamentally shaped by a Christological understanding of the polemical unity between the reality of God and the reality of the world. The double-sidedness and unity of this Christ-reality makes it possible for Bonhoeffer to argue for a specific Christological foundation of human reality while, at the same time, endorsing the affirmation of human reality as *human* reality. This is closely linked to Bonhoeffer's understanding of the mystery of Christ within reality. In Bonhoeffer the understanding of reality and the understanding of Christ are understood intimately in relation to each other.

In Bonhoeffer's understanding of *responsibility* we find the same understanding of a fundamental Christological basis of his whole thought, which implies that the relation to the other is always determined both by the concrete encounter with the other as a human being and, at the same time, an endorsement of this immediate encounter as always saturated by the Christ-reality. In that sense Bonhoeffer's notion of responsibility also may be read as an affirmation of both human reality and the reality of God – both in the Christ-reality. This also implies that the responsible person is held responsible before God and human beings at the same time. Bonhoeffer can even say that the responsible person represents Christ before human beings, and human beings before Christ.

Finally, in his concept of *autonomy*, we find the same motif returning. Bonhoeffer does not advocate a notion of autonomy separate from the Christ-reality. Rather, his Christologically shaped understanding of reality implies for him that he does not separate a 'Christian' and 'autonomous' ethic. Instead he maintains the idea of the polemical, contradictory unity of the Christ-reality. Therefore, when he argues for true worldliness he makes use of an analogy from the Holy Communion and says that this is only 'in, with, and under' the preaching of Christ. True worldliness depends upon the preaching of the cross of Christ. However, this does not imply a law, which is different from the law of creation. Rather, the law of Christ liberates creation for fulfilment of its own law.

Even if Zimmermann does not speak explicitly about a Chalcedonian Christology in Bonhoeffer – but rather a 'participatory Christological ontology'[73] – our findings with regard to Bonhoeffer's Christian humanism fundamentally are in accord with each other. I therefore agree with Zimmermann's following summary of his findings:

---

73. Jens Zimmermann, 'Dietrich Bonhoeffer's Christian Humanism in Philosophical and Theological Context', in *Dietrich Bonhoeffers Theologie heute* (Gütersloh: Gütersloher Verlagshaus, 2009), 369–86 (371).

Bonhoeffer's Christological humanism ties together his central ideas of one Christ reality (ultimate and penultimate), this-worldliness and realistic responsibility. The freedom of the Christian and his existence as a unified subject across the various areas of human activity are grounded in the fact that reality itself is directed toward the affirmation, reconciliation and renewal of humanity in Christ.[74]

In light of the analysis of these key concepts in Luther's and Bonhoeffer's ethical thought, I therefore argue that Luther's and Bonhoeffer's shared Chalcedonian understanding ties them together in shared fundamental premises for a Christian humanism in its polemical affirmation of the simultaneously divine and human reality.

The Lutheran Christian humanism derived from a Chalcedonian approach and its affirmation of a differentiated unity of universality and specificity holds several significant implications for the understanding of the world, natural life, the human being and social and political life. Some of the central implications of this understanding are:

- It affirms the attempt to argue for a third position between religious fundamentalism and secular liberalism. Schweiker, De Gruchy, Grenholm, Luther and Bonhoeffer all affirm such a 'third' position, even if their arguments for it and the terminology they use may differ.
- It endorses a legitimate role for religious voices in the public debate. However, it also maintains the necessity of a critical distance from the practices and beliefs of particular traditions. The universality implied in Christian humanism affirms its openness towards other traditions, and its awareness that truth may be found in diverse religious and philosophical traditions and outlooks.
- It maintains the validity and legitimacy of a specific *Christian* or *theological* outlook and/or assessment of worldly, scientific, public, cultural and political issues, even while arguing that this does not stand in contrast to the universal validity and implications of deliberations on such issues.
- The universal and specific dimensions of a Christian social ethic are not seen as being in contrast to one another; rather, they are seen as resting in a differentiated unity that can be seen as an expression of a Chalcedonian mode of thought.

---

74. Ibid., 380. See also Zimmermann's essay in the previously mentioned anthology, where he engages in a discussion with secular and theological objections to Bonhoeffer's Christological humanism: Jens Zimmermann, 'Being Human, Becoming Human: Dietrich Bonhoeffer's Christological Humanism', in *Being Human, Becoming Human: Dietrich Bonhoeffer and Social Thought* (ed. Jens Zimmerman and Brian Gregor; Eugene, OR: Pickwick, 2010), 25–48.

Communicative responsibility Christologically reshaped

The concept of responsibility is an approach to ethics which does not have quite the same long history as the deontological and teleological approaches.[75] It was particularly technological developments during the twentieth century that raised the demand for another understanding of the foundation and aim of ethics.[76] Bonhoeffer's ethic was one of the early theological contributions to this debate, as his ethic can be understood as an ethic of responsibility.[77] Also, within the Lutheran tradition the emphasis on responsiveness as a source of responsibility has played a significant role in the understanding of the relationship between God and the human being.[78] In this part of the book it is therefore the intention to turn to the constructive interplay between responsiveness and the concept of responsibility.

In continuation of the book's aim, I argue that the communication implied in the *communicatio idiomatum* of the Chalcedonian Christology leads to a constructive engagement with selected contemporary positions of communicative ethics (particularly Jeffrey Stout and Gary Simpson),[79] H. Richard Niebuhr's

---

75. The following section is a summary and revision of the main findings in Ulrik Nissen, 'Responsibility and Responsiveness: Reflections on the Communicative Dimension of Responsibility', *Neue Zeitschrift für systematische Theologie und Religionsphilosophie* 53, no. 1 (2011), 90–108.

76. Hans Jonas, *The Imperative of Responsibility: In Search of an Ethics for the Technological Age* (Chicago, IL: University of Chicago Press, 1984), 1–24; Schweiker, *Responsibility and Christian Ethics*, 24–30. Reed agrees that responsibility is a modern concept, even if she also points to earlier traces of this concept, see Esther D. Reed, *The Limit of Responsibility: Engaging Dietrich Bonhoeffer in a Globalizing Era* (ed. Brian Brock and Susan F. Parsons; T&T Clark Enquiries in Theological Ethics; London: T&T Clark, 2018), chapter 2 (47–86).

77. See e.g. Chapter 4, 'Responsibility and Christological Responsiveness'.

78. Oswald Bayer, *Freiheit als Antwort: zur theologischen Ethik* (Tübingen: Mohr, 1995); Peter Dabrock, 'Responding to "Wirklichkeit". Reclaiming Bonhoeffer's Approach to Theological Ethics Between Mystery and the Formation of the World', in *Mysteries in the Theology of Dietrich Bonhoeffer. A Copenhagen Bonhoeffer Symposium* (ed. Kirsten Busch Nielsen, Ulrik Nissen and Christiane Tietz; Göttingen: Vandenhoeck & Ruprecht, 2007), 49–80; Peter Dabrock, 'Wirklichkeit verantworten: der responsive Ansatz theologischer Ethik bei Dietrich Bonhoeffer', in *Verantwortungsethik als Theologie des Wirklichen* (ed. Wolfgang Nethöfel, Peter Dabrock and Siegfried Keil; Göttingen: Vandenhoeck & Ruprecht, 2009), 117–58; Wolfgang Huber, 'Sozialethik als Verantwortungsethik', in *Verantwortungsethik als Theologie des Wirklichen* (ed. Wolfgang Nethöfel, Peter Dabrock and Siegfried Keil; Göttingen: Vandenhoeck & Ruprecht, 2009), 74–100.

79. See Gary Simpson, 'Toward a Lutheran "Delight in the Law of the Lord": Church and State in the Context of Civil Society', in *Church & State. Lutheran Perspectives* (ed. John R. Stumme and Robert W. Tuttle; Minneapolis, MN: Fortress Press, 2003), 20–50; Jeffrey Stout, *Democracy and Tradition* (New Forum Books; Princeton, NJ: Princeton University Press, 2005).

understanding of responsibility as responsiveness and Bonhoeffer's Christological concept of responsibility. I will argue in this section that these positions sustain a responsive concept of responsibility based on a broadly conceived Chalcedonian Christology. I seek to appropriate the communicative exchange of Chalcedonian Christology as a figurative model for communicative exchange in public discourse. Just as the *communicatio idiomatum* implies that there is a communicative exchange between the two natures of Christ and yet the distinctiveness of both natures is maintained, the Chalcedonian understanding of public discourse entails a communicative exchange of different views and yet it upholds the distinctive characteristics of the common and particular approach.

As the concept of communication of properties between the two natures of Christ is a different concept of 'communication' than the one usually found in so-called 'communicative ethics', a brief elaboration on this concept is needed. Central to my argument is the contention that, with regard to both the relation between the two natures of Christ and the societal understanding of communication, we have a 'communicative exchange'. However, whereas the exchange in Christ pertains to his properties or attributes, the societal concept pertains to an argumentative or discursive exchange. Even if these two concepts are different, I argue that they share significant resemblances making it possible to endorse a Christologically saturated concept of communicative exchange in public discourse.

The concept of communication can be differentiated according to at least three different meanings: (1) the technical (where it is understood in light of the transmission between sender-code-receiver); (2) the interactive or reciprocal communication (related to everyday-life exchange); and (3) from the semantics of 'communion' (the transformative level). In this sense it pertains to 'intensive, interpersonal, existential communication'.[80] Whereas the theories of 'communicative ethics' are often read in light of the second, reciprocal level of communication, I contend that these positions also hold elements of the third level. Interactive communication in a public discourse is also (trans)formative in the sense that the participants in this discourse not only reason with each other but also are being shaped by particular values and beliefs embedded in this discursive, democratic practice (I believe this to be an important insight in Jeffrey Stout's position).[81] Thereby, they are also taking part in the third, transformative level. In connecting the concept of communication to the transformative understanding, I am also connecting it to the understanding found in the Lutheran concept of *communicatio idiomatum*.[82] As we have seen several times in the book, this concept is understood both as a Christological and sacramental concept in Luther and Bonhoeffer. As we have also seen, several of Bonhoeffer's key concepts may be understood in light of a broadly conceived Chalcedonian Christology related

---

80. Cf. Wannenwetsch, 'Communication as Transformation', 95.
81. See also Chapter 7.
82. Cf. also Wannenwetsch, 'Communication as Transformation', for a 'sacramental' appropriation of this concept with regard to communication.

to this concept. The implications of these findings imply that the concepts of reason, reality, the secular etc. are understood in light of the 'real presence' of Christ. Therefore, we may speak of an underlying Christological ontology (or a 'participatory Christological ontology') behind these concepts.[83] This also holds implications for the concept of communication as it is understood in light of the contention that the inner mystery of reality is Christ himself – why communication in the public discourse fundamentally is understood as communication in Christ. This implies (1) that the reciprocal and discursive communication in public discourse is acknowledged in its own right; and (2) that it is fundamentally understood as a communication 'in Christ'.

In Stout we find such a position, where the communicative emphasis allows him to argue for a recognition of differences and yet maintain a common democratic culture of reasoning. In his *Democracy and Tradition*, it is the aim to develop a position which maintains democratic virtues and includes the diversity of, for example, tradition-based views. Stout's approach is pragmatic, which allows him to emphasize the democratic practices. Rather than argue for a substantial understanding of already agreed upon values and ideals, Stout develops an expressivist understanding of the constitutive practices of modern democracy. He argues that there are certain democratic practices embedded in our tradition which imply an appreciation of our differences and yet an awareness of the importance of holding each other responsible. Partly inspired by a Hegelian understanding of reason as embodied in a social practice,[84] he develops a position between secular liberalism and new traditionalism. He maintains the idea that communities are essential for ethics as a social practice and that reason in this sense is socially embedded. At the same time, he emphasizes that it is as a community of reason-givers that the discursive exchange of democracy is upheld.[85] This places him between a communitarian understanding known from, for example, Hauerwas and the political liberalism found in Rawls.[86] 'I am trying to articulate a form of pluralism, one that citizens with strong religious commitments can accept and that welcomes their full participation in public life without fudging on its own premises. But I see this pluralism primarily as an existing feature of the political culture, not as a philosophical doctrine needing to be imposed on it. Our political culture is already pluralistic in the relevant sense.'[87] For this book it is important to note that this implies both the discursive exchange of reasons and the idea of holding each other responsible. Both of these ideas are seminal to the present argument. With regard to the former, Stout makes this explicit as a foundational

---

83. See also Chapter 4, 'Reality as the Contradictory Christ-Reality' and 'The Christological Ontology of Reason'.
84. Stout, *Democracy and Tradition*, 304.
85. Ibid., 293.
86. For his detailed discussion of these two authors, see also ibid., chapters 3 (63–91) and 6 (140–61).
87. Ibid., 296–97.

idea of his position. He argues that democracy is a tradition with certain 'enduring attitudes, concerns, dispositions, and patterns of conduct';[88] among these is a discursive practice of reasoning which is constitutive of democracy. This social practice implies the latter – holding each other responsible. The responsibility is integrated as a defining and meaning-giving characteristic of the discourse itself.

> The continuing social process of holding one another responsible is chiefly what I have in mind when I refer to the ethical life or inheritance of a people. Central to democratic thought as I understand it is the idea of a body of citizens who reason with one another about the ethical issues that divide them … It follows that one thing a democratic people had better have in common is a form of ethical discourse, a way of exchanging reasons about ethical and political topics.[89]

Even if Stout does not elaborate on this concept of responsibility, his understanding of the democratic discourse substantiates the motif of responsiveness which is central to this concept. He continuously refers to either this concept itself or the idea of accountability. Therefore, it can be argued that the idea of responsibility plays a much more central role in Stout than he has made explicit in his understanding of the discursive exchange of reasons in a democratic society. What is even more crucial is that this responsibility is closely connected with the motif of responsiveness implied in his alternative understanding of public reasoning, where he argues for a full recognition of religious views and arguments in the public debate understood as a mutual exchange of reasons.[90]

A similar communicative position, but argued from a Lutheran perspective, is found in Simpson.[91] Simpson reflects on the emergence of civil society as an 'order of creation' and outlines how this implies a communicative concept of reason. Simpson argues that the previous centuries' 'representative publicness' of the 'public sphere' is transformed into the civil society. Capitalism and the press called into existence a new public which over time began to regard itself as different from the public of the nation-state. Eventually this became the 'emerging public sphere of civil society'.[92] The emerging 'bourgeois' public sphere was accompanied by competing public spheres, the plurality of which can be called 'civil society': 'civil society is that great plurality of different kinds of associations, affiliations, movements, and institutions for the prevention and promotion of this, that, and the other thing'.[93] Simpson raises the question of whether this civil society can be understood as a new creational order of the triune God, in addition to the 'church',

---

88. Ibid., 3.
89. Ibid., 6.
90. Ibid., 10.
91. Simpson, 'Toward a Lutheran "Delight in the Law of the Lord"'.
92. Ibid., 45.
93. Ibid.

'state' and 'family' already recognized in the Lutheran tradition.[94] This is where Simpson's deliberations intersect with this book and its interest in responsibility. This is due to Simpson's attention to the concept of accountability, which may be understood as one of three central modes of responsibility (the other two being 'imputability' and 'liability').[95] Simpson argues that political accountability now is exercised by the civil society together with democratically constituted states. Hereby, civil society has taken on the accountability previously exercised through the preaching office. This implies that we can think beyond the differences and intersections of church and state, and rather see the political accountability task of civil society metaphorically expressed in the joint movement of the traffic circle.[96] Simpson takes these deliberations a step further when he reflects on the concept of reason. He rightly acknowledges the centrality of reason in Luther's political thought, and argues that reason must be understood as communicative reason with regard to civil society. It is in this communicative dimension that we find the link between Simpson's understanding and the communicative exchange depicted in the Chalcedonian Christology. The central point in Simpson's understanding of communicative reason is that 'claims to practical moral truth must be redeemed critically through participatory practices and public communicative reason... participatory procedures and practices of public communicative reason empower traditions and institutions that are affected by a moral claim to have a say in the formulation, stipulation, and adoption of moral norms'.[97] In the context of this book's argument, I contend that this communicative understanding of reason and its implied critical participatory redeeming of moral truth reflects a participatory exchange which holds figurative resemblance to the communication of attributes in the Chalcedonian Christology.

The communicative exchange in public discourse implies a response to the other. This role of the other plays a central part both in the relation between responsibility and responsiveness, and the Chalcedonian understanding of responsive responsibility. The concept of responsiveness in responsibility is closely related to the Latin root of responsibility, *respondeo*. Just as in the German *Verantwortung*, and in the Danish *an-svar*, this root meaning implies a responsive relationship between the moral agent and the other. The ethical question is what the moral response should be in a given situation. This responsive understanding of responsibility is also found, for example, in H. Richard Niebuhr.[98]

---

94. See also Chapter 2 on the Lutheran three estates and Chapter 5 on Bonhoeffer's mandates.

95. Gerald P. McKenny, 'Responsibility', in *The Oxford Handbook of Theological Ethics* (ed. Gilbert C. Meilaender and William Werpehowski; Oxford: Oxford University Press, 2005), 237–53.

96. Simpson, 'Toward a Lutheran "Delight in the Law of the Lord"', 46.

97. Ibid., 47.

98. H. Richard Niebuhr, *The Responsible Self: An Essay in Christian Moral Philosophy* (Louisville, KY: Westminster John Knox Press, 1999).

Niebuhr distinguishes between four central elements in responsibility, namely, response (to interpreted action upon us), interpretation (of the question to which an answer is being given), accountability (in anticipation of answers to our answers) and social solidarity (as a continuing discourse among beings forming a continuous society).[99] In a recent overview of the concept of responsibility, Gerald McKenny differentiates between three key elements in responsibility: imputability (that actions can be ascribed to one), accountability (that one is answerable to someone) and liability (that one is answerable for something or someone).[100] The primary difference between Niebuhr's and McKenny's terminology seems to be Niebuhr's stronger emphasis on responsiveness and social solidarity. With regard to the response to and interpretation of responsibility, Niebuhr argues that all action is in response to action upon us. This is the case for the natural response in our bodies, our social response in society and the more individual response between individual beings. But it is only moral responsibility that implies the dimension of interpretation which can be found in both social and individual contexts.[101] In these contexts, action is interpreted as being symbolic of larger meaning and the adequate response is given accordingly. When Niebuhr ponders accountability as an element of responsibility, he understands it as 'part of the response pattern of our self-conduct'.[102] It is important for Niebuhr that the response is given in anticipation of answers to our answers. In this sense it is not just a question of responsiveness. Rather, accountability is 'like a statement in a dialogue...It is made as part of a total conversation that leads forward and is to have meaning as a whole.'[103]

This emphasis on accountability is a central reason why Wannenwetsch criticizes Niebuhr's concept of responsibility for not being responsibility at all.[104] Wannenwetsch warns against the danger of moral self-justification in the theories of responsibility,[105] and instead argues for Bonhoeffer's theory of responsibility. Even if I concur with Wannenwetsch in these reservations, I follow Niebuhr – and I do believe Bonhoeffer would as well – in his understanding of the dialogical encounter with the other as an expression of the interrelatedness of human interaction. I do not see this as being at odds with Bonhoeffer's Christological understanding. Rather, I see it as an important implication of Bonhoeffer's Christological affirmation of reality that a Christologically saturated concept

99. Ibid., 61–68.
100. McKenny, 'Responsibility', 242–51. See also Schweiker, *Responsibility and Christian Ethics*, 55–58.
101. Niebuhr, *The Responsible Self*, 61–63.
102. Ibid., 64.
103. Ibid.
104. Bernd Wannenwetsch, '"Responsible Living" or "Responsible Self"? Bonhoefferian Reflections on a Vexed Moral Notion', *Studies in Christian Ethics* 18, no. 3 (2005), 125–40 (137).
105. Ibid., 125–37.

of reality implies a differentiated unity of human reality and God's reality.[106] Finally, social solidarity indicates that the response to action upon us takes place in 'a continuing discourse or interaction among beings forming a continuing society'.[107] So it is this continuous (responsive) interrelatedness with others that serves as the foundation of responsibility. I will not go into a further discussion of Niebuhr's concept of responsibility more generally, but instead refer to other works that take up parts of this discussion.[108]

These central motifs in Niebuhr's understanding of responsibility imply a responsiveness that constitutes a dialogical pattern resembling the communicative exchange found in Stout and Simpson. Just as in Stout and Simpson, Niebuhr argues that the continuing discourse is constitutive of the continuing society. I contend that this communicative dimension in Niebuhr establishes a link between him and the *communicatio idiomatum* of the Chalcedonian Christology. This becomes more apparent when he reflects explicitly on the figure of Jesus Christ. Even if Niebuhr does not mention the Chalcedonian Christology or the *communicatio idiomatum* motif, he ponders the relationship between the universal and the particular. Niebuhr argues that Jesus understands the universal as the will and action of God in all that nature and men do. The universal contains, transforms, includes and fashions every particular. 'The will of God is what God does in all that nature and men do. It is the universal that contains and transforms, includes and fashions, every particular.'[109] Jesus responds to all these actions and interprets them in the context of divine, universal action. This response serves as the foundation of universal responsibility. As Niebuhr describes how every particular is included in the universal – in Jesus' interpretation of particular events – he depicts a concept of differentiated unity which holds a resemblance to the aim of the present book. 'The Christian ethos so uniquely exemplified in Christ himself is an ethics of universal responsibility. It interprets every particular event as included in universal action. It is the ethos of citizenship in a universal society, in which no being that exists and no action that takes place is interpretable outside the universal context.'[110] Just as the universal and particular are different and yet cannot be separated from each other, the book continuously has attempted

---

106. See also Chapter 4, 'Reality as the Contradictory Christ-Reality' and 'The Secular as *Saeculum*'.

107. Niebuhr, *The Responsible Self*, 65.

108. See e.g. Ronald F. Thiemann, *The Legacy of H. Richard Niebuhr* (Minneapolis, MN: Augsburg Fortress, 1991); Glen Harold Stassen, Diane M. Yeager, John Howard Yoder and H. R. Niebuhr, *Authentic Transformation: A New Vision of Christ and Culture* (Nashville, TN: Abingdon Press, 1996); William Werpehowski, *American Protestant Ethics and the Legacy of H. Richard Niebuhr* (Moral Traditions Series; Washington, DC: Georgetown University Press, 2002).

109. Niebuhr, *The Responsible Self*, 164.

110. Ibid., 167.

to argue for a relationship of simultaneous difference and unity with regard to universality and specificity pertaining to the foundation of a Lutheran social ethic.

As I point to these possibilities of reading Niebuhr in continuity with the present book's argument, I readily admit that there are also fundamental differences. First, Niebuhr is using the concept of universality in a different sense than I have been doing during most of the book. In Chapter 2 on Luther's ethics, I argued that the universal moral law (natural law) is derived from the specific foundation in God's will. Likewise, in Chapters 3–5 on Bonhoeffer, I argued for the Christ-reality as a mysterious affirmation of the reality of God (as the specific) and the reality of the world (as the universal). In Niebuhr the particular are the concrete and historically conditioned events and these are interpreted in light of God's will as the universal. Second, Niebuhr does not base his understanding on a Chalcedonian Christology, just as we do not find a Christological ontology underlying his reflections. This is where Bonhoeffer and Niebuhr part ways. However, even if they have fundamentally different understandings of the Christ-reality, they share the understanding that the reality of God (Bonhoeffer) is an inseparable dimension of the universality (Niebuhr) underlying all concrete situations (Bonhoeffer) and particular events (Niebuhr). Whereas Bonhoeffer – in light of the one Christ-reality – interprets this as the foundation of responsibility in the response to Christ and to the other, Niebuhr understands this as the foundation of responsibility in response to the universal (divine action) behind the particular events. Both of them understand it as being affirmative of human reality and yet inseparable from the reality of God. Therefore, I also argue that for both Niebuhr and Bonhoeffer the universal and the particular/specific are not to be understood in contrast to each other but rather in a relationship of simultaneous difference and unity.

In conclusion, the communicative and responsive shaping of responsibility that we have seen in Stout, Simpson, Niebuhr and the Lutheran tradition points to an understanding of responsibility that holds important potential for the contemporary debate on the role of Christian ethics in public discourse. In the Chalcedonian affirmation of a differentiated unity of universality and specificity, it serves as the source of a third position beyond the futile antagonism of liberalism and communitarianism. Hereby, it maintains the reasonableness of a liberal democratic assertion of a common political discourse, and yet it also contends the necessity of authentic particular worldviews and outlooks. In its argument for such a third way of thinking it aims to contribute to an understanding whereby these positions are seen in a constructive relationship – rather than in contrast – with each other.

Conclusion

In this sixth chapter, we have seen how the book's findings substantiate an understanding of Christian ethics, where the Chalcedonian Christology leads to a Christologically saturated understanding of law and justice with an affirmation of both the universal and specific dimensions. We saw how both the universal understanding and the specific approach are essential for the Lutheran tradition. Both are necessary and yet neither is sufficient in itself. The Lutheran understanding of natural law was read as an example of how the universal and specific dimensions are related to each other in a differentiated unity. Likewise, the classical tradition of Christian humanism was seen as an expression of both dimensions. In light of contemporary advocates of a Christian humanism, we saw how the Lutheran tradition – not least Bonhoeffer – also can be read as being Christian humanist. Finally, we pondered the concept of responsibility as an idea that can be reformulated in communicative terms. The communicative reshaping of responsibility opens up the possibility of integrating the responsive understanding of responsibility found in dialogical approaches, and the communicative dimension implicit in the Chalcedonian understanding of the *communicatio idiomatum*.

Chapter 7

LIVING IN THE *SAECULUM* AND BEARING WITNESS TO CHRIST

Having seen how the findings of the book imply an affirmation of both the universal and specific dimensions of Christian ethics, we will now turn to the implications of these findings as they also transcend universality and specificity. This is the point where the book's contention of a Chalcedonian motif implies that, just as Bonhoeffer pointed to the strength of the formula of Chalcedon in its transgression of itself, the Chalcedonian contention of the differentiated (or polemical) unity of universality and specificity also implies that these concepts are affirmed and yet transcended at the same time. They are affirmed as they both express important and essential sides of a Christian ethic between these two opposites, and yet they are transcended as neither is sufficient in itself and each becomes problematic without the other. We need a new term for this position between these extremes. For lack of a better term, the book has used the idea of a 'differentiated unity of universality and specificity'.[1] We can also speak of a 'third position'. Several contemporary theologians and

---

1. Alternatives perhaps could be an ethic of authenticity or integrity. The idea would be the same – that there is a dynamic place for Christian ethics between a merely universalistic approach to Christian ethics (where we risk giving up on its identity) and a very specific (or distinct) approach (where we risk losing sight of all that holds us in bonds of care with fellow human beings irrespective of our different worldviews). I have briefly touched on the concept of authenticity in Chapter 6. For an outline of a Christian ethic of integrity, see Nigel Biggar, *Behaving in Public: How to Do Christian Ethics* (Grand Rapids, MI/Cambridge: W. B. Eerdmans, 2011), chapter 1 (1–23). Bretherton's recent book, in its general aim, also can be seen as a move in the same direction: Luke Bretherton, *Christ and the Common Life: Political Theology and the Case for Democracy* (Grand Rapids, MI: W. B. Eerdmans, 2019). In my own work in progress, I am pursuing what I call a 'responsive' ethic, which implies that we are living in common relations of responsivity and as Christians live our lives in response to Christ: Ulrik Nissen, *The Responsive Body: Beginning, Altering, and Fulfilling Human Life* (forthcoming).

philosophers argue for such a 'third position', and I briefly outlined the search for such a position in Chapter 1.[2] Klemm and Schweiker speak about theological humanism as a 'third-way thinking' beyond over-humanization and hypertheism;[3] Stout ponders his concept of ethics as a social practice as 'a third way' between moral objectivity and subjectivity;[4] and Biggar argues for 'a third way' between 'a "conservative" biblical and theological seriousness, which is shy of attending too closely to public policy; or "liberal" engagement with public policy, which is theologically thin and bland'.[5] We could, of course, also mention Bonhoeffer's argument for a Christian ethic between radicalism and accommodation.[6] In all of these positions we find arguments coming close to the aim of the present book, namely, trying to establish a position between universality and specificity. The present book, however, goes beyond the mentioned 'third positions' in its Chalcedonian approach to the 'differentiated unity' and the implied understanding that universality and specificity are maintained in their differences and yet they can be paradoxically reconciled.

In this chapter I will attempt to draw on some of the main findings of the book's constituent papers while attempting to demonstrate some of their implications pertaining to selected key issues in a contemporary debate on Christian ethics in public. I will do this by focusing on the Christian's dual citizenship and the concept of conversation in the polyphony of public life, and by pointing to some of the overall implications of the book's findings with regard to the question of bearing witness in debates over contentious issues. In pondering these last questions, there will also be occasional references to the Bible, as I share the understanding

---

2. When the current book was first presented as a doctoral thesis in Denmark, it gave rise to a debate in the theological journal, *Dansk teologisk tidsskrift*. I wish to express my gratitude for this debate. See Svend Andersen, 'En tredje vej for den teologiske etik?', *Dansk teologisk tidsskrift* 78, no. 2 (2015), 113–23; Jeppe Bach Nikolajsen, 'Kristen etik i et pluralistisk samfund', *Dansk teologisk tidsskrift* 79, no. 2 (2016), 105–21. I gave a provisional reply to these articles in a later issue: Ulrik Nissen, 'Kristen etik mellem kompromis og radikalitet. Om ansvarsetikken som en tredje vej inspireret af K. E. Løgstrup og Dietrich Bonhoeffer', *Dansk teologisk tidsskrift* 80, no. 2-3 (2017), 110–26.

3. David E. Klemm and William Schweiker, *Religion and the Human Future: An Essay on Theological Humanism* (Blackwell Manifestos; Malden, MA/Oxford: Wiley-Blackwell, 2008), 11–22.

4. Jeffrey Stout, *Democracy and Tradition* (New Forum Books; Princeton, NJ: Princeton University Press, 2005), 274.

5. Biggar, *Behaving in Public*, xvii.

6. Dietrich Bonhoeffer, *Ethik* (herausgegeben von Ilse Tödt, Heinz Eduard Tödt, Ernst Feil und Clifford Green; Dietrich Bonhoeffer Werke; band 6; Gütersloh: Chr. Kaiser, 2nd rev. edn, 1998) (DBW 6), 144–50. See also Chapter 5.

found in e.g. Oliver O'Donovan and Nigel Biggar that a Christian ethic must be formulated in light of Scripture.[7]

The Christian's dual citizenship

Throughout the book we have continuously returned to the concept of the differentiated unity of universality and specificity. In doing so, it has been the aim to argue for the foundations of a Christian ethic between these two opposites. In Bonhoeffer, the concept of reality has been a recurring theme, where we have pondered the reality of the world and the reality of God as reconciled in the Christ-reality. We have also seen how Bonhoeffer uses this idea to reformulate the Lutheran understanding of the two kingdoms. As we also have noted, Bonhoeffer wants to maintain Luther's two kingdoms doctrine, but he argues that it has been misunderstood among his contemporaries as two separate realms. It is important for Bonhoeffer that it is understood as a polemical or contradictory unity, resembling the relation between the natures of Christ. Hereby, Bonhoeffer moves beyond either a dualistic interpretation or a simple identification of the two realms. This is where Bonhoeffer can be read along the lines of the mentioned 'third way'.

Without referring to Bonhoeffer, Oliver O'Donovan makes a similar claim, when he contends that the relation between the two natures of Christ resembles the relation between the two kingdoms:

> [A]s in speaking of the Incarnation itself we cannot affirm the hypostatic union without the two natures, so with the Kingdom of God we cannot conceive the henosis of political and spiritual without the duality of the two terms held together in it… The unity of the kingdoms, we may say, is the heart of the Gospel, their duality is their pericardium. Proclaiming the unity of God's rule in Christ is the task of Christian witness; understanding the duality is the chief assistance rendered by Christian reflection.[8]

---

7. Oliver O'Donovan, *The Desire of the Nations: Rediscovering the Roots of Political Theology* (Cambridge: Cambridge University Press, 1996), 15; Biggar, *Behaving in Public*, 66. See also Brian Brock, *Singing the Ethos of God: On the Place of Christian Ethics in Scripture* (Grand Rapids, MI: W. B. Eerdmans, 2007). Brock's whole book is an attempt both to recognize the strangeness of the Bible and yet find ways to immerse ourselves into the universe of the biblical texts and thereby be shaped by them.

8. O'Donovan, *The Desire of the Nations*, 82. On the construction of 'the two' in Luther, see also Michael Richard Laffin, *The Promise of Martin Luther's Political Theology: Freeing Luther from the Modern Political Narrative* (ed. Brian Brock and Susan F. Parsons; T&T Clark Enquiries in Theological Ethics. London: T&T Clark, 2016), 98–111.

This 'differentiated unity' holds important implications for how to understand what we could call the 'dual citizenship' of the Christian.[9] Again, these are to be differentiated and yet not separated from each other. By introducing the concept of 'citizenship', I seek two things (partly following Wannenwetsch). First, I want to draw on a concept that expresses the idea of commitment (rather than just obedience) to a political reality, i.e. a communal reality, a polis. Second, I contend that this term substantiates a participatory and transformative understanding of the citizen's identification with the particular polis. In light of the book's findings, I contend that the Christian can be understood as having such a dual citizenship – and one lord, Jesus Christ. The Christian is a citizen of two political realities and yet has one lord. On the one hand, the Christian is a citizen of the nation or state where he lives and, on the other hand, he is a citizen in the kingdom of God, the heavenly city. This implies that the Christian recognizes the political rulers as ordained by God (Rom. 13), and yet keeps in mind that this is a limited authority, and that the ultimate ruler is the lord, Jesus Christ (Acts 5.29).

Therefore, I also concur with Tage Kurtén, in his article 'The Christian Living in Two Worlds?', when he argues that as Christians we fundamentally live in one world and have to move beyond a two-world dichotomy: 'I think we, following Hauerwas, can maintain that concrete human life is beyond such a two-world dichotomy… one lives in one world (not two) and looks upon life in a unifying way.'[10] This follows from the book's repeated critique of a dualistic interpretation of the two kingdoms doctrine and emphasis on Bonhoeffer's argument for the one Christ-reality. However, at the same time, Christian political thought today has to recognize the challenge of pluralism and has to maintain a Christian witness among the multitude of voices in a liberal democracy. Kurtén also recognizes this challenge and yet, instead of a consensus (understood as based on rational deliberation), he argues that '[i]t suffices if we can live together in peace.'[11]

Where I take a step beyond Kurtén, however, is in pondering the question: where is this peace to be found? It goes beyond the present book to engage with Augustine's political thought. But his thought is an important reminder of the provisional character of temporal peace. This follows from his understanding of the two loves characterizing the two cities: the earthly and the heavenly.[12] For the heavenly city, peace is the supreme good, which the citizens look forward to on the basis of faith and hope. This city is characterized by the love for God rather than lust for domination. The peace of the heavenly city is a peace of harmony

---

9. Bernd Wannenwetsch, 'Soul Citizens: How Christians Understand Their Political Role', *Political Theology* 9, no. 3 (2008), 373–94.

10. Tage Kurtén, 'The Christian Living in Two Worlds? Religious Contributions to the Legitimacy of a Democratic Society', *Studia theologica* 61, no. 2 (2007), 91–112 (107).

11. Ibid., 108.

12. Aurelius Augustine, *City of God* (ed. Henry Scowcroft Bettenson; Penguin Classics; Harmondsworth, Middlesex: Penguin Books, 1984), 14.28.

and enjoyment of God and each other in God.[13] This is in contrast to the earthly city, where the earthly peace is a harmonious compromise concerning things relevant for mortal life.[14] Hereby, the two cities have completely different aims and are characterized by fundamentally different loves. However, in the *saeculum* they coexist while remaining distinctly different from each other.[15] The Augustinian understanding of the *saeculum* as the provisional peace implies that the Christian can be understood as exiled. In this sense I share Luke Bretherton's use of the Augustinian reading of Jer. 29.4-7, which he has taken as a leading motif in his book on Christianity and contemporary politics.[16] Just as the Israelites were exiled in Babylon and still should pray for the welfare of the city, so the Christian can be understood as exiled and yet concerned with the welfare of the nation and the state, where he or she lives.[17]

It is this dual citizenship which implies that the Christian constantly oscillates between universality and specificity. The Christian lives in the world, but is not of the world (Jn 17.15-16). An identification of the Christian political life with the universal dimension (and the worldly reality, as Bonhoeffer would call it) would imply an accommodation that Bonhoeffer warns against. Likewise, an identification with specificity could imply a radicalism that he equally warns against.[18] Neither one nor the other is complete in itself and can be separated from the other; likewise the two cannot be identified as they rest in a polemical or paradoxical relation to each other. In this paradoxical tension – the differentiated unity between universality and specificity – the Christian lives in an appreciation of the secular and provisional peace and yet hopes for the full realization of the heavenly city, *civitas Dei*, in the world to be.

---

13. Ibid., 19.17.

14. Ibid.

15. See e.g. Eric Gregory, Charles Mathewes and Kristen Deede Johnson for recent studies on Augustine's political thought. Kristen Deede Johnson, *Theology, Political Theory, and Pluralism: Beyond Tolerance and Difference* (Cambridge Studies in Christian Doctrine; vol. 15; Cambridge: Cambridge University Press, 2007), 104–73; Charles T. Mathewes, *A Theology of Public Life* (Cambridge Studies in Christian Doctrine, 17; Cambridge: Cambridge University Press, 2007); Eric Gregory, *Politics & the Order of Love: An Augustinian Ethic of Democratic Citizenship* (Chicago, IL/London: University of Chicago Press, 2008).

16. Luke Bretherton, *Christianity and Contemporary Politics: The Conditions and Possibilities of Faithful Witness* (Chichester: Wiley, 2010), 3–6. This motif has not disappeared in his recent book, but the emphasis seems to have shifted towards how talk of God and talk of politics are mutually constitutive and shape each other: Bretherton, *Christ and the Common Life*, 2–4. In this book, Bretherton also argues in favour of the New Testament concept of *kosmos* instead of the Augustinian *saeculum*, as the latter is much more ambiguous, see ibid., 231–40.

17. See also O'Donovan, *The Desire of the Nations*, 83.

18. DBW 6, 144–50.

But in the end there will be a holy city (polis) without a temple, for God and the Lamb will themselves be the temple (Revelation 21), and the citizens of this city will be believers from the community of Jesus in all the world, and God and the Lamb will exercise dominion in this city. In the heavenly polis, state and church will be one.[19]

The double-sidedness of the Christian citizenship is also reflected in the two lines of thought that we have found in Bonhoeffer. On the one hand, there is an affirmation of the worldly reality. We could call this the '*etsi deus non daretur* principle'.

> [W]e cannot be honest unless we recognize that we have to live in the world – 'etsi deus non daretur'. And this is precisely what we do recognize – before God! God himself compels us to recognize it. Thus our coming of age leads us to a truer recognition of our situation before God. God would have us know that we must live as those who manage their lives without God. The same God who is with us is the God who forsakes us (Mark 15:34!). The same God who makes us to live in the world without the working hypothesis of God is the God before whom we stand continually. Before God, and with God, we live without God.[20]

There is a full affirmation of the secular, so that we can speak of Christian ethics *as if* God were not there. This is in line with the Lutheran natural law tradition, Bonhoeffer's affirmation of worldly reality and Bonhoeffer's secular theology in his prison letters. It is this side of the book's findings which substantiates the universalist approach to Christian ethics. And it is here that we find the Danish Løgstrup tradition which argues that the Christian must make ethical decisions on exactly the same bases as anyone else.

However, while recognizing this secular approach to Christian ethics, the book maintains that the Lutheran natural law is inseparable from God's will, that the Grotian claim in Bonhoeffer is hypothetical (as it was for Grotius) and that the affirmation of worldly reality is always understood in relation to the Christ-reality. Therefore, as important as this universal dimension is, it is equally important to remember that this should not be understood separately from its theological or Christological qualification. So the book affirms the secular, the profane and the worldly – but this is always done before God, in Christ.

On the other hand, there is an affirmation of the reality of God. This is the side that underlies the Christian life as a pilgrimage, the understanding of the Christian as not simply identified with democratic citizenship – or in the book's terminology,

---

19. Dietrich Bonhoeffer, *Conspiracy and Imprisonment* (ed. Mark S. Brocker; trans. Lisa E. Dahill; Dietrich Bonhoeffer Works; vol. 16; Minneapolis, MN: Fortress Press, 2006) (DBWE 16), 512.

20. Dietrich Bonhoeffer, *Letters and Papers from Prison* (ed. John W. De Gruchy; trans. Isabel Best, Lisa E. Dahill, Reinhard Krauss and Nancy Lukens; Dietrich Bonhoeffer Works; vol. 8; Minneapolis, MN: Fortress Press, 2010) (DBWE 8), 478–79.

the specific dimension of Christian ethics. There is more to Christian identity or Christian political life than simply being a liberal democratic citizen under the conditions of an 'overlapping consensus'. The eschatological dimension of the Christian ethic implies that, even if we have a vision of a peaceable kingdom, we recognize that we are not yet there. Therefore, a Christian ethic can approve of liberal democracy and its pursuit of a common discourse. It may be recognized as the best possible way of ensuring our common good. But it is always a provisional recognition, as the Christian ethic is saturated with hope for a peace that transcends the peace and stability established by procedural means. 'Pilgrims towards the heavenly *polis* can never be thoroughly claimed by any pledge of allegiance that an earthly polity requests. This marks not only a provision over against enforced commitment to a totalitarian state, but also over against the republican shaping of the soul's complete commitment to a free political society.'[21] Therefore, the Christian ethic recognizes the liberal democracy for being 'as good as it gets' (or a '*modus vivendi*', as Rawls would call it – and which is not enough for him) on this side of eternity, and yet the Christian always hopes for something 'more', something better – a peace and harmony beyond our imagination. I believe this to be an important implication of Bonhoeffer's distinction between the ultimate and the penultimate.[22]

Therefore, the dual citizenship of the Christian implies that the Bonhoefferian understanding of the polemical or contradictory unity of the reality of God and the reality of the world in Christ leads to a different understanding of what we have in common in public than we find in the Rawlsian understanding of 'overlapping consensus'. It maintains that this is constantly contradictory and in constant tension. Therefore, the differentiated unity that I have been arguing for leads to a tense (or polemical) unity (or consensus), where the continuous difference is maintained and recognized, even as the unity is upheld.[23]

Conversation and the polyphony of life

The dual citizenship of the Christian also implies that the Christian is undertaking a conversation in a land where it is not always clear where the church is, and where the public is. In this sense, where the church 'is' remains a mystery. The wheat and the weeds grow side by side (Mt. 13.24-30). There is a hiddenness to the church, which also implies that Bonhoeffer's understanding of the mystery of Christ becomes a hermeneutical key to an understanding of a Christologically saturated concept of reality. The real presence of Christ reaches beyond the institutional boundaries of the church, takes away all kinds of ecclesial prejudices and reminds

---

21. Wannenwetsch, 'Soul Citizens', 390.
22. DBW 6, 137–62.
23. Cf. also Biggar for an understanding along the same lines: Biggar, *Behaving in Public*, 43. Gilbert Meilaender also argues against a Rawlsian consensus and need for a *modus vivendi* with regard to bioethical issues, see Gilbert Meilaender, 'Against Consensus: Christians and Public Bioethics', *Studies in Christian Ethics* 18, no. 1 (2005), 75–88.

the Christian always to meet the other 'in Christ'. Responding to the other is simply responding to a fellow human being. In this sense there is nothing specific about this response – it is of a universal nature. On the other hand, the conversation is also a challenge, as the Christian is called to bear witness to the world of their reconciliation with God in Christ. This gives the Christian a call to speak with a clearly recognizable and distinctive voice when needed. This may be a voice that is sweet and comforting (Mt. 11.28), but it may also be a prophetic voice that speaks out against social injustices (cf. e.g. Amos 5.10-17) and tendencies towards political or other kinds of ideological blasphemy (Acts 5.29).

In holding this voice the Christian is seeking a conversation with others in public. This raises the question of what I mean by this conversation and public. In my argument for the conversation, I follow others who also emphasize this approach.[24] Biggar, Stout and Johnson hold different emphases in their understanding of this conversation. I will not go into a detailed reading of these differences here. Suffice it to state that Stout argues from the tradition of American pragmatism (primarily John Dewey) and, in this light, advocates a democratic discursive practice that is expressive of a democratic tradition:

> The continuing social process of holding one another responsible is chiefly what I have in mind when I refer to the ethical life or inheritance of a people. Central to democratic thought as I understand it is the idea of a body of citizens who reason with one another about the ethical issues that divide them, especially when deliberating on the justice or decency of political arrangements. It follows that one thing a democratic people had better have in common is a form of ethical discourse, a way of exchanging reasons about ethical and political topics.[25]

Biggar draws on a 'Barthian Thomism' which implies that the Christian's conversation in public is both rooted in an awareness of where it comes from and yet genuinely open to learn from people outside the church.[26] Johnson is inspired by Augustinian theology and argues that the conversation not only pertains to political issues, but is an 'ethos permeating our involvements with one another'.[27]

Common to them, however, is the aim to give more space to specific voices shaped by various traditions than they find possible in Rawlsian political liberalism.[28] The conversational approach opens up more for speaking from within the particular

---

24. Stout, *Democracy and Tradition*; Johnson, *Theology, Political Theory, and Pluralism*; Nigel Biggar, 'Not Translation, but Conversation: Theology in Public Debate about Euthanasia', in *Religious Voices in Public Spaces* (ed. Nigel Biggar and Linda Hogan; Oxford: Oxford University Press, 2009), 151–93; Biggar, *Behaving in Public*.

25. Stout, *Democracy and Tradition*, 6, see also 293.

26. Biggar, *Behaving in Public*, 83–89, 107–12.

27. Johnson, *Theology, Political Theory, and Pluralism*, 237.

28. Stout, *Democracy and Tradition*, 3; Johnson, *Theology, Political Theory, and Pluralism*, 235–36; Biggar, *Behaving in Public*, 42–43, 60–61.

tradition when engaging in public discourse. You may say what you wish to say. 'By this [i.e. conversation] I mean an exchange of views in which the respective parties express their premises in as much detail as they see fit and in whatever idiom they wish, try to make sense of each other's perspectives, and expose their own commitments to the possibility of criticism.'[29] 'Christians should tell it as they see it.'[30] However, even if you can say whatever you want to say – and precisely because of that – it is also important that this conversation is shaped by certain virtues. Stout emphasizes the democratic virtues of civility[31] and the formation of character following from being part of a democratic social praxis.[32] Biggar points to the virtues of docility, tolerance, charity, critical candor, (im)patience and forbearance that should guide the Christian's conversation in public.

> Docility, tolerance-as-care, charity-as-respect and charity-as-optimal-construal, critical candor (even in the ultimate form of denunciation), impatience with grave and shameless vice, patience with anything less, charity in granting forgiveness, and repentance in asking for it – these are among the virtues that should govern the manner of Christians' conversation and should cause them to *behave in public*.[33]

Johnson speaks of a deep conversation, where we partake just as much with our manner of lives as with our words.[34]

The conversational approach lies in immediate continuation of the book's findings. The centrality of the *communicatio idiomatum* in the book's Christological foundation of Christian ethics substantiates a communicative (or conversational) approach to Christian ethics in public.[35] This is understood in a triadic relation conceived as responding to the reality of God, the reality of the other, (polemically) unified in the Christ reality. As we have seen, this implies both a Christologically substantiated concept of communication, and a transformative understanding of letting the reality of Christ become real.

Concerning the public, it has proven necessary for the Rawlsian tradition to define the 'public' very precisely.[36] In the present book I understand the public

---

29. Stout, *Democracy and Tradition*, 10–11.
30. Biggar, *Behaving in Public*, 7.
31. Stout, *Democracy and Tradition*, 10.
32. Ibid., 303f.
33. Biggar, *Behaving in Public*, 75.
34. Johnson, *Theology, Political Theory, and Pluralism*, 235, 47.
35. See also Chapter 4, particularly the section entitled 'Responsibility and Christological Responsiveness'.
36. See e.g. Svend Andersen, *Macht aus Liebe. Zur Rekonstruktion einer lutherischen politischen Ethik* (Berlin/New York: W. de Gruyter, 2010), 257–59, 306–7. This is also the case in Rawls' own writings, where he has to make it very clear where his conditions of public reason apply. See e.g. John Rawls, 'The Idea of Public Reason Revisited', *The University of Chicago Law Review* 64, no. 3 (1997), 765–807.

in a broader sense. I understand it as the point where individuals with different viewpoints meet and where the underlying worldview (religious or otherwise) of the individuals may (or may not) have a (crucial) bearing upon the arguments put forward. The crucial point is that we in 'the public' aim to both understand the other and make ourselves understood in conversation with others. As a Christian (or simply a human being) we do our best in public to engage in this communicative exchange while remaining faithful to our traditions (or identity formative contexts). This implies two things. First, the Christian seeks meaningful conversation with others on the premises of exchanging reasons (this implies that I maintain the place of conversational reasoning in ethics) and yet as 'reasonable citizens' we come from somewhere (this implies that I likewise maintain the Christological and ecclesial understanding of Christian ethics). Second, the conversational understanding of 'the public' means that this is almost anywhere and everywhere. This could imply either that the values and ideology of secularistic politics should permeate all spheres of life, or that the kingdom of Christ is to shine through all of reality as there is no being apart from Christ. The present book takes the latter approach.

These last comments point towards another important qualification, namely, how the conversation is conducted. Fundamentally, I contend that all things may be said. Nothing is per definition excluded from the outset. However, it is also a conversation wherein we seek to understand each other. This holds implications both for the language itself and for the manner in which it is spoken. With regard to the language itself, I contend that Christian political thought acknowledges a multitude of voices in public, or – to speak with Bonhoeffer – a polyphony of life. As we saw, Bonhoeffer uses the musical metaphor of polyphonic music to express a fundamental reality of Christian life. As long as the love for God is the *cantus firmus*, all other areas of Christian life can be seen as contrapuntal voices. Further, Bonhoeffer understands this as an expression of the Chalcedonian mystery of human life. This metaphor in Bonhoeffer opens up a polyphonic understanding of the conversation in public.[37] The Christian can engage in and take part in a polyphony of voices in public conversation. This does not stand against the faithful witness. Rather, the polyphonic affirmation of public conversation should be seen as a confirmation of the real presence of Christ in all areas of the worldly reality of Christian life. We have seen this repeatedly as an expression of the Chalcedonian Christology underlying Bonhoeffer's ethic.

---

37. For another Bonhoeffer-inspired understanding of the polyphony of life, or 'polyphonic worldliness' as he calls it, see Barry Harvey, *Taking Hold of the Real: Dietrich Bonhoeffer and the Profound Worldliness of Christianity* (Eugene, OR: Cascade Books, 2015), chapter 8 (234–68). See also Reed for an understanding of polyphony in Christian ethics inspired by Mikhail Bakhtin. Reed also raises the discussion of the limits of polyphony and the problem of conflicting voices, see Esther D. Reed, *The Genesis of Ethics: On the Authority of God as the Origin of Christian Ethics* (London: Darton, Longman and Todd, 2000), chapter 3 (119–82).

The polyphonic conversation holds parallels to what Biggar has called a 'polyglot liberalism'. Biggar speaks affirmatively of the aim (of common understanding) in what he calls humane liberalism (that he finds in Habermas, Rawls and Stout) and yet he argues that they lack a sufficient recognition of the manner in which public discourse is conducted. Polyglot liberalism recognizes a plurality of voices in the public sphere in striving for a common understanding and yet it emphasizes the openness and willingness to learn from others.

> What this polyglot liberalism requires is not a single tongue, but a responsible manner – not so much public reason as public reasonableness. This amounts to an ethic of communication, and it depends on a certain anthropology, namely, a view of human beings as endowed with a special dignity – the dignity of beings who are equal in their capacity to open themselves to what is good, to discern what is right, and to bear witness to them.[38]

This understanding opens up for the theological contribution to the public conversation, and yet it reminds the Christian of the willingness to learn from others.

Christiane Tietz has argued for the bilinguality of the Christian in public. Tietz argues that the Christian, to a wide extent, should seek to translate his or her ethical views so that they can be a part of the ethical discourse in public. On the other hand – and this is the argument for the second language – she recognizes that there are situations where the Christian may speak with a clearly recognizable voice and where translation is not possible, so that it becomes clear '*who* speaks and *why*'.[39] My hesitation concerning Tietz's reading derives from the consequences of her Habermasian reading of the Lutheran tradition, which implies e.g. that she dismisses Luther's understanding of natural law and instead argues for a procedural reason.[40] Rather than the Habermasian emphasis on the need for translation, I maintain the conversation and contend that this is more in continuity with Bonhoeffer's understanding of the one reality, the Christ-reality. The Christian does not shift between languages. Rather, the Christian gives voice to different dimensions of the one and same reality. Rather than a shift in languages, it is a shift in argumentative modes or ways of conversing. Different contexts

---

38. Nigel Biggar, 'Saving the "Secular": The Public Vocation of Moral Theology', *Journal of Religious Ethics* 37, no. 1 (2009), 159–78 (168). Where Biggar writes about 'polyglot' liberalism, Reed also points to what she calls 'heteroglossia' and uses the story of the tower of Babel (Gen. 11.1–9) to illustrate how the different languages were also God's merciful limitation of the human being's potential harm to themselves from their increased self-sufficiency, see Reed, *The Genesis of Ethics*, 151–53.

39. Christiane Tietz, '...mit anderen Worten...Zur Überzetzbarkeit religiöser Überzeugungen in politischen Diskursen', *Evangelische Theologie* 72, no. 2 (2012), 86–100 (99) (my translation).

40. Ibid., 97.

may require different arguments, but not different languages.[41] At the same time, Bonhoeffer repeatedly maintains that this is a polemical and contradictory unity of the reality of God and the reality of the world. It is important for Bonhoeffer to maintain both sides of this reality at the same time. They are in unity, but remain so in a continuous tension. It is this constant tension which is expressed in my term: the 'differentiated unity' of universality and specificity.

Pertaining to manner, Bonhoeffer does not speak about virtues underlying the conversation in public, but he does speak about conformation with Christ with regard to the Christian life.[42] We have seen how these 'Christological virtues' primarily serve as an implicit argument for justifying an active participation in the resistance against a political regime that transgresses its proper limits.[43] However, if we ponder these traits with regard to the contemporary debate on the participation of Christians in public discourse, I contend that Bonhoeffer's understanding of 'ethics as formation' may give rise to a Christologically shaped virtue ethical understanding of the Christian's conversation in public.[44] It leads too far to elaborate in detail on this here. Suffice it to point to the characteristic Bonhoefferian move that we also saw earlier when Bonhoeffer argues for the unity between the life, death and resurrection of Christ. When Bonhoeffer argues for the formation of the Christian, he points to Christ as the incarnated, crucified and risen one. 'Formation occurs only by being drawn into the form of Jesus Christ, by *being conformed to the unique form of the one who became human, was crucified, and is risen.* This does not happen as we strive "to become like Jesus", as we customarily say, but as the form of Jesus Christ himself so works on us that it molds us, conforming our form to Christ's own (Gal. 4:9).'[45] This implies that it is not a formation that points towards an other-worldliness or away from the world. Rather, it is a formation to the one who became truly human. 'To be conformed to the one who has become human – that is what being really human means.'[46] At the same time, being conformed to the crucified one means to be a human

---

41. See also the anthology on the translation of religion more generally (with respect to several religious traditions) and Tietz's contribution 'Habermas' Call for Translating Religion into Secular Language' (104–22) in Michael P. DeJonge and Christiane Tietz, *Translating Religion: What Is Lost and Gained?* (Routledge Studies in Religion; vol. 47; New York: Routledge, 2015).

42. DBW 6, 62–90.

43. See Chapter 4.

44. For a reading of Bonhoeffer in light of virtue ethics, see Jennifer Moberly, *The Virtue of Bonhoeffer's Ethics: A Study of Dietrich Bonhoeffer's Ethics in Relation to Virtue Ethics* (Princeton Theological Monograph Series; vol. 194; Eugene, OR: Pickwick, 2013).

45. Dietrich Bonhoeffer, *Ethics* (ed. Clifford J. Green; trans. Reinhard Krauss, Charles C. West and Douglas W. Stott; Dietrich Bonhoeffer Works; vol. 6; Minneapolis, MN: Fortress Press, 2005) (DBWE 6), 93.

46. Ibid., 94.

7. Living in the Saeculum and Bearing Witness to Christ

being judged by God.[47] Finally, being conformed to the risen one means to be a new human being before God. The human being lives in the midst of death and sin. Yet, it is a life in Christ, with the mystery of Christ remaining hidden from the world.[48]

However – and this is where the conformation with Christ holds significant implications for the contemporary discussion on conversation in public – even if the Christian in many respects does not differ from fellow human beings (i.e. the Christian shares common concerns with fellow human beings), they partake in this conversation as the ones who have become one with Christ and therefore witness to this reality and Jesus Christ as their lord.

> The new human beings live in the world like anyone else. They often differ very little from other people. They are not concerned to promote themselves, but to lift up Christ for the sake of their brothers and sisters. Transfigured into the form of the risen one, they bear here only the sign of the cross and judgment. In bearing them willingly, they show themselves as those who have received the Holy Spirit and are united with Jesus Christ in incomparable love and community.[49]

This is the point where Bonhoeffer also turns to the church. The conformation with Christ is a conformation with the one who became a real, concrete human being.[50] And yet, this is a formation which takes place in the church as the body of Christ.[51]

This is not a conversation that the Christian enters into with a set of given norms and principles, nor is this the aim of the conversation. Rather, as we have seen, the responsibility – and thereby the responsive dimension of this conversation – requires a continuous openness of the conversation. Nor is the primary question whether the Christian expresses him- or herself in a universal or a specific language. Rather, the primary issue is faithfulness. In Chapter 4 I used the concept of authenticity, Biggar speaks of integrity.[52] When I use the concept of faithfulness here, it is to emphasize the Christian's discipleship and how the Christian is called to follow his or her Lord (Mt. 9.9).[53] This follows from the Bonhoefferian contention that the Christian only has one lord – Jesus Christ. It is the lordship of Christ and the call to follow Christ faithfully which is the primary issue for the Christian. This is particularly

---

47. DBW 6, 82.
48. Ibid.
49. DBWE 6, 95.
50. DBW 6, 86.
51. Ibid., 84, 90.
52. Biggar, *Behaving in Public*, 1–23.
53. The emphasis on faithfulness is also central in Bretherton's work, see Bretherton, *Christianity and Contemporary Politics*, 16–22; Bretherton, *Christ and the Common Life*, 1–15.

emphasized in Bonhoeffer's *Discipleship*.[54] Therefore – and due to the Chalcedonian Christology seen throughout the book – the book takes a crucial step beyond universality and specificity. The differentiated unity of universality and specificity implies that (1) each is confirmed in itself; (2) each is insufficient separate from the other; and (3) the differentiated unity calls for a position beyond either of these extremes. The book has pointed to the Chalcedonian Christology in the Lutheran tradition (most notably in Luther and Bonhoeffer) and its implied affirmation of the real presence and contemporaneity of Christ as one way to go for such a reshaped understanding of the differentiated unity of universality and specificity.

Bearing witness over contentious issues

Throughout the book the main focus has been on foundational issues with regard to social ethics and political theology. It has been the aim to investigate whether the Lutheran tradition holds the potential for a differentiated unity of universality and specificity based on Chalcedonian motifs. In the previous two sections we have seen what this position implies with regard to some key discussions in a contemporary context. In this last section we will turn to a brief outlook pertaining to the implications of this position for concrete questions. Hereby, we are moving more towards applied (or practical) ethics, even if I am hesitant about too narrow an understanding of applying ethics.[55] We will take two examples, where the first is taken as an example of how the contribution of a theological insight may further the understanding of a complicated concept: human dignity. Here, the theological voice contributes constructively to the public discourse. The second is taken as an example of an issue where a Christian understanding may be at odds with the common understanding in public: abortion. This may be seen as an example of the prophetic dimension of a Christian ethic, where it criticizes the prevailing wrongs of a society's praxis.

---

54. Dietrich Bonhoeffer, *Nachfolge* (herausgegeben von Martin Kuske und Ilse Tödt; Dietrich Bonhoeffer Werke; band 4; Gütersloh: Chr. Kaiser, 1994) (DBW 4), 45–67.

55. I will not go into detail with this discussion here, but I share the reservation with regard to applied ethics as a discipline, where we first establish ethical principles and then attempt to solve ethical issues in light of these principles. Such an understanding of practical ethics could be called a 'top-down approach'. My reservation with regard to such an approach also lies in continuity of Bonhoeffer's rejection of a principle-oriented ethic. On the other hand, I am also reluctant to accept a purely situationist ethic, where we have no prior ground for coming to a judgement on difficult issues that we have to reflect upon. The most suitable description for my understanding probably would be 'an ethic of responsiveness', meaning that there is a form of dialogical or responsive formation in coming to a certain degree of clarity about what is the moral good with relation to a particular issue. However, in the present book this leads too far. Here, I only attempt to reflect on a few issues in light of the book's findings.

Human dignity

First we turn to an issue where the universal and specific approaches largely converge, even if they argue from different premises – i.e. the question of human dignity. This is a contested concept in contemporary ethics and can be maintained from both a strictly philosophical and a theological approach. Adam Schulman points to at least four sources of human dignity in his contribution to the report on *Human Dignity and Bioethics* delivered by the US Presidential Council on Bioethics in 2008:

1. Classical antiquity. The concept itself is derived from the Latin *dignitus* and *dignitas*, just as Greek and Roman literature use the idea of dignity as describing the honourable and highly esteemed. In the Stoic tradition, dignity was understood in relation to the human being's ability to lead a life according to reason.
2. Biblical religion. This is particularly the idea of man as created in the image of God. This supports both a progressive understanding, where the emphasis is laid on human responsibility for creation, and a more conservative position that argues for the protection of life.
3. Kantian moral philosophy. In Kant's moral philosophy, dignity is particularly related to the human being as a rational being. Dignity is derived from the human being's ability to be an autonomous moral being, to be its own lawgiver. This dignity on rational grounds serves as the background for the influential understanding that the human being should never be used merely as a means to one's own end (i.e. one should never instrumentalize another human being).
4. Twentieth-century constitutions and international declarations. After the Second World War, the concept of human dignity has been invoked in several UN declarations and at least thirty-seven national constitutions. Often dignity here is associated with human rights and has the role of protecting against atrocities such as those happening during war.[56]

I cannot go into each of these traditions here, but refer to Schulman's account and discussion of them. The important point is that the Judaeo-Christian tradition is counted among these sources. This implies both that this tradition has something to contribute to this conversation, and that this is a contribution in conversation with the other approaches. Hereby, it both acknowledges that which it holds in common with these other approaches (and the openness and willingness to learn from these understandings) (the universal dimension) and it maintains its specific

---

56. Adam Schulman, 'Bioethics and the Question of Human Dignity', in *Human Dignity and Bioethics: Essays Commissioned by the President's Council on Bioethics* (ed. Adam Schulman and Thomas W. Merrill; Washington, DC: President's Council on Bioethics, 2008), 3–18.

contribution in this conversation, as it is aware that the reason why it is interesting to listen to is that it has something substantial to say. So the aim here is not that the Christian ethic necessarily speaks with a highly specific or distinctive voice in the conversation. Indeed, this is only done when the conversation calls upon such a distinctive contribution – be it from a Christian or e.g. a Kantian approach. The aim is rather to understand the concept of human dignity as a normative idea that cuts across these different traditions of thought and expresses a shared understanding of something dear that we hold in common. The concept of human dignity is not the exclusive possession of either of these traditions and therefore they benefit from each other in the conversation on how to understand and make use of this concept in the debate on contemporary ethical issues.

This conversation implies that the contribution from Christian ethics is important, not for the sake of distinctiveness or specificity in itself, but for the sake of understanding this concept. This follows from both its assertion of Christian humanism (see Chapter 4) and the tradition of natural law (see Chapter 1). So in this sense it is open to learning as much as possible from the conversation with other sciences and from the debates in the public sphere in general. But at the same time it maintains that it comes from somewhere. It is aware of its embeddedness in a particular Christian tradition and ecclesial context. To take it apart from this context would reduce it to an empty abstraction. Cf. e.g. Huber and Tietz who also argue for the contribution of theological ethics in furthering the understanding of this concept.[57] It would lead too far to go into the details of the contribution that Christian ethics brings to this conversation. Suffice it therefore to point to a few ideas that would be part of the Christian understanding of human dignity:

1. The human being as created in the image of God. As Schulman pointed out, this implies both a special responsibility and a special status. The responsibility holds implications for bioethical issues and the role of the human being in advancing new biotechnologies, where the progressive approach can imply that the human being has a responsibility to advance these technologies in cooperation with God (*cooperatio Dei*) in the *creatio continua*. It also holds significant implications with regard to the understanding of the human being as either master or steward of creation. The 'mastership' and 'stewardship' traditions are both derived from biblical sources and hold significantly different implications for the understanding of how to use or care for creation.
2. The finitude of human beings. Human beings are created in the image of God, but at the same time they are understood as finite beings. They are made of soil (Gen. 2.7) and the Hebrew root meaning of the human being

---

57. Wolfgang Huber, 'Freiheit als Form der Liebe. Die Aktualität christlicher Freiheit in den gesellschaftlichen Herausforderungen unserer Zeit', in *Religion im Erbe. Dietrich Bonhoeffer und die Zukunftsfähigkeit des Christentums* (ed. Christian Gremmels and Wolfgang Huber; Gütersloh: Chr. Kaiser/Gütersloher Verlagshaus, 2002), 17–36 (25ff.); Tietz, '… mit anderen Worten', 98.

as *ha'adamah* literally means a being made of soil, an earthly being. This is an important side of human dignity, as the Christian understanding is not that human dignity is only that which makes the human being different from all other life forms. Rather, the human being is understood both as the only creature made in the image of God and at the same time as a living being sharing life conditions with all other living beings. Hereby, the biological, finite and limited dimension of the human being is emphasized.
3. The human being as a bodily being. For a Christian understanding, human dignity is not just placed in reason, consciousness or awareness of personhood. Rather, the human being is a bodily being, which is why the bodily dimension is inseparable from a proper understanding of the human being. Bonhoeffer also emphasizes this aspect when he argues for the rights of the bodily life.[58] He also ties this to the understanding of human dignity: 'Bodily life, which we receive through no action of our own, intrinsically bears the right to its preservation... Since by God's will human life on earth exists only as bodily life, the body has a right to be preserved for the sake of the whole person.'[59]

In order to understand a concrete topic like human dignity, a Christian ethic in light of the differentiated unity of universality and specificity, therefore, does two things. (1) It enters into the conversation with other disciplines to learn as much as possible from them and hopefully also contribute to furthering their insights; and (2) it seeks the deeper understanding of such a concept in light of the specific Christian tradition. The latter step implies (i) a thorough engagement with the historical sources of specific Christian thought – not least in the Bible and the Christian tradition; (ii) a reflection on what this implies in a contemporary, ecclesial context (i.e. the Christian community) and how this community shapes this concept; and (iii) a reflection on how one can maintain these insights in faithful witness to the Lordship of Christ in a contemporary context.

Christian bioethics in public

During the last two decades, the question of religion in public pertaining to bioethical issues has received renewed attention. Suffice it to mention two relatively recent books[60] and two thematic issues of established journals: *Studies*

---

58. DBW 6, 179–92. See also Ulrik Nissen, 'What Is a Human Body? Moving Towards a Responsive Body', in *What Is Human? Theological Encounters with Anthropology* (ed. Eve-Marie Becker, Jan Dietrich and Bo Kristian Holm; Göttingen: Vandenhoeck & Ruprecht, 2017), 311–35.

59. DBWE 6, 185.

60. David E. Guinn, ed., *Handbook of Bioethics and Religion* (New York: Oxford University Press, 2006); Friedemann Voigt, ed., *Religion in bioethischen Diskursen: interdisziplinäre, internationale und interreligiöse Perspektiven* (Berlin/New York: W. de Gruyter, 2010).

in *Christian Ethics* (2005.18) and *Christian Bioethics* (2007.13) (the last journal continuously publishes on this theme, but the mentioned issue has a special collection of contributions on this topic by several distinguished authors). This discussion more or less concerns many of the same themes I have been pondering in the present book, only with focused attention on bioethics. Therefore, I will not go into this debate here. Instead I will point to one question within bioethics where I will highlight the implications of the book's position.

The question of *abortion* remains a contested issue within bioethics. First, this is due to the emotional feelings arising from this question, which we are reminded of continuously through the public media. This is the case for advocates of both the so-called 'pro life' and 'pro choice' movements – especially as we see it in the US debate. Second, it is due to the fundamental disagreement both (i) on the question of when life begins (and whether it is life or personhood that is the determining criteria for protection); and (ii) how one should balance protection of the unborn life versus women's rights over their bodies. These questions remain controversial and the prospect of the opposing positions ever coming to a consensus is not very likely.

This raises the question of how we should approach a debate over such controversial issues. One approach is to take the course of a Rawlsian liberalism, the other could be to take the approach of the differentiated unity described in the present book. The Rawlsian approach would imply a balancing of political values and an argument for a discussion within the premises of public reason, when we debate this issue in public. The aim here would be to reach an overlapping consensus in the public sphere concerning abortion. This may lead to the implication that the Christian in public will set aside the recognizably theological contribution to this debate.[61] Rawls raises this question himself, both in *Political Liberalism* and in his 'The Idea of Public Reason Revisited'.[62] In its original statement, Rawls uses it to illustrate the reasonable balancing of political values that is an expression of public reason. Here he argues that when we balance the question of abortion in light of the political values of 'the due respect for human life, the ordered reproduction of political society over time, including the family in some form, and finally the equality of women as equal citizens', a reasonable balancing of these values will 'give a woman a duly qualified right to decide whether or not to end her pregnancy during the first trimester'. A comprehensive doctrine which does not recognize this right is to that extent unreasonable.[63] Whereas Rawls uses this example to demonstrate what it means to aim for 'a reasonable balance of political values',[64] I read it as an illustration of the limits

---

61. Svend Andersen, 'Christliche Bioethik in Europa', in *Religion in bioethischen Diskursen* (ed. Friedemann Voigt; Berlin/New York: W. de Gruyter, 2010), 293–311.

62. John Rawls, *Political Liberalism* (Columbia Classics in Philosophy; New York: Columbia University Press, paperback edn, 1996), lvff., 243 (footnote 32); Rawls, 'The Idea of Public Reason Revisited', 798–99.

63. Rawls, *Political Liberalism*, 243 (footnote 32).

64. Ibid., 243.

of Rawls' concept of reasonableness. It is not clear to me why the reasonable comprehensible doctrine ends at the balancing that Rawls proposes. I do not find any convincing arguments why Rawls' balancing is particularly reasonable, compared to another balancing of these political values. Rawls also seems to grant this in some of his later comments on this passage, when he acknowledges that an elaboration of these reflections may not even be 'the most reasonable or decisive argument'.[65] Therefore, he even goes so far as to say that political liberalism should not always end with 'a general agreement of views, nor is it a fault when it does'. The disagreement and the subsequent discussion may even lead to a deepened mutual understanding even when agreement cannot be reached.[66]

The other concept is the conversational approach for which I have been arguing. This view contends a deliberative conversation, where anything may be said, and where both the content and the manner in which it is said reflect both (1) the recognition of and respect for the other; and (2) the tradition and the community out of which it arises. This is the approach taken in the present book. This implies that the Christian listens to the other and seeks to learn from the other. But it also implies that the Christian can maintain a faithful witness in this conversation. The aim is that we reach a shared understanding (the universal dimension) – be it in public or elsewhere – but if the Christian (in the course of this conversation) finds it necessary to be explicit or specific about the premises of his or her convictions, this is fully justified (the specific dimension).

To state it even more concretely – if the Christian believes that the fertilized egg has a dignity equivalent with a new-born baby, he or she is justified to argue for this viewpoint in public discourse. And if the Christian (or anyone else) is of the opinion that the termination of a pregnancy in its very early stages, or the use of embryonic stem cells for scientific purposes, fundamentally is to be regarded as the termination of human life, he or she may say so as part of the public conversation on this topic. We find such a viewpoint e.g. in Bonhoeffer, when he states that injuring the developing life in the mother's womb is deliberately to take away life from a developing human being.

> To kill the fruit in the mother's womb is to injure the right to life that God has bestowed on the developing life. Discussion of the question whether a human being is already present confuses the simple fact that, in any case, God wills to create a human being and that the life of this developing human being has been deliberately taken. And this is nothing but murder.[67]

Holding such a viewpoint in public is a controversial standpoint – at least in a Danish setting, which is my own national context. But the fact that it is controversial does not necessarily imply that it is not true. Of course, the opposite is also the

---

65. Ibid., lvi (footnote 31).
66. Rawls, 'The Idea of Public Reason Revisited', 799.
67. DBWE 6, 206.

case, that its controversiality is not a guarantee of its truthfulness. The point is, however, that it is a standpoint which should not be deemed out of the public conversation from the outset. For the conversation actually to be a conversation it requires that one enters into it with the aim of talking with one another, which requires a mutual respect and the attempt to make one's standpoint as convincing as possible. This should be an important goal for the Christian. Here I concur with Biggar.[68] However, the findings of the present book also imply that there are fundamental differences that may prevent an overlapping consensus. In this case, the Christian will accept that the overlapping consensus cannot be reached and will settle for the *modus vivendi* being 'as good as it gets', while admitting a sense of alienation and the justification of speaking out against the prevailing attitudes in public pertaining to this particular question (or other contested moral issues).

In this outline of the implications of my position pertaining to abortion, I have focused on just this one question. The outlined implications also touch on several other bioethical issues. The differentiated unity of universality and specificity also here implies both that (1) the aim is to reach a shared understanding based on a conversational approach; and (2) that this conversation implies a multitude of voices where the differences also may be made explicit when (for various reasons) this is found either expedient or necessary.

Conclusion

In this last chapter of the book we have attempted to take a step beyond the Chalcedonian understanding of the differentiated unity between universality and specificity and thereby transcend these concepts. This is done in continuation of Bonhoeffer's recognition of the formulations of Chalcedon and yet he points to its strength in transcending itself. The book hereby points to these concepts as coming to their limits. Even if both of them express important dimensions of a Christian ethic, both of them are also insufficient in themselves. This points to the necessity for a 'third position'. The chapter has focused on the contemporary implications of this differentiated unity pertaining to the question of the Christian's dual citizenship, the conversation in public and how the Christian is called to bear witness also over contentious issues. Hereby, it was shown how this position maintains both universality and specificity as essential and yet attempts to go beyond these concepts. In the last section of this chapter, it was demonstrated what some of the implications of the book's findings are with regard to two concrete questions: human dignity and the question of bioethics in public (with particular reference to the debate on abortion). The first topic was seen as an example, where the book substantiates a constructive conversation with other views and thereby furthers the understanding of human dignity in public. This was seen as an expression of the book's recognition of the universal dimension. The second topic was taken as a

---

68. Biggar, *Behaving in Public*, 59.

controversial question, where it is unlikely that the understanding of this question will be significantly furthered in the foreseeable future, even if we aim to engage in a constructive conversation with each other. To a large extent it seems that the significant arguments have been put forward. However, this does not mean that the Christian voice no longer plays a role. The book has argued that a Christian voice in public may still play an important role in a specific and distinctive critique of prevailing wrongs. Hereby, these two last examples demonstrate how the book's findings lead to a position between universality and specificity and how these dimensions are understood as being in a differentiated unity with each other.

CONCLUSION

The time has now come to draw this book to a close and conclude our findings. The book was initiated with the question of whether it is possible – on the basis of select theorists (primarily from within the Lutheran tradition) – to determine a foundation for a Christian social ethic that enables us simultaneously to maintain the unity and the difference between universal and specific validity. Hereby, the book pondered the possibility of overcoming the traditional dichotomy between a universal and a more specific foundation of a Christian social ethic by endorsing a differentiated unity between the two. In approaching this question, the book was oriented by the thesis that there are central Chalcedonian motifs in the Lutheran tradition – not least in Bonhoeffer's Christological ethic – that may provide a basis for reformulating the foundation of a Lutheran social ethic pertaining to the crucial question of how the relationship between the universal and the specific dimension of a Christian social ethic can be understood; and that these motifs may be appropriated for the purpose of endorsing a differentiated unity of the universal and specific foundation, and hence validity of a Christian social ethic.

We can now conclude affirmatively on this thesis and sustain the findings of the book in recognizing the presence of such Chalcedonian motifs in the Lutheran tradition and the subsequent possibility of endorsing a differentiated unity of universality and specificity pertaining to the foundation of a Christian social ethic. Accordingly, universality and specificity are maintained as opposites and yet both of these dimensions are affirmed. Neither of these is understood separately from the other, rather, they are necessarily related to each other. Hereby, they are both affirmed and yet transcended at the same time. The foundation of the Christian social ethic is found in a differentiated unity between these two dimensions which finds a figurative expression in the Chalcedonian understanding of the relation between the two natures of Christ. Just as the divine and human nature are one in Christ and yet 'without confusion, without change, without division, without separation',[1] so it is with these two dimensions of a Christian social ethic. Hereby, the differentiated unity also transcends universality and specificity and points to

---

1. John Macquarrie, *Jesus Christ in Modern Thought* (London: SCM Press, 3rd impr. edn, 1993), 165.

a 'third position' where these two dimensions are in continuous communication with and exchange between each other.

In the present conclusion I will point to the main contributions of the book as a whole, rather than summarizing the findings once again. I will do so by pointing to five contributions where I believe the present book contributes with new insights.

- The book demonstrates the Chalcedonian motifs in Luther's political thought and how these serve as the basis for a differentiated unity of divinity and humanity in the foundation of his social ethics. Other studies have also shown how the Chalcedonian Christology – not least the *communicatio idiomatum* – is central for Luther's theology. The present book contributes to these studies by showing the significance this has for Luther's political thought.

We saw in Chapter 2 how there is a simultaneity of divinity and humanity in Luther's social ethics. This forms an underlying idea behind several core concepts in his theology, ethics and political thought. In the same chapter, it was shown explicitly how this reflects a Chalcedonian mode of thought, particularly pertaining to the *communicatio idiomatum*. The exchange of properties between the two natures of Christ is seen as a model for Luther's theology as a whole and shapes central ideas such as the doctrine of justification, his Christology, understanding of the Holy Communion, ethics etc. We saw how Luther also has this simultaneity of divinity and humanity as an important background for his political thought and how this served as the argument for God's presence in the political order and how this shaped his political thought.

- The book demonstrates the contemporary tendency to think in antagonistic terms pertaining to universality and specificity with regard to the debate on the relation between religion and politics. This implies that a Christian ethic in the public sphere is often either accommodated or seen in contrast to liberal democracy. The book places itself in continuation of other positions by arguing for a 'third position' beyond either accommodation or confrontation. As a contribution to these positions, the present book develops a Christologically founded understanding of a differentiated unity between universality and specificity.

In Chapters 6 and 7, the book ponders the tendency in contemporary Christian ethics to think in dichotomous ways about the relation between universality and specificity. It is argued that the Lutheran two kingdoms doctrine is particularly prone to this tendency. As an alternative, the book argues for the differentiated unity of universality and specificity, where these two dimensions are in an exchange or are communicating with each other. Hereby, the book argues for a communicative and responsive third position between universality and specificity. In Chapter 6 we saw how this shapes the concept of responsibility, and in Chapter 4 how Bonhoeffer's concept of responsibility may be understood as a responsive concept. In Chapter 7 we saw how this position substantiates a conversational approach to Christian ethics in public. The significant contribution of the book lies in its demonstration that this conversational position may be seen as a reflection of the exchange and communication of attributes between the divine and human natures in Christ. As we saw in Luther's ethics and repeatedly in Bonhoeffer's Christological ethic (throughout Chapters 3–5), the Chalcedonian Christology is understood broadly and the figurative meaning of the relation and communication between the two natures of Christ are seen as comprising a mode of thought which becomes a hermeneutical key to their theology and ethics. This figurative understanding of the relation between the two natures of Christ, for the issue in focus in the present book, implies that it makes no sense to separate universality and specificity from each other. Rather, they are to be seen in a differentiated unity with each other. Pertaining to representatives of either a universalistic approach (e.g. Løgstrup) or a specific understanding (e.g. Søe) of Christian ethics, or with regard to Christian ethics in public (Rawls versus Hauerwas), the book has argued for a Christologically founded position transcending these opposites.

- The book demonstrates Bonhoeffer's ethic as a basis for moving beyond accommodation and radicalization. Bonhoeffer's Christological ethic makes it possible to speak of a differentiated unity of universality and specificity derived from the polemical unity of the reality of God and the reality of the world in the Christ-reality. The book illustrates this in an analysis of several core concepts in Bonhoeffer's ethic. Other studies have also shown the centrality of Christology for Bonhoeffer's ethic. The present book contributes to these studies by demonstrating (1) the importance of the Chalcedonian Christology for Bonhoeffer's ethic; and (2) how central concepts in his ethic are formed on this basis.

In Chapter 4, we have seen this Christological foundation of Bonhoeffer's ethic and how it sustains a differentiated unity of universality and specificity with regard to his concept of reality, the secular, Christonomy, reason and responsibility. We have seen how the Christology in Bonhoeffer is shaped by a Chalcedonian Christology, even if he also argues for transcending its limits. Bonhoeffer's reservation primarily concerns the risk of objectifying the Christology and thereby losing the personal encounter with Christ (the *who* Christ is). Bonhoeffer's affirmative reading of Chalcedon implies that Bonhoeffer's concept of reality shapes his other concepts. Bonhoeffer has a participatory, Christological ontology which implies that there is no being apart from Christ. This leads to a Christologically saturated concept of reality which shapes all other concepts in Bonhoeffer's ethic. Therefore, in these core concepts, Bonhoeffer's Christological concept of reality implies a polemical unity between the reality of God and the reality of the world founded in the incarnation of Christ. This double-sidedness of Bonhoeffer's ethic implies that, on the one hand, he can speak affirmatively of both the worldly, secular and godless reality and, on the other hand, be equally affirmative of the revelatory, ecclesial and proclamatory dimension of the Christ-reality. Bonhoeffer's ethic hereby becomes central to the book's aim to establish a foundation between universality and specificity pertaining to Christian social ethics. Bonhoeffer's ethic as a whole may be understood as a Christologically founded position between radicalism and compromise, whereby Bonhoeffer places himself between oppositional pairs of immediate resemblance with the book's universality (compromise) and specificity (radicalism).

- The book contributes constructively to the understanding of Christian humanism and responsibility in light of the differentiated unity of universality and specificity. Bonhoeffer especially has also been read by others as a Christian humanist and the concept of responsibility has been demonstrated as central to him. The contribution of the book lies in its demonstration of the Chalcedonian Christology and its implications for the religious and political debate pertaining to Christian humanism and responsibility.

In Chapter 6, the book contributes constructively to the reshaping of Christian humanism and responsibility. With regard to the former, the book shows how Luther's concept of natural law, reason and his political thought may be seen as expressive of a Christian humanism. Bonhoeffer is also read by others as a Christian humanist, but the contribution of the book lies in its argument for a Chalcedonian understanding of Christian humanism. With regard to the reshaping of a Chalcedonian understanding of responsibility, the book demonstrates how the *communicatio idiomatum* sustains a communicative and responsive concept of responsibility which is seen in light of the book's contention of a differentiated unity of universality and specificity. This chapter also constructively engages with Niebuhr's responsive concept of responsibility.

- The book exemplifies what the differentiated unity of universality and specificity implies for the contemporary debate on Christian political thought – pertaining to both foundational issues such as the question about the Christian's dual citizenship and the conversational approach to Christian political thought, and more concrete questions such as the debate on human dignity and the role of Christian bioethics in public.

In the final Chapter 7, the implications of the book's findings are exemplified with regard to (1) the question about the Christian being both a national citizen and a citizen in the kingdom of God; and (2) the conversational approach to the question about religion in the public sphere. With regard to the former, the paradoxical understanding of the unity between the reality of God and the reality of the world implies an affirmative understanding of the Christian's national citizenship, even if this is maintained as provisional and relative. The conversational approach is understood in light of the Chalcedonian affirmation of reality and how Bonhoeffer speaks of the polyphony of life, with the love for God as the *cantus firmus* against which all other areas of human life can be seen as contrapuntal voices. Bonhoeffer sees this as an expression of the Chalcedonian mystery of human life. The book argues that this may be seen as a polyphonic affirmation of the public conversation and confirmation of the real presence of Christ in all areas of worldly reality. In the last sections, the book shows how its differentiated unity of universality and specificity implies both how it can contribute constructively to a debate such as the one on human dignity and how there may be situations where the Christian ethic is called to speak out against prevailing wrongs.

Having summarized its main conclusions and contributions, we can now close the book. And yet, the closure is at the same time an opening. The continuous exchange and dynamic interplay between universality and specificity mean that the Christian ethic in the *saeculum* continuously is on its way (a *peregrinatio*). It is in a continuous conversation and openness so that it may learn from others and contribute with insights from its own tradition. On this journey it is a living response to the reconciliation of the world with God in Christ, and it rejoices in its call to bear faithful witness to Christ, while always reminding itself that this is the Christ who was one of us, who was wholly human and wholly divine. SDG.

BIBLIOGRAPHY

Abromeit, Hans-Jürgen. *Das Geheimnis Christi: Dietrich Bonhoeffers erfahrungsbezogene Christologie*. Neukirchener Beiträge zur Systematischen Theologie, 8. Neukirchen-Vluyn: Neukirchener, 1991.

Allen, J. W. *A History of Political Thought in the Sixteenth Century*. Repr. edn. London: Methuen, 1977.

Althaus, Paul. *Die Ethik Martin Luthers*. Gütersloh: Gütersloher Verlagshaus Gerd Mohn, 1965.

Amelung, Eberhard. 'Autonomie'. In *Theologische Realenzyklopädie*. Autokephalie-Biandrata. Band V. Edited by James K. CameronHorst Balz et al., 4–17. Berlin/New York: W. de Gruyter, 1980.

Andersen, Svend. 'Christliche Bioethik in Europa'. In *Religion in bioethischen Diskursen*. Edited by Friedemann Voigt, 293–311. Berlin/New York: W. de Gruyter, 2010.

Andersen, Svend. 'Democracy and Modernity – A Lutheran Perspective'. In *Religion and Normativity*. Edited by Peter Lodberg, 14–29. Religion, Politics, and Law. Vol. 3. Aarhus: Aarhus University Press, 2009.

Andersen, Svend. 'Die Rolle theologischer Argumentation im öffentlichen Leben'. In *Religion und Theologie im öffentlichen Diskurs. Hermeneutische und ethische Perspektiven*. Edited by G. Ulshöfer, 9–23. Frankfurt am Main: Haag, 2005.

Andersen, Svend. 'En tredje vej for den teologiske etik?' *Dansk teologisk tidsskrift* 78, no. 2 (2015): 113–23.

Andersen, Svend. *Løgstrup*. 2nd edn. Frederiksberg: Anis, 2005.

Andersen, Svend. 'Lutheran Political Theology in the Twenty-First Century'. In *Transformations in Luther's Theology. Historical and Contemporary Reflections*. Edited by Christine Helmer and Bo Kristian Holm, 245–63. Arbeiten zur Kirchen- und Theologiegeschichte. Leipzig: Evangelische Verlagsanstalt, 2011.

Andersen, Svend. *Macht aus Liebe. Zur Rekonstruktion einer lutherischen politischen Ethik*. Berlin/New York: W. de Gruyter, 2010.

Andersen, Svend. 'Theological Ethics, Moral Philosophy, and Natural Law'. *Ethical Theory and Moral Practice* 4 (2001): 349–64.

Asheim, Ivar (ed.). *Christ and Humanity*. Philadelphia, PA: Fortress Press, 1970.

Assel, Heinrich. 'Er luthersk politisk teologi valgbeslægtet med liberalisme og republikanisme?' *Dansk Teologisk Tidsskrift* 74 (2011): 313–18.

Augustine, Aurelius. *City of God*. Edited by Henry Scowcroft Bettenson. Penguin Classics. Harmondsworth, Middlesex: Penguin Books, 1984.

Barth, Friederike. *Die Wirklichkeit des Guten: Dietrich Bonhoeffers 'Ethik' und ihr philosophischer Hintergrund*. Beiträge zur historischen Theologie, 156. Tübingen: Mohr Siebeck, 2011.

Bayer, Oswald. 'Christus als Mitte. Bonhoeffers Ethik im Banne der Religionsphilosophie Hegels'. *Berliner Theologische Zeitschrift* 2 (1985): 259–76.

Bayer, Oswald. *Creator est creatura: Luthers Christologie als Lehre von der Idiomenkommunikation*. Theologische Bibliothek Töpelmann, 138. Berlin/New York: W. de Gruyter, 2007.

Bayer, Oswald. *Freiheit als Antwort: zur theologischen Ethik*. Tübingen: Mohr, 1995.
Bayer, Oswald. *Martin Luther's Theology: A Contemporary Interpretation* [Martin Luther's Theologie]. Translated by Thomas H. Trapp. Grand Rapids, MI: W. B. Eerdmans, 2008.
BBC.com. 'Europe and Right-Wing Nationalism: A Country-by-Country Guide'. https://www.bbc.com/news/world-europe-36130006 (accessed 22 July 2019).
Bethge, Eberhard. *Dietrich Bonhoeffer. Theologe – Christ – Zeitgenosse. Eine Biographie*. 8th rev. edn. Gütersloh: Gütersloher Verlagshaus, 2004.
Bethge, Eberhard. 'Freiheit und Gehorsam bei Bonhoeffer'. In *Schöpferische Nachfolge*, 331–61. Heidelberg: FEST, 1978.
Biggar, Nigel. *Behaving in Public: How to Do Christian Ethics*. Grand Rapids, MI/Cambridge: W. B. Eerdmans, 2011.
Biggar, Nigel. 'Not Translation, but Conversation: Theology in Public Debate about Euthanasia'. In *Religious Voices in Public Spaces*. Edited by Nigel Biggar and Linda Hogan, 151–93. Oxford: Oxford University Press, 2009.
Biggar, Nigel. 'Saving the "Secular": The Public Vocation of Moral Theology'. *Journal of Religious Ethics* 37, no. 1 (2009): 159–78.
Binder, Hans-Otto. 'Säkularisation'. In *Theologische Realenzyklopädie*. Edited by James K. Cameron, Horst Balz et al., 597–602. Religionspsychologie – Samaritaner. Band XXIX. Berlin/New York: W. de Gruyter, 1998.
Bloomquist, Karen L., and John R. Stumme. *The Promise of Lutheran Ethics*. Minneapolis, MN: Fortress Press, 1998.
Bonhoeffer, Dietrich. *Act and Being: Transcendental Philosophy and Ontology in Systematic Theology*. Edited by Wayne Whitson Floyd, Jr. Translated by Martin Rumscheidt. Dietrich Bonhoeffer Works. Vol. 2. Minneapolis, MN: Fortress Press, 1996 (DBWE 2).
Bonhoeffer, Dietrich. *Akt und Sein. Transcendentalphilosophie und Ontologie in der systematischen Theologie*. Herausgegeben von Hans-Richard Reuter. Zweite, durchgesehene und aktualisierte Auflage. Dietrich Bonhoeffer Werke. Band 2. Gütersloh: Chr. Kaiser, 2002 (DBW 2).
Bonhoeffer, Dietrich. *Barcelona, Berlin, Amerika. 1928–1931*. Herausgegeben von Reinhart Staats und Hans Christoph von Hase in zusammenarbeit mit Holger Roggelin und Matthias Wünsche. Dietrich Bonhoeffer Werke. Band 10. München: Chr. Kaiser, 1991 (DBW 10).
Bonhoeffer, Dietrich. *Berlin. 1932–1933*. Herausgegeben von Carsten Nikolaisen und Ernst-Albert Scharffenorth. Dietrich Bonhoeffer Werke. Band 12. Gütersloh: Chr. Kaiser, 1997 (DBW 12).
Bonhoeffer, Dietrich. *Berlin, 1932–1933*. Edited by Larry L. Rasmussen. Translated by Isabel Best and David Higgins. Dietrich Bonhoeffer Works. Vol. 12. Minneapolis, MN: Fortress Press, 2009 (DBWE 12).
Bonhoeffer, Dietrich. *Conspiracy and Imprisonment*. Edited by Mark S. Brocker. Translated by Lisa E. Dahill. Dietrich Bonhoeffer Works. Vol. 16. Minneapolis, MN: Fortress Press, 2006 (DBWE 16).
Bonhoeffer, Dietrich. *Creation and Fall: A Theological Exposition of Genesis 1–3*. Edited by John W. De Gruchy. Translated by Douglas Stephen Bax. Dietrich Bonhoeffer Works. Vol. 3. Minneapolis, MN: Fortress Press, 1997 (DBWE 3).
Bonhoeffer, Dietrich. *Dietrich Bonhoeffer Werke*. Herausgegeben von Eberhard Bethge, Ernst Feil, Christian Gremmels, Wolfgang Huber, Hans Pfeifer, Albrecht Schönherr und Heinz Eduard Tödt. Band 1–17. Gütersloh: Chr. Kaiser, 1986–99 (DBW).
Bonhoeffer, Dietrich. *Dietrich Bonhoeffer Works*. General editor, Wayne Whitson Floyd, Jr. Vols 1–17. Minneapolis, MN: Fortress Press, 1995–2014 (DBWE).

Bonhoeffer, Dietrich. *Discipleship*. Edited by Geffrey B. Kelly and John D. Godsey. Translated by Barbara Green and Reinhard Krauss. Dietrich Bonhoeffer Works. Vol. 4. Minneapolis, MN: Fortress Press, 2003 (DBWE 4).

Bonhoeffer, Dietrich. *Ecumenical, Academic, and Pastoral Work: 1931–1932*. Edited by Victoria J. Barnett, Mark S. Brocker and Michael B. Lukens. Translated by Anne Schmidt-Lange, Isabel Best, Nicolas Humphrey and Marion Pauck. Dietrich Bonhoeffer Works. Vol. 11. Minneapolis, MN: Fortress Press, 2012 (DBWE 11).

Bonhoeffer, Dietrich. *Ethics*. Edited by Clifford J. Green. Translated by Reinhard Krauss, Charles C. West and Douglas W. Stott. Dietrich Bonhoeffer Works. Vol. 6. Minneapolis, MN: Fortress Press, 2005 (DBWE 6).

Bonhoeffer, Dietrich. *Ethik*. Herausgegeben von Ilse Tödt, Heinz Eduard Tödt, Ernst Feil und Clifford Green. Dietrich Bonhoeffer Werke. Band 6. 2nd rev. edn. Gütersloh: Chr. Kaiser, 1998 (DBW 6).

Bonhoeffer, Dietrich. *Illegale Theologen-Ausbildung: Sammelvikariate 1937–1940*. Herausgegeben von Dirk Schulz. Dietrich Bonhoeffer Werke. Band 15. Gütersloh: Chr. Kaiser, 1998 (DBW 15).

Bonhoeffer, Dietrich. *Konspiration und Haft. 1940–1945*. Herausgegeben von Jørgen Glenthøj, Ulrich Kabitz und Wolf Krötke. Dietrich Bonhoeffer Werke. Band 16. Gütersloh: Chr. Kaiser, 1996 (DBW 16).

Bonhoeffer, Dietrich. *Letters and Papers from Prison*. Edited by John W. De Gruchy. Translated by Isabel Best, Lisa E. Dahill, Reinhard Krauss and Nancy Lukens. Dietrich Bonhoeffer Works. Vol. 8. Minneapolis, MN: Fortress Press, 2010 (DBWE 8).

Bonhoeffer, Dietrich. *London. 1933–1935*. Herausgegeben von Hans Goedeking, Martin Heimbucher und Hans-Walther Schleicher. Dietrich Bonhoeffer Werke. Band 13. Gütersloh: Chr. Kaiser, 1994 (DBW 13).

Bonhoeffer, Dietrich. *London, 1933–1935*. Edited by Keith Clements. Translated by Isabel Best. Dietrich Bonhoeffer Works. Vol. 13. Minneapolis, MN: Fortress Press, 2007 (DBWE 13).

Bonhoeffer, Dietrich. *Nachfolge*. Herausgegeben von Martin Kuske und Ilse Tödt. Dietrich Bonhoeffer Werke. Band 4. Gütersloh: Chr. Kaiser, 1994 (DBW 4).

Bonhoeffer, Dietrich. *Ökumene, Universität, Pfarramt. 1931–1932*. Herausgegeben von Eberhard Amelung und Christoph Strohm. Dietrich Bonhoeffer Werke. Band 11. Gütersloh: Chr. Kaiser, 1994 (DBW 11).

Bonhoeffer, Dietrich. *Sanctorum Communio. Eine dogmatische Untersuchung zur Soziologie der Kirche*. Herausgegeben von Joachim von Soosten. Dietrich Bonhoeffer Werke. Band 1. Gütersloh: Chr. Kaiser, 1986 (DBW 1).

Bonhoeffer, Dietrich. *Sanctorum Communio: A Theological Study of the Sociology of the Church*. Edited by Clifford J. Green. Translated by Reinhard Krauss and Nancy Lukens. Dietrich Bonhoeffer Works. Vol. 1. Minneapolis, MN: Fortress Press, 1998 (DBWE 1).

Bonhoeffer, Dietrich. *Schöpfung und Fall*. Herausgegeben von Martin Rüter und Ilse Tödt. Dietrich Bonhoeffer Werke. Band 3. 2nd rev. edn. Gütersloh: Chr. Kaiser, 2002 (DBW 3).

Bonhoeffer, Dietrich. *Theological Education Underground, 1937–1940*. Edited by Victoria J. Barnett. Translated by Victoria J. Barnett, Claudia D. Bergmann, Peter Frick and Scott A. Moore. Dietrich Bonhoeffer Works. Vol. 15. Minneapolis, MN: Fortress Press, 2012 (DBWE 15).

Bonhoeffer, Dietrich. *Widerstand und Ergebung. Briefe und Aufzeichnungen aus der Haft*. Herausgegeben von Christian Gremmels, Eberhard Bethge und Renate Bethge in zusammenarbeit mit Ilse Tödt. Dietrich Bonhoeffer Werke. Band 8. Gütersloh: Chr. Kaiser, 1998 (DBW 8).

Boomgaarden, Jürgen. *Das Verständnis der Wirklichkeit: Dietrich Bonhoeffers systematische Theologie und ihr philosophischer Hintergrund in 'Akt und Sein'*. Gütersloh: Chr. Kaiser/ Gütersloher Verlagshaus, 1999.

Braaten, Carl E. 'Natural Law in Theology and Ethics'. In *Two Cities of God*. Edited by Carl E. Braaten and Robert W. Jenson, 42–58. Grand Rapids, MI: W. B. Eerdmans, 1997.

Bretherton, Luke. *Christ and the Common Life. Political Theology and the Case for Democracy*. Grand Rapids, MI: W. B. Eerdmans, 2019.

Bretherton, Luke. *Christianity and Contemporary Politics: The Conditions and Possibilities of Faithful Witness*. Chichester: Wiley, 2010.

Brock, Brian. *Singing the Ethos of God: On the Place of Christian Ethics in Scripture*. Grand Rapids, MI: W. B. Eerdmans, 2007.

Burtness, James H. *Shaping the Future: The Ethics of Dietrich Bonhoeffer*. Philadelphia, PA: Fortress Press, 1985.

Cahill, Lisa Sowle. *Global Justice, Christology and Christian Ethics*. New Studies in Christian Ethics. Vol. 32. Cambridge: Cambridge University Press, 2013.

Carson, Ronald A. 'Motifs of Kenosis and Imitatio in the Work of Dietrich Bonhoeffer, with an Excursus on the Communicatio Idiomatum'. *Journal of the American Academy of Religion* 43, no. 3 (1975): 542–53.

Conner, William F. 'Laws of Life: A Bonhoeffer Theme with Variations'. *Andover Newton Quarterly* 18, no. 2 (1977): 101–10.

Coors, Michael. 'Macht aus Liebe: zur Rekonstruktion einer lutherischen politischen Ethik'. *Theologische Literaturzeitung* 136, no. 2 (2011): 198–200.

Craig, Edward. 'Ontology'. London: Routledge, 1998.

Crisp, Oliver. *Divinity and Humanity: The Incarnation Reconsidered*. Current Issues in Theology. Cambridge: Cambridge University Press, 2007.

Dabrock, Peter. 'Responding to "Wirklichkeit". Reclaiming Bonhoeffer's Approach to Theological Ethics Between Mystery and the Formation of the World'. In *Mysteries in the Theology of Dietrich Bonhoeffer. A Copenhagen Bonhoeffer Symposium*. Edited by Kirsten Busch Nielsen, Ulrik Nissen and Christiane Tietz, 49–80. Göttingen: Vandenhoeck & Ruprecht, 2007.

Dabrock, Peter. 'Wirklichkeit verantworten: der responsive Ansatz theologischer Ethik bei Dietrich Bonhoeffer'. In *Verantwortungsethik als Theologie des Wirklichen*. Edited by Wolfgang Nethöfel, Peter Dabrock and Siegfried Keil, 117–58. Göttingen: Vandenhoeck & Ruprecht, 2009.

De Gruchy, John W. *Confessions of a Christian Humanist*. Minneapolis, MN: Fortress Press, 2006.

De Gruchy, John W., Stephen Plant and Christiane Tietz. *Dietrich Bonhoeffers Theologie heute: Ein Weg zwischen Fundamentalismus und Säkularismus?/Dietrich Bonhoeffer's Theology Today: A Way Between Fundamentalism and Secularism?* Gütersloh: Gütersloher Verlagshaus, 2009.

DeJonge, Michael P., and Christiane Tietz. *Translating Religion: What Is Lost and Gained?* Routledge Studies in Religion. Vol. 47. New York: Routledge, 2015.

Dumas, André. *Une théologie de la réalité: Dietrich Bonhoeffer*. Geneva: Labor et Fides, 1968.

Elmelund Petersen, Carsten. 'Etik mellem Luther og Barth: en analyse af N.H. Søes teologiske etik'. *Dansk teologisk tidsskrift* 59, no. 2 (1996): 106–24.

Feil, Ernst. *Die Theologie Dietrich Bonhoeffers: Hermeneutik, Christologie, Weltverständnis*. Studien zur systematischen Theologie und Ethik. Band 45. 5th ext. edn. Berlin: LIT, 2005.

Fergusson, David. 'Beyond Theologies of Resentment: An Appreciation of Jeffrey Stout's *Democracy and Tradition*'. *Scottish Journal of Theology* 59, no. 2 (2006): 183–97.

Fergusson, David. *Community, Liberalism and Christian Ethics*. New Studies in Christian Ethics. Cambridge: Cambridge University Press, 1998.

Fink, Hans, and Robert Stern (eds). *What Is Ethically Demanded? K. E. Løgstrup's Philosophy of Moral Life*. Notre Dame, IN: University of Notre Dame Press, 2017.

Floyd, Wayne Whitson, and Charles Marsh. *Theology and the Practice of Responsibility: Essays on Dietrich Bonhoeffer*. Valley Forge, PA: Trinity Press International, 1994.

Forrester, Duncan B. 'Social Justice and Welfare'. In *The Cambridge Companion to Christian Ethics*. Edited by Robin Gill, 195–208. Cambridge: Cambridge University Press, 2000.

Frey, Christofer. 'Gottesdienst als Lebensform: Ethik für Christenbürger'. *Zeitschrift für evangelische Ethik* 44, no. 1 (2000): 70–72.

Funamoto, Hiroki. 'Penultimate and Ultimate in Dietrich Bonhoeffer's Ethics'. In *Being and Truth*, 376–92. London: SCM Press, 1986.

Godsey, John D., and Geffrey B. Kelly. *Ethical Responsibility: Bonhoeffer's Legacy to the Churches*. Toronto Studies in Theology. New York/Toronto: Edwin Mellen Press, 1981.

Green, Clifford J. *Bonhoeffer. A Theology of Sociality*. Rev. edn. Grand Rapids, MI: W. B. Eerdmans, 1999.

Green, Clifford J. 'Ethical Theology and Contextual Ethics. New Perspectives on Bonhoeffer's Ethics'. In *Religion im Erbe. Dietrich Bonhoeffer und die Zukunftsfähigkeit des Christentums*. Edited by Christian Gremmels and Wolfgang Huber, 255–69. Gütersloh: Chr. Kaiser, 2002.

Greenawalt, Kent. *Religious Convictions and Political Choice*. New York: Oxford University Press, 1988.

Greggs, Tom. 'Religionless Christianity in a Complexly Religious and Secular World: Thinking Through and Beyond Bonhoeffer'. In *Religion, Religionlessness and Contemporary Western Culture*, 111–25. Frankfurt am Main: Peter Lang, 2008.

Gregory, Eric. *Politics & the Order of Love. An Augustinian Ethic of Democratic Citizenship*. Chicago, IL/London: University of Chicago Press, 2008.

Grenholm, Carl-Henric. *Bortom humanismen. En studie i kristen etik*. Stockholm: Verbum, 2003.

Grobien, Gifford A. *Christian Character Formation: Lutheran Studies of the Law, Anthropology, Worship and Virtue*. Oxford Studies in Theological Ethics. Oxford: Oxford University Press, 2019.

Grotefeld, Stefan. 'Rationalität, Vernunft und Moralbegründung'. In *Ethik, Vernunft und Rationalität/Ethics, Reason and Rationality*. Edited by Alberto Bondolfi, Stefan Grotefeld and Rudi Neuberth, 55–89. Münster: LIT, 1997.

Grotius, Hugo. *Prolegomena to the Law of War and Peace*. Library of Liberal Arts. Indianapolis, IN: Bobbs-Merrill Co., 1957.

Guinn, David E. (ed.). *Handbook of Bioethics and Religion*. New York: Oxford University Press, 2006.

Gustafson, James M. *Christ and the Moral Life*. Library of Theological Ethics. Louisville, KY: Westminster John Knox Press, 2009.

Hale, Lori Brandt, and Reggie L. Williams. 'Is this a Bonhoeffer Moment?' https://sojo.net/magazine/february-2018/bonhoeffer-moment (accessed 22 July 2019).

Harvey, Barry. 'Preserving the World for Christ: Toward a Theological Engagement with the "Secular"'. *Scottish Journal of Theology* 61, no. 1 (2008): 64–82.
Harvey, Barry. *Taking Hold of the Real: Dietrich Bonhoeffer and the Profound Worldliness of Christianity*. Eugene, OR: Cascade Books, 2015.
Hauerwas, Stanley. 'Dietrich Bonhoeffer'. In *The Blackwell Companion to Political Theology*. Edited by Peter Scott and William T. Cavanaugh, 136–49. Malden, MA: Blackwell, 2004.
Hauerwas, Stanley. *Performing the Faith: Bonhoeffer and the Practice of Nonviolence*. London: SPCK, 2004.
Hebblethwaite, Brian. 'Sozialethik'. In *Theologische Realenzyklopädie*. Edited by James K. Cameron Horst Balz et al., 497–527. Vol. 31. Berlin/New York: W. de Gruyter, 2000.
Henry, Michel. *I Am the Truth: Toward a Philosophy of Christianity [C'est moi la vérité]*. Cultural Memory in the Present. Stanford, CA: Stanford University Press, 2003.
Holm, Bo Kristian. *Gabe und Geben bei Luther. Das Verhältnis zwischen Reziprozität und reformatorischer Rechtfertigungslehre*. Theologische Bibliothek Töpelmann, 134. Berlin/New York: W. de Gruyter, 2006.
Holmes, Christopher R. J. *Ethics in the Presence of Christ*. London/New York: T&T Clark, 2012.
Holmes, Christopher R. J. '"The Indivisible Whole of God's Reality": On the Agency of Jesus in Bonhoeffer's Ethics'. *International Journal of Systematic Theology* 12 (2010): 283–301.
Holmes, Christopher R. J. 'Wholly Human and Wholly Divine, Humiliated and Exalted: Some Reformed Explorations in Bonhoeffer's Christology Lectures'. *Scottish Bulletin of Evangelical Theology* 25, no. 2 (2007): 210–25.
Honecker, Martin. 'Christologie und Ethik: zu Dietrich Bonhoeffers Ethik'. In *Altes Testament und christliche Verkündigung*, 148–64. Stuttgart/Ithaca, NY: Snow Lion Publications/W. Kohlhammer, 1987.
Huber, Wolfgang. 'Freiheit als Form der Liebe. Die Aktualität christlicher Freiheit in den gesellschaftlichen Herausforderungen unserer Zeit'. In *Religion im Erbe. Dietrich Bonhoeffer und die Zukunftsfähigkeit des Christentums*. Edited by Christian Gremmels and Wolfgang Huber, 17–36. Gütersloh: Chr. Kaiser/Gütersloher Verlagshaus, 2002.
Huber, Wolfgang. 'Sozialethik als Verantwortungsethik'. In *Verantwortungsethik als Theologie des Wirklichen*. Edited by Wolfgang Nethöfel, Peter Dabrock and Siegfried Keil, 74–100. Göttingen: Vandenhoeck & Ruprecht, 2009.
Janke, Wolfgang. 'Wirklichkeit. I. Philosophisch'. In *Theologische Realenzyklopädie*, 114. Berlin/New York: W. de Gruyter, 2004.
Johnson, Kristen Deede. *Theology, Political Theory, and Pluralism: Beyond Tolerance and Difference*. Cambridge Studies in Christian Doctrine. Vol. 15. Cambridge: Cambridge University Press, 2007.
Jonas, Hans. *The Imperative of Responsibility: In Search of an Ethics for the Technological Age*. Chicago, IL: University of Chicago Press, 1984.
Kant, Immanuel. *Grundlegung zur Metaphysik der Sitten*. Edited by Karl Vorländer Philosophische Bibliothek. Vol. 41. Hamburg: Felix Meiner, 1994.
Kärkkäinen, Veli-Matti. '"The Christian as Christ to the Neighbour": On Luther's Theology of Love'. *International Journal of Systematic Theology* 6, no. 2 (2004): 101–17.
Kelly, J. N. D. *Early Christian Doctrines*. 5th rev. edn. London: A. & C. Black, 1993.
Klemm, David E., and William Schweiker. *Religion and the Human Future: An Essay on Theological Humanism*. Blackwell Manifestos. Malden, MA/Oxford: Wiley-Blackwell, 2008.

Kohler, R. F. 'Christocentric Ethics of Dietrich Bonhoeffer'. *Scottish Journal of Theology* 23, no. 1 (1970): 27–40.
Kremer, K. 'Ontologie'. In *Historisches Wörterbuch der Philosophie*. Edited by Joachim Ritter and Karlfried Gründer, 1189–98. Basel/Stuttgart: Schwabe & Co., 1984.
Krötke, Wolf. 'Wirklichkeit'. In *Religion in Geschichte und Gegenwart. Handwörterbuch für Theologie und Religionswissenschaft*. Edited by Hans Dieter Betz, Don S. Browning, Bernd Janowski and Eberhard Jüngel, 1594–96. Tübingen: Mohr Siebeck, 2005.
Kunstmann, Joachim. 'Wirklichkeit II. Praktisch-theologisch'. In *Theologische Realenzyklopädie*. Edited by James K. CameronHorst Balz et al., 120–23. Band XXXVI. Wiedergeburt-Zypern. Berlin/New York: W. de Gruyter, 2004.
Kurtén, Tage. 'Kärlekens lag eller den naturliga lagen? Biblisk moraltradition i dag'. In *Bibeln och kyrkans tro i dag. Synodalavhandling 2004*. Edited by Maarit Hytönen, 178–95. Tammerfors: Kyrkans forskningscentral, 2004.
Kurtén, Tage. 'The Christian Living in Two Worlds? Religious Contributions to the Legitimacy of a Democratic Society'. *Studia theologica* 61, no. 2 (2007): 91–112.
Laffin, Michael Richard. *The Promise of Martin Luther's Political Theology: Freeing Luther from the Modern Political Narrative*. Edited by Brian Brock and Susan F. Parsons. T&T Clark Enquiries in Theological Ethics. London: T&T Clark, 2016.
Lage, Dietmar. *Martin Luther's Christology and Ethics*. Texts and Studies in Religion. Lewiston, NY: Edwin Mellen Press, 1990.
Lanczkowski, G. 'Saeculum'. In *Die Religion in Geschichte und Gegenwart. Handwörterbuch für Theologie und Religionswissenschaft*. Edited by Wilfrid Werbeck, 1279–80. Tübingen: J. C. B. Mohr (Siebeck), 1961.
Lehmkühler, Karsten. 'Christologie'. In *Bonhoeffer und Luther. Zentrale Themen ihrer Theologie*. Edited by Klaus Grünwaldt, Christiane Tietz and Udo Hahn, 55–78. Hannover: VELKD, 2007.
Lienhard, Marc. *Martin Luthers christologisches Zeugnis: Entwicklung und Grundzüge seiner Christologie*. Göttingen: Vandenhoeck & Ruprecht, 1980.
Lodberg, Peter. *Sammenhængskraften: replikker til Fogh*. Højbjerg: Univers, 2007.
Løgstrup, K. E. *Den etiske fordring*. Løgstrup biblioteket. 4th edn. Århus: Klim, [1956] 2010.
Løgstrup, K. E. *Etiske begreber og problemer*. Løgstrup biblioteket. 3rd edn. Aarhus: Klim, 2014.
Løgstrup, Knud Ejler. *The Ethical Demand* [Den etiske fordring]. Revisions. Notre Dame, IN: University of Notre Dame Press, 1997.
Luther, Martin. *Auslegung des 101. Psalms*. Herausgegeben von E. Thiele und O. Brenner. Weimar: H. Böhlau, [1534–35] 1914 (WA 51, 197–264).
Luther, Martin. *Confession Concerning Christ's Supper*. Luther's Works 37: Word and Sacrament 3. Edited and translated by Robert H. Fischer. Philadelphia, PA: Fortress Press, [1528] 1961 (LW 37, 151–372).
Luther, Martin. *Der 82. Psalm ausgelegt*. Herausgegeben von E. Thiele. Weimar: H. Böhlau, [1530] 1913 (WA 31 I, 189–218).
Luther, Martin. *Der 127. Psalm ausgelegt an die Christen zu Riga in Liesland*. Weimar: H. Böhlau, [1524] 1899 (WA 15, 348–79).
Luther, Martin. *Der Große Katechismus*. Bearbeitet von Robert Kolb (BSELK, 912–1162).
Luther, Martin. *Deudsch Catechismus (Der Große Katechismus)*. Weimar: H. Böhlau, [1529] 1910 (WA 30 I, 125–238).

Luther, Martin. *Die Bekenntnisschriften der Evangelisch-Lutherischen Kirche*. Herausgegeben von Irene Dingel im Auftrag der Evangelischen Kirche in Deutschland. New edn. Göttingen: Vandenhoeck & Ruprecht, 2014 (BSELK).

Luther, Martin. *Die Disputation de divinitate et humanitate Christi*. Weimar: H. Böhlau, [28 February 1540] 1932 (WA 39 II, 92–121).

Luther, Martin. *Die Konkordienformel*. Bearbeitet von Irene Dingel. Göttingen: Vandenhoeck & Ruprecht, 2014 (BSELK, 1163–607).

Luther, Martin. *Die zweite Disputation gegen die Antinomer*. 12 January 1538 (WA 39 I, 418–85).

Luther, Martin. *D. Martin Luthers Werke: Schriften*. Band 1–73. Kritische Gesamtausgabe. Weimarer Ausgabe. 1883ff. Weimar: H. Böhlau (WA).

Luther, Martin. *Ein Sendbrief von dem harten Büchlein wider die Bauern*. Weimar: H. Böhlau, [1525] 1908 (WA 18, 375–401).

Luther, Martin. *Ein unterrichtung wie sich die Christen ynn Mosen sollen schicken, gepredigt durch Mart. Luther*. Weimar: H. Böhlau, [1527] 1900 (WA 24, 2–16).

Luther, Martin. *Fastenpostille. Am Vierden Sonntag nach Epiphanie. Epistel S. Pauli zu den Romern ca. xiii*. Begonnen von E. Thiele, vollendet von G. Buchwald. Weimar: H. Böhlau, [1525] 1927 (WA 17 II, 88–104).

Luther, Martin. *In epistolam S. Pauli ad Galatas commentarius ex praelectione*. Herausgegeben von U. Freitag. Weimar: H. Böhlau, [1531, 1535] 1911 (WA 40 I, 1–688; 40 II, 1–184).

Luther, Martin. *Lectures on Genesis, Chapters 1–5*. Edited by Jaroslav Pelikan. Translated by George V. Schick. Luther's Works 1. Saint Louis, MO: Concordia Publishing House, 1964 (LW 1).

Luther, Martin. *Luther's Works*. Edited by Jaroslav Pelikan et al. Vols 1–55. US edn. St Louis, MO/Philadelphia, PA: Concordia/Fortress Press, 1955 (LW).

Luther, Martin. *Ob Kriegsleute auch in seligem Stande sein können*. Weimar: H. Böhlau, [1526] 1908 (WA 19, 616–62).

Luther, Martin. *Psalm 82*. Edited by Jaroslav Pelikan. Translated by C. M. Jacobs. Revised by Walther I. Brandt. Luther's Works 13: Selected Psalms II. Saint Louis, MO: Concordia Publishing House, 1956 (LW 13, 39–72).

Luther, Martin. *Temporal Authority: To What Extent It Should Be Obeyed*. Edited and revised by Walther I. Brandt. Translated by J. J. Schindel. Luther's Works 45: The Christian in Society II. Philadelphia, PA: Mühlenberg Press, [1523] 1962 (LW 45, 75–129).

Luther, Martin. *The Freedom of a Christian*. Edited by Harold J. Grimm. Translated by W. A. Lambert and revised by Harold J. Grimm. Luther's Works 31: Career of the Reformer 1. Philadelphia, PA: Fortress Press, [1520] 1957 (LW 31, 327–77).

Luther, Martin. *Vom Abendmahl Christi, Bekenntnis*. Herausgegeben von E. Thiele und O. Brenner. Weimar: H. Böhlau, [1528] 1909 (WA 26, 241–509).

Luther, Martin. *Von den Konziliis und Kirchen*. Herausgegeben von F. Cohrs und O. Brenner. Weimar: H. Böhlau, [1539] 1914 (WA 50, 488–653).

Luther, Martin. *Von der Freiheit eines Christenmenschen*. Weimar: H. Böhlau, [1520] 1897 (WA 7, 12–38).

Luther, Martin. *Von Jhesu Christo Warem Gott und Menschen und von seinem Ampt und Reich, so er führt in der Christenheit. Die Ander Predigt, Von der Menschheit Christi und seinem Ampt*. Weimar: H. Böhlau, [1537] 1911 (WA 45, 297–324).

Luther, Martin. *Von weltlicher Oberkeit, wie weit man ihr Gehorsam schuldig sei*. Weimar: H. Böhlau, [1523] 1900 (WA 11, 229–81).

Luther, Martin. *Vorlesungen über 1. Mose von 1535-45. Kap. 2, 16–17*. Herausgegeben von G. Koffmane und O. Reichert (WA 42, 79–87).

Luther, Martin. *Vorlesung über die Stufenpsalmen. Psalmus CXXVII*. Herausgegeben von U. Freitag. Weimar: H. Böhlau, [1532/33, 1540] 1930 (WA 40 III, 202–69).

Luther, Martin. *Whether Soldiers, Too, Can Be Saved*. Luther's Works 46: The Christian in Society III. Edited and revised by Robert C. Schultz. Translated by Charles M. Jacobs. Philadelphia, PA: Fortress Press, [1526] 1967 (LW 46, 87–137).

Luther, Martin. *Wider die himmlischen Propheten, von den Bildern und Sakrament*. Herausgegeben von O. Brenner und H. Barge. Weimar: H. Böhlau, [1525] 1908 (WA 18, 37–125).

MacIntyre, Alasdair. *Whose Justice? Which Rationality?* London: Duckworth, 1988.

Macquarrie, John. *Jesus Christ in Modern Thought*. 3rd impr. edn. London: SCM Press, 1993.

Mannermaa, Tuomo. *Der im Glauben gegenwärtige Christus. Rechtfertigung und Vergottung. Zum ökumenischen Dialog*. Arbeiten zur Geschichte und Theologie des Luthertums, N.F. Band 8. Hannover: Lutherisches Verlagshaus, 1989.

Markus, Robert A. *Christianity and the Secular*. Notre Dame, IN: University of Notre Dame Press, 2006.

Mathewes, Charles T. *A Theology of Public Life*. Cambridge Studies in Christian Doctrine, 17. Cambridge: Cambridge University Press, 2007.

Mawson, Michael. *Christ Existing as Community: Bonhoeffer's Ecclesiology*. Oxford: Oxford University Press, 2018.

Mawson, Michael, and Philip G. Ziegler (eds). *Christ, Church, and World: New Studies in Bonhoeffer's Theology and Ethics*. London: T&T Clark, 2016.

Mayer, Rainer. *Christuswirklichkeit. Grundlagen, Entwicklung und Konsequenzen der Theologie Dietrich Bonhoeffers*. Arbeiten zur Theologie. Vol. 15. 2nd edn. Stuttgart: Calwer, 1969.

McBride, Jennifer M. *The Church for the World: A Theology of Public Witness*. Oxford: Oxford University Press, 2012.

McGrath, Alister E. *Reformation Thought: An Introduction*. 2nd edn. Oxford, UK/Cambridge, MA: Basil Blackwell, 1993.

McKenny, Gerald P. 'Responsibility'. In *The Oxford Handbook of Theological Ethics*. Edited by Gilbert C. Meilaender and William Werpehowski, 237–53. Oxford: Oxford University Press, 2005.

Mehl, Roger. 'La notion du naturel dans l'ethique de Bonhoeffer'. In *Evangile hier et aujourd'hui; melanges offerts au Franz J. Leenhardt*, 205–16. Geneva: Editions Labor et Fides, 1968.

Meilaender, Gilbert. 'Against Consensus: Christians and Public Bioethics'. *Studies in Christian Ethics* 18, no. 1 (2005): 75–88.

Messer, Neil. *Respecting Life: Theology and Bioethics*. London: SCM Press, 2011.

Messer, Neil. *Theological Neuroethics: Christian Ethics Meets the Science of the Human Brain*. Edited by Brian Brock and Susan F. Parsons. Enquiries in Theological Ethics. London: T&T Clark, 2017.

Milbank, John. *Being Reconciled: Ontology and Pardon*. Radical Orthodoxy Series. London: Routledge, 2003.

Milbank, John. *Theology and Social Theory: Beyond Secular Reason*. Signposts in Theology. Repr. edn. Oxford: Blackwell, 1997.

Miller, Mark C. *Living Ethically in Christ: Is Christian Ethics Unique?* American University Studies. Series VII, Theology and Religion. Vol. 173. New York: P. Lang, 1999.
Moberly, Jennifer. *The Virtue of Bonhoeffer's Ethics: A Study of Dietrich Bonhoeffer's Ethics in Relation to Virtue Ethics.* Princeton Theological Monograph Series. Vol. 194. Eugene, OR: Pickwick, 2013.
Moltmann, Jürgen. *Herrschaft Christi und soziale Wirklichkeit nach Dietrich Bonhoeffer.* Theologische Existenz heute. Vol. 71. München: Chr. Kaiser, 1959.
Ngien, Dennis. 'Chalcedonian Christology and Beyond: Luther's Understanding of the Communicatio Idiomatum'. *The Heythrop Journal* 45, no. 1 (2004): 54–68.
Nickson, Ann L. *Bonhoeffer on Freedom: Courageously Grasping Reality.* Oxford: Ashgate, 2002.
Niebuhr, H. Richard. *Christ & Culture.* New York: HarperOne, 2001.
Niebuhr, H. Richard. *The Responsible Self: An Essay in Christian Moral Philosophy.* Louisville, KY: Westminster John Knox Press, 1999.
Niebuhr, Reinhold. *Moral Man and Immoral Society: A Study in Ethics and Politics.* New York: Charles Scribner, 1960.
Nielsen, Kirsten Busch. 'Critique of Church and Critique of Religion in Bonhoeffer's Late Writings'. In *Dietrich Bonhoeffers Theologie heute*, 319–34. Gütersloh: Gütersloher Verlagshaus, 2009.
Nielsen, Kirsten Busch. *Die gebrochene Macht der Sünde: der Beitrag Dietrich Bonhoeffers zur Hamartologie.* Arbeiten zur systematischen Theologie. Vol. 2. Leipzig: Evangelische Verlagsanstalt, 2010.
Nielsen, Kirsten Busch. *Syndens brudte magt: en undersøgelse af Dietrich Bonhoeffers syndsforståelse.* Publikationer fra Det Teologiske Fakultet, 1. Københavns: Det Teologiske Fakultet, Københavns Universitet, 2008.
Nielsen, Kirsten Busch. 'The Concept of Religion and Christian Doctrine: The Theology of Dietrich Bonhoeffer Reconsidered'. *Studia theologica* 57, no. 1 (2003): 4–19.
Nielsen, Kirsten Busch. 'Überlegungen zum Religionsverständnis Dietrich Bonhoeffers: Zwischen Kritik und Konstruktion'. *Dietrich Bonhoeffer Jahrbuch* 1 (2003): 93–106.
Nielsen, Kirsten Busch, Ulrik Nissen and Christiane Tietz (eds). *Mysteries in the Theology of Dietrich Bonhoeffer: A Copenhagen Bonhoeffer Symposium* Forschungen zur systematischen und ökumenischen Theologie. Vol. 119. Göttingen: Vandenhoeck & Ruprecht, 2007.
Nielsen, Kirsten Busch, Ralf Karolus Wüstenberg and Jens Zimmermann (eds). *Dem Rad in die Speichen fallen: Das Politische in der Theologie Dietrich Bonhoeffers/A Spoke in the Wheel: The Political in the Theology of Dietrich Bonhoeffer.* Gütersloh: Gütersloher Verlagshaus, 2013.
Nikolajsen, Jeppe Bach. 'Kristen etik i et pluralistisk samfund'. *Dansk teologisk tidsskrift* 79, no. 2 (2016): 105–21.
Nilsson, Kjell Ove. *Simul. Das Miteinander von Göttlichem und Menschlichem in Luthers Theologie.* Göttingen: Vandenhoeck & Ruprecht, 1966.
Nissen, Ulrik. 'Being Christ for the Other: A Lutheran Affirmation of Christian Humanism'. *Studia theologica* 64, no. 2 (2010): 177–98.
Nissen, Ulrik. 'Between Unity and Differentiation. On the Identity of Lutheran Social Ethics'. In *The Sources of Public Morality – On the Ethics and Religion Debate.* Edited by Ulrik Nissen, Svend Andersen and Lars Reuter, 152–71. Societas Ethica. Europäische Forschungsgesellschaft für Ethik. Münster: LIT, 2003.
Nissen, Ulrik. *Between Universality and Specificity. A Study of Christian Social Ethics with Particular Emphasis on Dietrich Bonhoeffer's Ethics.* Aarhus: Aarhus University, 2014.

Nissen, Ulrik. 'Dietrich Bonhoeffer: A Journey from Pacifism to Resistance'. In *Christianity and Resistance in the 20th Century*, 147–74. Leiden/Boston, MA: Brill, 2009.
Nissen, Ulrik. 'Dietrich Bonhoeffer and the Ethics of Plenitude'. *Journal of the Society of Christian Ethics* 26, no. 1 (2006): 97–114.
Nissen, Ulrik. 'Dietrich Bonhoeffer's Ethik in einer säkularen Welt des Terrors'. In *Bonhoeffer weiterdenken…* Edited by Andreas Klein and Matthias Geist, 17–32. Münster: LIT, 2006.
Nissen, Ulrik. 'Disbelief and Christonomy of the World'. *Studia theologica* 60, no. 1 (2006): 91–110.
Nissen, Ulrik. 'Kristen etik mellem kompromis og radikalitet. Om ansvarsetikken som en tredje vej inspireret af K. E. Løgstrup og Dietrich Bonhoeffer'. *Dansk Teologisk Tidsskrift* 80, no. 2–3 (2017): 110–26.
Nissen, Ulrik. 'Letting Reality Become Real: On Mystery and Reality in Dietrich Bonhoeffer's Ethics'. *Journal of Religious Ethics* 39, no. 2 (2011): 321–43.
Nissen, Ulrik. 'Martin Luthers und Philipp Melanchthons Verständnis vom natürlichen Gesetz'. In *Luther Between Present and Past. Studies in Luther and Lutheranism*. Edited by Ulrik Nissen, Anna Vind, Bo Holm and Olli-Pekka Vainio, 208–34. Helsinki: Luther-Agricola-Society, 2004.
Nissen, Ulrik. *Nature and Reason. A Study on Natural Law and Environmental Ethics*. Aarhus: Aarhus Universitet Library Scholarly Publishing Services, 2019. doi:10.7146/aul.334.226.
Nissen, Ulrik. *Påberåbelsen af lex naturalis i diskussionen om statsmagtens legitimitet i det 16. århundredes lutherske, reformerte og anglikanske teologi, og denne diskussions betydning for opkomsten af den moderne idé om samfunds-kontrakten*. Aarhus: Aarhus Universitet Library Scholarly Publishing Services, 2019. doi:10.7146/aul.330.224.
Nissen, Ulrik. 'Reconciliation and Public Law. Christian Reflections about the Sources of Public Law'. *Studia theologica* 58, no. 1 (2004): 27–44.
Nissen, Ulrik. 'Responding to Human Reality. Responsibility and Responsiveness in Bonhoeffer's Ethics'. In *Being Human, Becoming Human: Dietrich Bonhoeffer and Social Thought*. Edited by Brian Gregor and Jens Zimmerman, 203–25. Eugene, OR: Wipf & Stock, 2010.
Nissen, Ulrik. 'Responsibility and Responsiveness: Reflections on the Communicative Dimension of Responsibility'. *Neue Zeitschrift für systematische Theologie und Religionsphilosophie* 53, no. 1 (2011): 90–108.
Nissen, Ulrik. 'Saeculum og fyldens etik. en radikal læsning af Dietrich Bonhoeffer'. *Dansk teologisk tidsskrift* 68, no. 4 (2005): 285–304.
Nissen, Ulrik. 'Social Ethics Between Universality and Specificity. Outline of a Chalcedonian Social Ethic'. *Dialog* 51, no. 1 (2012): 83–91.
Nissen, Ulrik. 'The Christological Ontology of Reason'. *Neue Zeitschrift für systematische Theologie und Religionsphilosophie* 48, no. 4 (2006): 460–78.
Nissen, Ulrik. *The Responsive Body. Beginning, Altering, and Fulfilling Human Life*. Forthcoming.
Nissen, Ulrik. 'What Is a Human Body? Moving Towards a Responsive Body'. In *What Is Human? Theological Encounters with Anthropology*. Edited by Eve-Marie Becker, Jan Dietrich and Bo Kristian Holm, 311–35. Göttingen: Vandenhoeck & Ruprecht, 2017.
O'Donovan, Oliver. *Resurrection and Moral Order. An Outline for Evangelical Ethics*. 2nd edn. Leicester/Grand Rapids, MI: Apollos/W. B. Eerdmans, 1994.

O'Donovan, Oliver. *The Desire of the Nations: Rediscovering the Roots of Political Theology.* Cambridge: Cambridge University Press, 1996.
Ott, Heinrich. *Wirklichkeit und Glaube.* Erster Band. Zum theologischen Erbe Dietrich Bonhoeffers. Zürich: Vandenhoeck & Ruprecht, 1966.
Pannenberg, Wolfhart. *Grundzüge der Christologie.* 5th ext. edn. Gütersloh: Mohn, 1976.
Peters, Tiemo Rainer. 'Jenseits von Radikalismus und Kompromiss: die politische Verantwortung der Christen nach Dietrich Bonhoeffer'. In *Verspieltes Erbe*, 94–115. Munich: Chr. Kaiser, 1979.
Phillips, John A. *The Form of Christ in the World: A Study of Bonhoeffer's Christology.* London: Collins, 1967.
Prüller-Jagenteufel, Gunter M. *Befreit zur Verantwortung: Sünde und Versöhnung in der Ethik Dietrich Bonhoeffers.* Ethik im Theologischen Diskurs. Münster: LIT, 2004.
Rasmussen, Anders Fogh. 'Fogh: Hold religionen indendørs'. *Politiken* (2006): 6.
Rasmussen, Larry. 'The Ethics of Responsible Action'. In *The Cambridge Companion to Dietrich Bonhoeffer.* Edited by John W. De Gruchy, 206–25. Cambridge: Cambridge University Press, 1999.
Rasmussen, Larry L. *Dietrich Bonhoeffer: Reality and Resistance.* Studies in Christian Ethics. Nashville, TN: Abingdon, 1972.
Raunio, Antti. 'Faith and Christian Living in Luther's Confession Concerning Christ's Supper (1528)'. *Lutherjahrbuch* 76 (2009): 19–56.
Raunio, Antti. 'Natural Law and Faith: The Forgotten Foundations of Ethics in Luther's Theology'. In *Union with Christ*, 96–124. Grand Rapids, MI: W. B. Eerdmans, 1998.
Raunio, Antti. *Summe des christlichen Lebens: die 'Goldene Regel' als Gesetz der Liebe in der Theologie Martin Luthers von 1510 bis 1527.* Reports from the Department of Systematic Theology. Vol. 13. Helsinki: University of Helsinki, 1993.
Raunio, Antti. *Summe des Christlichen Lebens: die 'Goldene Regel' als Gesetz der Liebe in der Theologie Martin Luthers von 1510–1527.* Veröffentlichungen des Instituts für Europäische Geschichte Mainz. Abteilung für abendländische Religionsgeschichte, 160. Mainz: Philipp von Zabern, 2001.
Rawls, John. *Political Liberalism.* Columbia Classics in Philosophy. Paperback edn. New York: Columbia University Press, 1996.
Rawls, John. 'The Idea of Public Reason Revisited'. *The University of Chicago Law Review* 64, no. 3 (1997): 765–807.
Reed, Esther D. *The Genesis of Ethics: On the Authority of God as the Origin of Christian Ethics.* London: Darton, Longman and Todd, 2000.
Reed, Esther D. *The Limit of Responsibility: Engaging Dietrich Bonhoeffer in a Globalizing Era.* Edited by Brian Brock and Susan F. Parsons. T&T Clark Enquiries in Theological Ethics. London: T&T Clark, 2018.
Reicke, S. 'Säkularisation'. In *Die Religion in Geschichte und Gegenwart. Handwörterbuch für Theologie und Religionswissenschaft.* Edited by Wilfrid Werbeck, 1280–88. Tübingen: J. C. B. Mohr (Siebeck), 1961.
Schliesser, Christine. 'Accepting Guilt for the Sake of Germany: An Analysis of Bonhoeffer's Concept of Accepting Guilt and Its Implications for Bonhoeffer's Political Resistance'. *Union Seminary Quarterly Review* 60, no. 1–2 (2006): 56–68.
Schliesser, Christine. *Everyone Who Acts Responsibly Becomes Guilty: Bonhoeffer's Concept of Accepting Guilt.* Louisville, KY: Westminster John Knox, 2008.
Schliesser, Christine. '"The First Theological-Ethical Doctrine of Basic Human Rights Developed by a Twentieth-Century German Protestant Theologian" – Dietrich Bonhoeffer and Human Rights'. In *Dem Rad in die Speichen fallen. Das Politische in*

der Theologie Dietrich Bonhoeffers/A Spoke in the Wheel. The Political in the Theology of Dietrich Bonhoeffer. Edited by Kirsten Busch Nielsen, Ralf K. Wüstenberg and Jens Zimmermann, 369–84. Gütersloh: Gütersloher Verlagshaus, 2013.

Schneider, Edward D. 'Bonhoeffer and a Secular Theology'. *Lutheran Quarterly* 15, no. 2 (1963): 151–57.

Schuele, Andreas, and Günter Thomas (eds). *Who Is Jesus Christ for Us Today? Pathways to Contemporary Christology.* Louisville, KY: Westminster John Knox Press, 2009.

Schulman, Adam. 'Bioethics and the Question of Human Dignity'. In *Human Dignity and Bioethics. Essays Commissioned by the President's Council on Bioethics.* Edited by Adam Schulman and Thomas W. Merrill, 3–18. Washington, DC: President's Council on Bioethics, 2008.

Schweiker, William. 'Freedom within Religion (with Response by John W. De Gruchy)'. *Conversations in Religion and Theology* 6, no. 1 (2008): 100–19.

Schweiker, William. *Responsibility and Christian Ethics.* New Studies in Christian Ethics. Cambridge: Cambridge University Press, 1995.

Schweiker, William. *Theological Ethics and Global Dynamics in the Time of Many Worlds.* Oxford: Blackwell, 2006.

Schweiker, William. 'Theological Ethics and the Question of Humanism'. *Journal of Religion* 83, no. 4 (2003): 539–61.

Sherman, Franklin. 'The Vital Center: Toward a Chalcedonian Social Ethic'. In *The Scope of Grace. Essays on Nature and Grace in Honor of Josep Sittler.* Edited by Philip J. Hefner, 233–56. Philadelphia, PA: Fortress Press, 1964.

Shults, F. LeRon, and Brent Waters (eds). *Christology and Ethics.* Grand Rapids, MI/ Cambridge: W. B. Eerdmans, 2010.

Simpson, Gary. 'Toward a Lutheran "Delight in the Law of the Lord": Church and State in the Context of Civil Society'. In *Church & State: Lutheran Perspectives.* Edited by John R. Stumme and Robert W. Tuttle, 20–50. Minneapolis, MN: Fortress Press, 2003.

Stassen, Glen Harold. *A Thicker Jesus: Incarnational Discipleship in a Secular Age.* Louisville, KY: Westminster John Knox Press, 2012.

Stassen, Glen Harold, Diane M. Yeager, John Howard Yoder and H. R. Niebuhr. *Authentic Transformation: A New Vision of Christ and Culture.* Nashville, TN: Abingdon Press, 1996.

Steiger, Johann Anselm. 'Die communicatio idiomatum als Achse und Motor der Theologie Luthers: Der "fröhliche Wechsel" als hermeneutischer Schlüssel zu Abendmahlslehre, Anthropologie, Seelsorge, Naturtheologie, Rhetorik und Humor'. *Neue Zeitschrift für systematische Theologie und Religionsphilosophie* 38, no. 1 (1996): 1–28.

Steiger, Johann Anselm. *Fünf Zentralthemen der Theologie Luthers und seiner Erben: Communicatio, Imago, Figura, Maria, Exempla.* Studies in the History of Christian Thought. Vol. 104. Leiden: Brill, 2002.

Steiger, Johann Anselm. 'The Communicatio Idiomatum as the Axle and Motor of Luther's Theology'. *Lutheran Quarterly* 14, no. 2 (2000): 125–58.

Stern, Robert. *The Radical Demand in Løgstrup's Ethics.* Oxford: Oxford University Press, 2019.

Stout, Jeffrey. *Democracy and Tradition.* New Forum Books. Princeton, NJ: Princeton University Press, 2005.

Suda, Max Josef. *Die Ethik Martin Luthers.* Forschungen zur systematischen und ökumenischen Theologie, 108. Göttingen: Vandenhoeck & Ruprecht, 2006.

Sullivan, Roger J. *Immanuel Kant's Moral Theory*. Cambridge: Cambridge University Press, 1989.
Søe, N. H. *Kristelig etik*. 2nd edn. København: G. E. C. Gads, 1946.
Taylor, Charles. *The Ethics of Authenticity*. Cambridge, MA: Harvard University Press, 1991.
Thiemann, Ronald F. *Religion in Public Life: A Dilemma for Democracy*. A Twentieth Century Fund Book. Washington, DC: Georgetown University Press, 1996.
Thiemann, Ronald F. *The Legacy of H. Richard Niebuhr*. Minneapolis, MN: Augsburg Fortress, 1991.
Tietz, Christiane. '... mit anderen Worten ... Zur Überzetzbarkeit religiöser Überzeugungen in politischen Diskursen'. *Evangelische Theologie* 72, no. 2 (2012): 86–100.
Tietz, Christiane. '"The Church Is the Limit of Politics": Bonhoeffer on the Political Task of the Church'. *Union Seminary Quarterly Review* 60, no. 1–2 (2006): 23–36.
Tietz, Christiane. 'The Role of Jesus Christ for Christian Theology'. In *Christ, Church and World. New Studies in Bonhoeffer's Theology and Ethics*. Edited by Michael Mawson and Philip G. Ziegler, 9–28. London: T&T Clark, 2016.
Tietz-Steiding, Christiane. *Bonhoeffers Kritik der verkrümmten Vernunft: Eine erkenntnistheoretische Untersuchung*. Beiträge zur historischen Theologie, 112. Tübingen: Mohr Siebeck, 1999.
Tietz-Steiding, Christiane. 'Verkrümmte Vernunft und intellektuelle Redlichkeit. Dietrich Bonhoeffers Erkenntnistheorie'. In *Religion im Erbe. Dietrich Bonhoeffer und die Zukunftsfähigkeit des Christentums*. Edited by Christian Gremmels and Wolfgang Huber, 293–307. Gütersloh: Chr. Kaiser, 2002.
Tödt, Heinz Eduard. 'Conscientious Resistance: Ethical Responsibility of the Individual, the Group, and the Church'. In *Ethical Responsibility: Bonhoeffer's Legacy to the Churches*. Edited by John D. Godsey and Geffrey B. Kelly, 17–42. New York/Toronto: Edwin Mellen Press, 1981.
Ulrich, Hans G. *Wie Geschöpfe leben. Konturen evangelischer Ethik*. Münster: LIT, 2005.
Voigt, Friedemann (ed.). *Religion in bioethischen Diskursen: interdisziplinäre, internationale und interreligiöse Perspektiven*. Berlin/New York: W. de Gruyter, 2010.
Walzer, Michael. *Spheres of Justice: A Defense of Pluralism and Equality*. New York: Basic Books, 1983.
Wannenwetsch, Bernd. 'Communication as Transformation: Worship and the Media'. *Studies in Christian Ethics* 13 (2000): 93–106.
Wannenwetsch, Bernd. *Gottesdienst als Lebensform: Ethik für Christenbürger*. Stuttgart: W. Kohlhammer, 1997.
Wannenwetsch, Bernd. 'Liturgy'. In *The Blackwell Companion to Political Theology*. Edited by Peter Scott and William T. Cavanaugh, 76–90. Malden, MA/Oxford: Blackwell, 2004.
Wannenwetsch, Bernd. 'Luther's Moral Theology'. In *The Cambridge Companion to Martin Luther*. Edited by Donald K. McKim, 120–35. Cambridge: Cambridge University Press, 2003.
Wannenwetsch, Bernd. *Political Worship: Ethics for Christian Citizens*. Translated by Margaret Kohl. Oxford/New York: Oxford University Press, 2004.
Wannenwetsch, Bernd. '"Responsible Living" or "Responsible Self"? Bonhoefferian Reflections on a Vexed Moral Notion'. *Studies in Christian Ethics* 18, no. 3 (2005): 125–40.

Wannenwetsch, Bernd. 'Soul Citizens: How Christians Understand Their Political Role'. *Political Theology* 9, no. 3 (2008): 373-94.
Wannenwetsch, Bernd. 'The Political Worship of the Church: A Critical and Empowering Practice'. *Modern Theology* 12, no. 3 (1996): 269-99.
Wannenwetsch, Bernd. 'The Whole Christ and the Whole Human Being: Dietrich Bonhoeffer's Inspiration for the "Christology and Ethics" Discourse'. In *Christology and Ethics*. Edited by F. LeRon Shults and Brent Waters, 75-98. Grand Rapids, MI: W. B. Eerdmans, 2010.
Wannenwetsch, Bernd. 'Trygve Wyller: Glaube und Autonome Welt. Rezension'. *Theologische Literaturzeitung* 124 (1999): 799-803.
Weissbach, Jürgen. *Christologie und Ethik bei Dietrich Bonhoeffer*. Theologische Existenz heute. Vol. 131. München: Chr. Kaiser, 1966.
Werpehowski, William. *American Protestant Ethics and the Legacy of H. Richard Niebuhr*. Moral Traditions Series. Washington, DC: Georgetown University Press, 2002.
Wilson, Bryan. 'Secularization'. In *Encyclopedia of Religion*. Edited by Lindsay Jones, 8214-20. Detroit, MI: Macmillan Reference USA, 2005.
WMA Declaration of Helsinki – Ethical Principles for Medical Research Involving Human Subjects.
Wolf, Ernst. 'Politia Christi: Das Problem der Sozialethik im Luthertum'. In *Peregrinatio*. Edited by Ernst Wolf, 214-42. München: Chr. Kaiser, 1962.
Wüstenberg, Ralf K. *Glauben als Leben: Dietrich Bonhoeffer und die nichtreligiöse Interpretation biblischer Begriffe*. Kontexte. Frankfurt am Main: Peter Lang, 1996.
Wüstenberg, Ralf K. 'Religionless Christianity: Dietrich Bonhoeffer's Tegel Theology'. In *Bonhoeffer for a New Day*, 57-71. Grand Rapids, MI: W. B. Eerdmans, 1997.
Wüstenberg, Ralf K., Stefan Heuser and Esther Hornung. *Bonhoeffer and the Biosciences: An Initial Exploration*. Frankfurt: Peter Lang, 2010.
Wyller, Trygve. *Glaube und autonome Welt: Diskussion eines Grundproblems der neueren systematischen Theologie mit Blick auf Dietrich Bonhoeffer, Oswald Bayer und K. E. Løgstrup*. Theologische Bibliothek Töpelmann, 91. Berlin/New York: W. de Gruyter, 1998.
Zimmermann, Jens. 'Being Human, Becoming Human: Dietrich Bonhoeffer's Christological Humanism'. In *Being Human, Becoming Human. Dietrich Bonhoeffer and Social Thought*. Edited by Jens Zimmerman and Brian Gregor, 25-48. Eugene, OR: Pickwick, 2010.
Zimmermann, Jens. 'Bonhoeffer's "Realistic Responsibility": Religion as the Foundation for Liberal Democratic Societies'. In *Dem Rad in die Speichen fallen. Das Politische in der Theologie Dietrich Bonhoeffers/A Spoke in the Wheel. The Political in the Theology of Dietrich Bonhoeffer*. Edited by Kirsten Busch Nielsen, Ralf K. Wüstenberg and Jens Zimmermann, 395-414. Gütersloh: Gütersloher Verlagshaus, 2013.
Zimmermann, Jens. *Dietrich Bonhoeffer's Christian Humanism*. Oxford: Oxford University Press, 2019.
Zimmermann, Jens. 'Dietrich Bonhoeffer's Christian Humanism in Philosophical and Theological Context'. In *Dietrich Bonhoeffers Theologie heute*, 369-86. Gütersloh: Gütersloher Verlagshaus, 2009.
Zimmermann, Jens. *Humanism and Religion. A Call for the Renewal of Western Culture*. Oxford: Oxford University Press, 2012.
Zimmermann, Jens, and Brian Gregor. *Being Human, Becoming Human: Dietrich Bonhoeffer and Social Thought*. Edited by K. C. Hanson, Charles M. Collier and D. Christopher Spinks. Princeton Theological Monograph Series. Eugene, OR: Pickwick, 2010.

INDEX

Althaus, Paul 8
Andersen, Svend 97–9
Augustine, Aurelius 124
autonomy (*see under* Bonhoeffer, autonomy and Christological, autonomy)

Bethge, Eberhard 13, 47
Biggar, Nigel 121 n.1, 122–3, 128–9, 131, 133, 140
Bonhoeffer, Dietrich
    autonomy 60–5
    ethics as hermeneutical starting point (*see under* ethics)
    mandate(s) 64, 81, 86–8
    reality 50–5
    reason 65–70
    responsibility 70–7
    secular(ism) 55–60
Bonhoeffer moment 2
Boomgaarden, Jürgen 50
Braaten, Carl E. 105
Bretherton, Luke 104 n.45, 107 n.60, 121 n.1, 125
Brexit 2
Brock, Brian 34 n.63, 123 n.7

calling 26, 63, 87–9, (*see also* Christological, calling)
cantus firmus 13, 47, 48, 130, 146
cartoon crisis 2
Chalcedon, formula of 16–19, 22, 29, 34, 40–3, 46–8, 77, 121, 140, 145
Chalcedonian
    autonomy, shaping of 60–5
    Christian humanism 106–11
    Christology 13–19
    Christology in Bonhoeffer ethics 17, 19, 39–48
    Christology in Luther's ethics 20, 23–38
    Christology, differentiated unity 4–8, 15, 19
    Christology as a foundation for social ethics 8–13
    communicative responsibility reshaped 112–19
    figurative and metaphorical sense 19
    law and justice 95–106
    motifs in the Lutheran tradition 4
    mystery of human life 130, 147
    political thought 95–120
    reality, shaping of 50–55
    reason, shaping of 65–70
    responsibility, shaping of 70–7
    secular, shaping of 55–60
    transgression of it 121–41
Christ, Jesus
    in Bonhoeffer's ethics (significance of Christ) 39–94
    call to Christians to bear witness of 121–141
    in Luther's ethics (significance of Christ) 23–38
    origin of reason, culture, humanity and tolerance 66
    political thought (significance of Christ) 95–120
    real presence of 30, 44, 57, 102, 114, 127, 130, 134, 147
    who Christ actually is 18, 41, 145
Christian bioethics in public 137–40
Christian ethics
    between universality and specificity 1–19, 143–7
    as conversational 7 (*see also* Conversation(al) approach)
    in public (*see under* Public, Christian voice(s) in)
    as witness (*see under* Witness, Christian)
Christian humanism (*see under* Chalcedonian, Christian humanism)

Index

Christianity
  amoral 7
  and contemporary politics 125
  early 15
  not serious as a pure idea 80
  origin of reason, culture, humanity and tolerance 66
  religionless 55–60
  what it is 41
Christological
  autonomy, understanding of 60–5
  Bonhoeffer's ethic as 4–5, 8, 11, 15–17, 20–1, 39–48, 62
  calling, foundation of 88–89
  conversation and polyphony of life (see also Conversation(al) approach) 127–34
  humanism 106–12
  interpretation of Luther's political thought 20
  motifs secondary 8
  motifs in Luther's ethics 8–10, 27, 37–8
  mystery of reality 44–8, 102
  natural law 90–3
  ontology 110, 114
  reality, understanding of 50–5, 82–5, 102, 110, 117–18
  reason, ontology of 65–70
  responsibility, understanding of 70–7, 110, 112–19
  secular, understanding of the 55–60, 126
  shaping of central concepts in Bonhoeffer's ethics 49–78
  social ethic as Chalcedonian 12–13
  thought in Christian ethics 14
  visible church 86
Christology
  Chalcedonian (see Chalcedon and Chalcedonian)
  lectures on (Bonhoeffer's) 41–6
  Luther's and Bonhoeffer's ethics 8–13
  core of any Christian theology 14
  revived Christology and ethics discourse 14
Christ-reality 50–5, 59, 63, 69–70, 72, 76–8, 80, 86–7, 89, 95, 110, 119, 123–4, 126, 131, 145–6

communicatio idiomatum 10, 17–21, 27–37, 40, 41–7, 101–2, 112–13, 118, 120, 129, 144, 146
conversation(al) approach 7, 22, 127–34, 135–7, 139–40, 146–7
Crisp, Oliver 17–18

De Gruchy, John W. 106–11
differentiated unity 3–4, 19
  Christian ethics, origins of 4
  Luther's social ethics, in 32–7
  third position 3–8
  universality and specificity, of 4–8, 15
dignity, human (*see under* human dignity)
divinity and humanity, simultaneity of in Luther's social ethics 23–38
dual citizenship 22 123–7, 140, 146

ethics
  between participation and witness 85–9
  Bonhoeffer's political thought 82–5
  central concepts in Bonhoeffer's 49–78
  Chalcedonian Christology in Bonhoeffer's 39–48
  Christian, between universality and specificity (*see under* Christian ethics)
  hermeneutical starting point (with Bonhoeffer's *Ethics*) 20
  life, death and resurrection of Jesus Christ 14
  living in the saeculum and bearing witness to Christ 121–41
  luther's social ethics 23–38
  political thought 95–120
etsi deus non daretur 4, 58, 68, 126

Feil, Ernst 56
Fergusson, David 97 n.7
foundation 2–3, 14, 19, 21, 27, 28, 32–4, 41, 45, 52, 59, 60, 62, 64–5, 67, 74–5, 77, 79, 83, 88–92, 94, 95, 100, 108–10, 112, 118–19, 129, 143–6
  Chalcedonian Christology for social ethics 8–13
  Christonomy for the human condition 60–5
  third position 4–8 (*see also* third position)

foundational 134, 146
foundationalist temptation 40

God and world, unity in Jesus Christ 1
Green, Clifford J. 40
Gregory, Eric 125 n.15
Grenholm, Carl-Henric 107, 111
Grobien, Gifford A. 100 n.23
Grotefeld, Stefan 78
Grotius, Hugo 4, 68, 126

Harvey, Barry 57 n.35, 130 n.37
Hauerwas, Stanley 19, 86, 99–100, 106, 114, 124
Henry, Michel 85 n.36
Holm, Bo Kristian 31
Holmes, Christopher R. J. 11
Huber, Wolfgang 136
human dignity 135–7
Humanism (*see under* Chalcedonian, Christian humanism)

Johnson, Kristen Deede 128–9

Kant, Immanuel 61, 135
Kantian 99, 135–6
Kelly, J. N. D. 15
Klemm, David E. 106, 122
Kurtén, Tage 105–6, 124

Laffin, Michael Richard 10 n.35, 23 n.1, 25 n.10, 98 n.12
Lehmkühler, Karsten 39–42
Lienhard, Marc 27
Luther, Martin
  Chalcedonian Christology (*see under* Chalcedon and Chalcedonian)
  communicatio idiomatum (*see under communicatio idiomatum*)
  simultaneity of divinity and humanity 23–38
  three estates 20, 24–27, 37, 87
  two kingdoms doctrine 8, 20, 24–7, 37, 64, 89, 96, 98, 123–4, 144
Løgstrup, K. E. 68, 95, 98–9, 106, 126, 145

MacIntyre, Alasdair 67, 102–3
Macquarrie, John 15–19

mandate(s) (*see under* Bonhoeffer, mandate(s))
Markus, Robert A. 60
Mathewes, Charles T. 125 n.15
Mawson, Michael 73 n.132
Mayer, Rainer 69
McBride, Jennifer M. 81 n.7, 85 n.37
McKenny, Gerald P. 117
Meilaender, Gilbert 127 n.23
Messer, Neil 93 n.95
Milbank, John 57, 59, 99
mystery (*see also* Chalcedonian, mystery of human life)
  of Christ 1, 18, 20, 43, 45, 110, 114, 127, 133
  of Christmas 46–7
  of reality 54, 110

nationalist movements 2
natural law
  Christologically reshaped 90–3
  grounded in Christ 90–1
  Lutheran understanding 3–4, 32–7, 95–101, 105, 109, 120, 126, 131
  simultaneously 'natural' and 'divine' 3–4, 32–7
  universality and specificity 1–4, 90–3, 95, 97
natural life
  in Bonhoeffer's *Ethics*) 67–8, 78, 91–3,
  in Christian humanism 107, 111
natural rights 68, 91–3
Nickson, Ann 50
Niebuhr, H. Richard 112, 116–19
Nielsen, Kirsten Busch 56, 60, 63
Nikolajsen, Jeppe Bach 122 n.2
Nilsson, Kjell Ove 10 n.37, 28 n.27, 33

O'Donovan, Oliver 14 n.48, 60 n.50, 97 n.8, 99, 123
ontological (*see under* ontology)
ontology (*see also* Christological, ontology)
  Christological, of reason (*see under* Christological)
  of reality 70
  participatory Christological 110, 114, 145
Ott, Heinrich 69–70

polity of Christ 21, 95–120
political thought
    Bonhoeffer 79–94
    contemporary 95–141
    as contradictory affirmation of reality 82–5
    foundation 3 (*see also* Foundation)
    Luther 10, 23–38
    in the polity of Christ 95–120
polyphony 47–48, 122, 127–134, 146
Prüller-Jagenteufel, Gunter 71–72
public, Christian voice(s) in 1, 21–2, 141

Raunio, Antti 105
Rawls, John 19, 66, 97–98, 114, 127, 131, 138–9, 145
Rawlsian 98, 127–9, 138
reality (*see under* Bonhoeffer, reality and Christological, reality)
    of Christ (*see under* Christ-reality)
    of God 1
    of the world 1
reason, Christological ontology (*see under* Bonhoeffer, reason and Christological)
reconciliation of the world and God 1
Reed, Esther 12 n.41, 72, 112 n.76, 130 n.37, 131 n.38
religion, private matter 1
responsibility (*see under* Bonhoeffer, responsibility and Chalcedonian, responsibility)
responsive(ness) 21, 70, 72, 75, 77, 70–7, 112–19, 120, 133, 144–6
responsivity 85 (*see also* Responsive(ness))

saeculum 55–60, 78, 121–41, 147
Schliesser, Christine 71, 76
Schulman, Adam 135–6
Schweiker, William 106–11, 122
secular(ism) (*see under* Bonhoeffer, secular(ism) and Christological, secular)
September 11th, 2001 1
Sherman, Franklin 12–13
Simpson, Gary 112, 115–16, 118–19
simultaneity 20, 23, 33, 37–8, 46, 69, 95, 101, 106, 144

Steiger, Johann Anselm 28 n.27, 31
Stout, Jeffrey 97 n.7, 112, 114–15, 118–19, 122, 128–9, 131
Søe, N. H. 99–100, 145

Taylor, Charles 104 n.43
Thiemann, Ronald 105
third position 3, 4–8, 19, 22, 111, 119, 121–2, 140, 144
    beyond liberalism and communitarianism 97, 119
Tietz, Christiane 131, 136

Ulrich, Hans G. 9
universality and specificity
    beyond liberalism and communitarianism 119
    Bonhoeffer's social ethics 20, 79–94
    Bonhoeffer's ethics (*see under* Bonhoeffer, Dietrich)
    Bonhoeffer's political thought 21
    Chalcedonian Christology 8, 19–20, 41, 49–78, 119, 134
    Christ, real presence and contemporaneity 134
    Christian ethics (*see under* Christian ethics)
    Christian humanism 106–11
    Christian's dual citizenship (*see under* Dual citizenship)
    Christology and ethics 19
    Christological shaping in Bonhoeffer's ethics 49–78
    common and particular 7
    communicatio idiomatum 18 (see also *communicatio idiomatum*)
    conversation 137, 140, 147 (*see also* conversation(al) approach)
    differentiated unity 24, 38, 79–94, 95, 99, 119, 121–22, 132, 134, 140–1, 143–7
    dynamic interplay 147
    human dignity 135–7
    law and justice 95–106
    Lutheran social ethics 8–9
    Luther's social ethics 20, 23–38
    natural law (*see under* Natural law)
    political thought 95–120

polity of Christ 95–120
rejection of a foundation 100
reshaped understanding 134
responsibility 112–19
radicalism and compromise 80
tension 132
third position(s) 4, 122
transcending the differentiated unity 22, 121–41
witness, bearing 134–41, 147 (*see also* Witness, Christian)

Walzer, Michael 102–3
Wannenwetsch, Bernd 40–1, 62, 71, 100–2, 117, 124
Witness, Christian 4, 9, 19, 21–2, 55, 75, 77, 83–4, 85–90, 94, 121–41
Wolf, Ernst 5, 9
Wüstenberg, Ralf K. 56
Wyller, Trygve 56, 62

Zimmermann, Jens 106, 107 n.58, 110

www.ingramcontent.com/pod-product-compliance
Lightning Source LLC
Chambersburg PA
CBHW050328020526
44117CB00031B/2030